THE BOOK OF MOVIE LISTS

An Offbeat, Provocative Collection of the Best
and Worst of Everything in Movies

Joseph McBride

CB
CONTEMPORARY BOOKS

Library of Congress Cataloging-in-Publication Data

McBride, Joseph.
    The book of movie lists : an offbeat, provocative collection of the best
and worst of everything in movies / Joseph McBride.
       p.   cm.
    Includes index.
    ISBN 0-8092-2891-2
    1. Motion pictures—Miscellanea.   I. Title.
PN1994.9.M39   1998
791.43—dc21   98-15254
                                                                  CIP

Cover design by Todd Peterson
Interior design by Nick Panos

Published by Contemporary Books
A division of NTC/Contemporary Publishing Group, Inc.
4255 West Touhy Avenue, Lincolnwood (Chicago), Illinois 60646-1975 U.S.A.
Copyright © 1999 by Joseph McBride
Printed in the United States of America
International Standard Book Number: 0-8092-2891-2

98   99   00   01   02   03   04   05   QP   9   8   7   6   5   4   3   2   1

For John McBride,
whose dad and pal I'm proud to be

Other Books by Joseph McBride

High and Inside: An A-to-Z Guide to the Language of Baseball

Steven Spielberg: A Biography

Orson Welles

Frank Capra: The Catastrophe of Success

Filmmakers on Filmmaking: Vols. I and II   (EDITOR)

Hawks on Hawks

Orson Welles: Actor and Director

Kirk Douglas

John Ford   (WITH MICHAEL WILMINGTON)

Focus on Howard Hawks   (EDITOR)

Persistence of Vision: A Collection of Film Criticism   (EDITOR)

CONTENTS

INTRODUCTION

A Thousand Clowns is a movie that meant a lot to me when I was starting college in the 1960s, just before the Vietnam War and the sexual revolution called into question everything my generation of baby boomers had been taught about life. It's a movie about the importance of following the beat of your own, stubbornly different drummer even when society tries its damnedest to make you march in line. There's one scene in *A Thousand Clowns* I often think about, all these years later. It comes when Murray, the nonconformist TV writer played by Jason Robards, worries that his influence over his adolescent nephew, who lives with him, might be starting to slip. "He started to make *lists* this year," Murray rants. "Lists of everything—subway stops! underwear! what he's gonna do next week! If he doesn't watch out, he'll start making lists of what he's gonna do next year and for the next *ten* years. . . . No, no, I haven't spent six years with him so he'd turn into a *list maker*!"

An eminently reasonable warning, but what movie buff can resist the making of lists? Whether we want to be or not, we're all list makers at heart. Anyone who's obsessed with movies brings to the theater a deep-seated need to bring order and coherence to a world outside that often seems unmanageable, even out of control. As F. Scott Fitzgerald writes in his essay "The Crack-Up," there's something profoundly soothing about the making of lists. When he was facing the collapse of all his illusions about life, he "made lists—made lists and tore them up, hundreds of lists: of cavalry leaders and football players and cities, and popular tunes and pitchers, and happy times, and hobbies and houses lived in. . . . And then, suddenly, surprisingly, I got better."

Perhaps there's also something troubling about the movies themselves that drives us to make lists. The evanescent nature of the moving image makes us want to capture and memorialize it. We're compelled to pin down our favorite moments in the movies and take them home to marvel at in solitude, like rare butterflies. Otherwise they flutter away, their memory begins to fade, and they no longer belong to us. So we make and collect lists of everything we like in the movies and everything we don't like. Then we can't help sharing our lists with other movie fanatics, with a mixture of embarrassment and pride, like Robert de La Chesnaye (Marcel Dalio) displaying his prized mechanical organ to his guests in Jean Renoir's *The Rules of the Game* (see this book's list of "My 17 Favorite Close-Ups in Movies").

Since movies are dreamlike and appeal largely to our subconscious, lists of movies function like Rorschach blots. Probably the quickest way to get to know someone is to ask for a list of his or her ten favorite movies. It's such a direct window into someone's psyche that it's almost unfair to ask the question until the person knows you well enough to trust you with such intimacies. Film critics and historians, however, don't have the luxury of holding back on our likes and dislikes. We can run, but we can't hide; by telling you what we think of the movies we watch for a living, we are letting you in on some of our deepest secrets.

This book is an extended Rorschach blot of one movie-haunted psyche—a psyche that has been busy recording the impressions of thousands of movies at the rate of twenty-four frames a second for almost fifty years. I have been studying and writing about movies and talking to people who make them for more than thirty of those years, and I've grown accustomed to letting people see what's inside my movie-addled brain. Tennessee Williams counseled his fellow writers never to be ashamed of sharing their thoughts, feelings, and experiences, and I've tried my best to follow his advice. (See my list entitled "Sister Superior: The 10 Sexiest Nuns in Movies.")

I've shared my discoveries, joys, and disappointments about movies in a dozen books, mostly dealing with great American directors, including Steven Spielberg, Frank Capra, Orson Welles, John Ford, and Howard Hawks. Along the way, I've written hundreds of movie reviews and articles for a wide range of newspapers, magazines, and Internet outlets, from *Sight and Sound*, *Film Quarterly*, and *Film Comment* to *Daily Variety*, *Boxoffice* magazine, and *Cinemania Online*. But despite that vast outflow of words and thoughts, there's still much about my moviegoing memory that, until now, has never found a home in print. This is finally my opportunity to round up and collect many of the funny stories about movies and odd, vagrant bits of movie lore that have been rattling around inside my head since I first visited a movie house at the age of two to see Walt Disney's *Fantasia*.

Putting together this book has turned out to be a real kick, not only because I've been able to get a lot off my chest, but also because, in the process, I've learned much about what I really think and feel about a wide range of movies. My taste in movies has always been popular and eclectic. While I've tried to carry my film scholarship into fresh and uncharted waters, I've also tried never to become so abstruse that I lose sight of what made me love movies in the first place. As a critic and historian, I've always followed my own individual path, freely admitting what I like and don't like, defiantly disregarding fashion, and not letting any doctrine or theory blind me to the irreducible complexities of movies or of life itself. (Such independence does not come without a price. See "The Jedediah Leland Memorial Award: To 6 Critics Who Lost Their Jobs Because of Their Reviews.")

I hope you'll find in this book much that's revealing, humorous, joyous, contentious, quirky, surprising, outrageous, and (for better or worse) unashamedly personal. You'll find things that make you smile in agreement and things that make you mutter in disagreement. To begin the list-making process right here, my four goals in *The Book of Movie Lists* are

1. To lead you to movies you haven't seen

2. To bring a fresh light to movies you have seen

3. To make a bit more sense of the jumble of movie history

4. And, most of all, to provoke a stimulating dialogue between us as you turn the pages

The numbered lists are ranked in order of my preferences. Others are arranged in either chronological or alphabetical order. The names of the movies' directors and the years of original release usually are included in parentheses after the titles. I've added whatever comments, anecdotes, quotations, and other pieces of information I've thought helpful to rationalize my choices and to tell you why I find these movies so fascinating. You can write your own additions and comments in the margins or scratch out my titles and replace them with your own. Better still, you can drop me a letter in care of the publisher to let me know when you think I'm right or wrong and what I should have included but didn't. I welcome your responses, which will be a great help in putting together future editions.

I see *The Book of Movie Lists* as a crowded, uproarious party filled with as many of my favorite movie people and fellow movie buffs as I can squeeze through the doors. In that spirit, I've asked several fellow film aficionados—critics, biographers, novelists, friends, and family members—to contribute "guest lists." I'm grateful to them all for agreeing to join the festivities and for taking my suggestion to be as revealingly personal as it is possible for guests to be at someone else's party. The contributors of these entertaining and informative lists, which you'll find scattered throughout the book, are Charles Champlin, Ray Greene, Gavin Lambert, Jonathan Lethem, Leonard Maltin, Jessica McBride, John McBride, Noel O'Hara, Ruth O'Hara, Patricia Scott Rodney, Jonathan Rosenbaum, and Bob Thomas.

I also am grateful to the following people for their generous advice and suggestions about this book, as well as for their many other kindnesses: Ruth O'Hara, John McBride, Jessica McBride, Mark McBride, Kendall Hailey, Elaine Jones, F. X. Feeney, Gary and Jillian Graver, and Lou and Judy Race. Like so many other film scholars, I would find it unthinkable to do research without the facilities of the Margaret Herrick Library of the Academy of Motion Picture Arts and Sciences; many thanks to Linda Harris Mehr and her devoted and knowledgeable staff. And for their help, friendship, and stimulating conversation, I thank Michael and Kerin McBride, Harrison Engle, Nadine Goff, Virginia Clark, Mary Mallory, Julia Sweeney, Henry Sheehan, Myron Meisel, Gene Kraft, and Charles Horton.

For giving me regular forums in which to write about movies, I am grateful to Ray Greene, Kim Williamson, and Christine James of *Boxoffice*; Jim Emerson, Rudy Brueggemann, and Kris Kaiyala of *Cinemania Online*; and Jeff Schwager of *Mr. Showbiz*.

Special thanks are due to my loyal, imaginative, and indefatigable agent, Richard Parks. And I'm delighted to be working again with my astute and infallibly amiable editors at Contemporary Books, Kara Leverte and Craig Bolt. I also thank copyeditor Regina Wells and the other talented and dedicated people with NTC/Contemporary Publishing Company.

Enjoy.

Two Cheers for Hollywood
Lists About the Movie Business

The Wisest Line About the Movie Business

"NOBODY KNOWS ANYTHING."

> —Novelist and screenwriter William Goldman, in his 1983
> book *Adventures in the Screen Trade: A Personal View
> of Hollywood and Screenwriting*

The 10 Most Profound Hollywood Jokes

1. Steven Spielberg (or whoever is the biggest director du jour)
goes to heaven and presents himself at the pearly gates. "As
a reward for your many good deeds," Saint Peter tells him,
"God wants to give you the opportunity to make the greatest movie ever made. You will have an unlimited budget
and shooting schedule. You can use any writer you want—

1

Shakespeare, Tolstoy, Dickens, Mark Twain—you name 'em, we have 'em. We have all the great stars with us, too—Garbo, Marilyn Monroe, Bogart, Cagney, Jimmy Stewart. We have the world's best cameramen—Gregg Toland, Billy Bitzer, James Wong Howe—and the finest musicians, from Bach and Beethoven to Strauss and Stravinsky. Oh, yes, I almost forgot. There's just one thing—God has this girl . . ."

2. At a 1986 Directors Guild of America press conference to protest Ted Turner's colorization of *The Maltese Falcon*, John Huston opened his prepared remarks by saying, "A couple of generations back, screenwriters used to tell a story about two producers lost in the desert and dying of thirst. About to give up the ghost, they crawl into view of a miraculous spring of pure effervescent water and they go joyously to drink, when one says, 'No, wait. Don't drink. Wait till I piss in it.' To bring the story up to date, one has only to add that, in my opinion, both producers are members of the Turner organization."

3. When MGM made its 1935 film version of the classic Charles Dickens novel *David Copperfield*, Frank Whitbeck of the studio's advertising department was checking the credits with an executive to ensure that everyone's billing was correct. As Max Wilk tells the story in his 1971 book *The Wit and Wisdom of Hollywood*, after they had run down the list of talent involved in the picture, Whitbeck said, "There's a lot of credit there. But one name that should get credit doesn't." "Who's that?" the executive demanded. "Probably the most important of all," Whitbeck replied. "The guy who wrote the book, Dickens." "He's dead, isn't

he?" the executive asked. "Yes," conceded Whitbeck. "Well," said the executive, "screw him!"

4. In his later years, so the story goes, veteran director Fred Zinnemann "took a meeting" in Hollywood with one of the young studio executives. After the initial pleasantries were exchanged, the executive said, "Well, Mr. Zinnemann, before we start, tell me a little bit about yourself. What have you done?" Zinnemann looked at him coldly and replied, "You first." (In the same vein, screenwriter Larry Gelbart recently reported pitching a movie idea to "a fetus in a three-piece suit.")

5. A screenwriter awakens in the middle of the night and tells his wife, "I've just had a dream with the best movie idea anyone's ever had!" At her suggestion, he writes the idea down so he'll be sure to remember it in the morning. When he wakes up, he looks at the piece of paper on his bedside table. It reads: "Boy meets girl."

6. "Goodbye, Mr. Zanuck, it certainly has been a pleasure working at Sixteenth-Century Fox"—Jean Renoir.

7. In 1925, the Hollywood screenwriter Herman J. Mankiewicz sent a telegram to his friend Ben Hecht, a former newspaperman who was then a struggling New York writer: "WILL YOU ACCEPT THREE HUNDRED PER WEEK TO WORK FOR PARAMOUNT PICTURES. ALL EXPENSES PAID. THE THREE HUNDRED IS PEANUTS. MILLIONS ARE TO BE GRABBED OUT HERE AND YOUR ONLY COMPETITION IS IDIOTS. DON'T LET THIS GET AROUND."

8. As Maurice Zolotow records in his 1977 biography *Billy Wilder in Hollywood*, "Billy was having a late-afternoon libation at the Tennis Club with some friends [in 1958] when a waiter brought over the late edition of the paper which headlined the news that [producer] Mike Todd had crashed to death in a plane accident. Art Cohn, a screenwriter who had been working on an adaptation of *Don Quixote* to star Mrs. Todd (Elizabeth Taylor), also died in that crash. Wilder began reading the story. Two columns on page one, telling of Todd's stage and movie triumphs, his wives, his rise from poverty. The story, with pictures, ran over to several more columns on page ten. At the bottom of the story were three lines about Art Cohn's credits. Wilder pointed out the disparity to fellow director Rouben Mamoulian, bitterly observing, 'Additional Dying by Art Cohn.' "

9. "In most places, you lie on the sand and look at the stars. In Hollywood, you lie on the stars and look at the sand"—Anonymous.

10. When Jesus (Max von Sydow) dies on the cross in *The Greatest Story Ever Told* (1965), director George Stevens gets an unintentional laugh by cutting to John Wayne playing The Centurion at the foot of the cross, wearing a helmet and short skirt and intoning, "Truly this man was . . . the son of *God*." According to Hollywood legend, when Wayne first read the line, Stevens pondered a moment and said, "Duke, try it again. And this time put a little more awe into it." The camera rolled again, and Wayne said, "*Aw*, truly this man was the son of God." (I asked George Stevens if that actually happened, and he replied, "No, but it's a damn good story.")

4

Two Cheers for Hollywood
15 of the Best Movies About Movies

Show People (KING VIDOR, 1928) Vidor's delightful spoof of Hollywood is a showcase for the considerable comic talents of the much-maligned Marion Davies. Expert pantomime carries Davies's hick character to stardom in silent comedy, while such Hollywood celebrities as Charlie Chaplin, John Gilbert, and Vidor himself add convincing atmosphere with cameo appearances.

What Price Hollywood? (GEORGE CUKOR, 1932) This unusually realistic account of the ill-fated relationship between a rising star (Constance Bennett) and her alcoholic director (brilliantly played by Lowell Sherman, a director himself) was the prototype for the later *Star Is Born* movies.

Bombshell (VICTOR FLEMING, 1933) A raucous Jean Harlow comedy about the life of a movie star, which screenwriters John Lee Mahin and Jules Furthman based on an unproduced play by Caroline Francke and Mack Crane, but also in part on Harlow's own messy personal life, *Bombshell* wittily captures the wide discrepancies between image and reality in Hollywood mythmaking.

Sullivan's Travels (PRESTON STURGES, 1941) Writer-director Sturges's self-reflexive fable stars Joel McCrea as a dissatisfied comedy director who leaves Hollywood in search of deeper meaning. His seriocomic odyssey ironically leads him back full circle to an appreciation of comedy's vital importance in the lives of his audience: "It's all some people have in this cock-eyed caravan."

Sunset Boulevard (BILLY WILDER, 1950)   The tragic story of the death of a hack screenwriter (William Holden) at the hands of a silent-movie queen (Gloria Swanson), *Sunset Boulevard* chronicles the destruction of a flamboyant art form and its replacement by faceless mediocrity. Before I went to Hollywood, I thought *Sunset Boulevard* was too cynical a portrait of the movie business, but after living there for a while, I realized that the movie is a "valentine," as Wilder described it to me. By eerie coincidence, my first apartment in Hollywood was four blocks from the one where Holden's Joe Gillis lived.

The Bad and the Beautiful (VINCENTE MINNELLI, 1952) This scathing saga of a ruthlessly ambitious producer (Kirk Douglas) and the careers he affects is compounded of equal parts David O. Selznick and Val Lewton.

Singin' in the Rain (GENE KELLY AND STANLEY DONEN, 1952) This glorious MGM musical about the coming of sound and the upheavals it brought to Hollywood is hugely entertaining while also serving as a virtual documentary of that era.

A Star Is Born (GEORGE CUKOR, 1954)   A heartrending dramatic musical about an alcoholic actor's decline while his wife rises to stardom, *A Star Is Born* represents the career summit of its director and its stars, James Mason and Judy Garland. Severely truncated after its premiere engagements, it was partially restored by Ronald Haver in 1983.

8½ (FEDERICO FELLINI, 1963)   Fellini's thinly disguised autobiographical account of an Italian director with a creative block stars Marcello Mastroianni as the filmmaker's alter ego.

This ingenious, vastly influential interweaving of fantasy and reality still casts a hypnotic spell.

Day for Night (FRANÇOIS TRUFFAUT, 1973)   Truffaut's affectionate tribute to the filmmaking process, with the director holding together a company torn by the tragicomic vicissitudes of life. The cast is headed by Jacqueline Bisset and Jean-Pierre Léaud, and Valentina Cortese and Jean-Pierre Aumont are especially moving as aging stars.

Hollywood Boulevard (JOE DANTE AND ALLAN ARKUSH, 1976)   This low-rent version of *Sunset Boulevard* is an uproarious self-satire of Roger Corman's schlocky New World Pictures, disguised as Miracle Pictures ("If It's a Good Picture, It's a Miracle"). Watch for the author of this book as the "Drive-In Rapist."

S.O.B. (BLAKE EDWARDS, 1981)   A wicked satire on modern Hollywood, as seen through the desperate attempts of a producer (Richard Mulligan) to turn a turkey into a hit by showing his wife's breasts on-screen (she is played by Edwards's own wife, Julie Andrews). A jeremiad in the form of a comedy, with William Holden playing the jaded director of the film-within-the-film, *S.O.B.* vents Edwards's righteous wrath at Hollywood's heartless venality.

The Stunt Man (RICHARD RUSH, 1980)   This black comedy about a ruthless director (Peter O'Toole) who plays God with the life of a stunt man (Steve Railsback) brims over with visual energy and diabolical wit. O'Toole sends up David Lean with sly relish in this story about the cinema's ability to dissolve the line between illusion and reality.

The Player (ROBERT ALTMAN, 1992)   A vitriolic black comedy adapted by Michael Tolkin from his novel about a studio executive (Tim Robbins) who tries to cover up his murder of a screenwriter. Altman's canny verisimilitude, which includes cameos by many Hollywood notables, helped make this film popular with the town it skewers.

Ed Wood (TIM BURTON, 1994)   Burton's black-and-white valentine to transvestite 1950s filmmaker Ed Wood (Johnny Depp) captures both the mind-boggling ineptitude of Wood's movies and the sincerity of his blinkered passion for the medium. Martin Landau's towering performance as the despairing, drug-addicted Bela Lugosi won him a richly deserved Oscar.

. . . Plus a Lost Classic About Movies

Hollywood (JAMES CRUZE, 1923)   A slice-of-life look at filmmaking in the silent era, with cameos by many stars of the day, including the tragically ostracized Roscoe (Fatty) Arbuckle. (See "10 Important Lost Movies.")

. . . And the 5 Worst Movies About Movies

The Last Movie (DENNIS HOPPER, 1971)   After the runaway success of *Easy Rider*, Universal made the mistake of letting Hopper go to Peru, with complete creative freedom, to film this obscure meditation on the art of cinema. The effects of chemical substances on creativity are clearer than anything the movie is trying to say, but as the director of the film-within-the-film, Samuel Fuller stands out like a rose in a garbage dump.

The Day of the Locust (JOHN SCHLESINGER, 1975) Nathanael West's great novella about Hollywood fringe people and a premiere that turns nightmarishly violent was transformed into a heavy-handed dud of a movie. Schlesinger's artsy, overheated visual style becomes a symptom of the ostentatious vulgarity the book attacks.

The Wild Party (JAMES IVORY, 1975) Other than Shakespeare adaptations, this is probably the only movie narrated in iambic pentameter. A pretentious Merchant Ivory mishmash, *The Wild Party* is an adaptation of a Joseph Moncure March poem loosely based on the Fatty Arbuckle scandal. This handsome but lifeless film, shot at the bizarre Mission Inn in Riverside, California, is directed with supercilious disdain for the Hollywood decadence it exploits. (I play a guest at the 1920s party and the orgy that follows. But since it's an orgy directed by James Ivory, I play that entire scene in bed . . . asleep.)

Won Ton Ton, the Dog Who Saved Hollywood (MICHAEL WINNER, 1976) British director Winner's distasteful send-up of Rin Tin Tin and 1920s Hollywood shows no trace of genuine affection for his subject matter, only a nasty smugness in ridiculing silent movies and the many aging actors who make ill-advised cameo appearances. (See "Where Have You Gone, Nathanael West?: The Strangest Event I've Ever Witnessed in All My Years of Covering Hollywood.")

Under the Rainbow (STEVE RASH, 1981) Utterly devoid of wit, this appalling farrago is truly one of the worst movies ever made. Taking off on the legends about the raucous misbehavior of midget actors housed in a Culver City hotel to play Munchkins in MGM's *The Wizard of Oz, Under the Rainbow* goes beyond offensiveness into mind-numbing idiocy.

10 Reasons People Today Miss the Studio System

1. The old moguls were guys with the common touch who had started at the bottom and loved movies.

2. Those executives could make decisions.

3. Because the studios made so many movies each year to feed their own theater chains, they had virtually guaranteed profits, which meant they could afford to make a few offbeat movies every year.

4. Because the studios had their own sources of financing, filmmakers didn't have the headaches and delays involved in raising money for pictures today. Studio control over budgets kept inefficiency and waste at a minimum.

5. Unlike today's widely dispersed and fragmented pool of filmmaking talent, creative people in the old days were brought together in a communal atmosphere on studio lots.

6. The studios had efficient story departments that scoured the world for literary properties, often hiring the world's greatest writers to work on them.

7. The studios nurtured and developed talent and carefully planned their careers, keeping them from making foolish mistakes in their choices of material.

8. Because the studios had people under long-term contracts, talent was guaranteed employment and didn't have to run around constantly, anxiously scrambling for work.

9. The studios had great crafts departments, with the best technicians in the industry under contract. Studio tech shops functioned as research-and-development facilities for the industry.

10. The studios had short-film departments that helped them develop new writers, directors, and actors.

10 Reasons People Today DON'T Miss the Studio System

1. Unlike the old moguls, who exercised tyrannical control over their employees' personal and professional lives, today's more laissez-faire employers couldn't care less, as long as the talent shows up on time and makes money for them.

2. The homogeneity of the old studios' output has been replaced by a richer and more diverse range of subjects and filmmaking styles, with a corresponding increase in opportunities for women and members of ethnic minority groups.

3. Freedom from onerous long-term contracts allows creative people to seek the best deals their talent can demand.

4. People aren't forced to work on assignment as often as they were under the old studio system.

5. Directors and actors have far more control over their own careers, running their own independent companies to develop material before presenting it to the studios for financing.

6. The most successful filmmakers have more opportunity to demand and receive a percentage of the distributor's gross receipts, making them the studio's partners in a film's success.

7. Producers, directors, and writers no longer have to work under humiliating supervision on studio lots, but instead can work out of their homes and private offices.

8. Filmmakers today don't even have to live in Los Angeles; they can be quite successful living in places such as northern California (e.g., George Lucas) and Chicago (e.g., John Hughes). This is partly due to new forms of electronic communication—for instance, screenwriters can collaborate via computer modem.

9. Location filming, which allows for greater authenticity, is much more common than it was in the days when studios had to justify their high overhead by filming as much as possible on the lot.

10. Independent sources of funding from outside the Hollywood system allow for greater freedom to make unusual films.

Credit-Card Movies
Some Really Cheap Well-Known Movies and What They Cost

Rock-bottom filmmaking is sometimes referred to as making "credit-card movies." Some of the following figures are approximate, and some do not include additional costs for postproduction and marketing, which even in the case of an ultra-cheap movie such as *El Mariachi* totaled about $1 million.

Four Men on a Raft (ORSON WELLES, 1942; a 48-minute segment of *It's All True*, posthumously completed and released in 1993 as part of the documentary *It's All True: Based on an Unfinished Film by Orson Welles*) $10,000

Rashomon (AKIRA KUROSAWA, 1950) $40,000

Breathless (JEAN-LUC GODARD, 1959) $120,000

The 400 Blows (FRANÇOIS TRUFFAUT, 1959) $80,000

The Immoral Mr. Teas (RUSS MEYER, 1959) $24,000

Shadows (JOHN CASSAVETES, 1959) $40,000

Il Posto (ERMANNO OLMI, 1961) $15,000

David Holzman's Diary (JIM McBRIDE, 1967) $2,500

Night of the Living Dead (GEORGE A. ROMERO, 1968) $114,000

Targets (PETER BOGDANOVICH, 1968) $130,000

Pink Flamingos (JOHN WATERS, 1972) $12,000

Hollywood Boulevard (JOE DANTE AND ALLAN ARKUSH,

1976) $64,000 (Producer Jon Davison made Roger Corman a bet he could bring in the film for under $60,000; the cost would have been $56,000, but it was decided to add $8,000 for the climactic special effect of a collapsing Hollywood sign.)

Tunnelvision (NEAL ISRAEL AND BRAD SWIRNOFF, 1976) $25,000

Return of the Secaucus Seven (JOHN SAYLES, 1980) $60,000

She's Gotta Have It (SPIKE LEE, 1986) $114,333

Hollywood Shuffle (ROBERT TOWNSEND, 1987) $100,000

Slacker (RICHARD LINKLATER, 1991) $23,000

El Mariachi (ROBERT RODRIGUEZ, 1992) $7,000

The Living End (GREGG ARAKI, 1992) $20,000

Clerks (KEVIN SMITH, 1994) $26,685

The Brothers McMullen (EDWARD BURNS, 1995) $27,500

Gravesend (SALVATORE STABILE, 1997) $5,000

In the Company of Men (NEAL LABUTE, 1997) $25,000

The 7 Best Ad Lines for Movies

1. *"Gable's back and Garson's got him"*   ADVENTURE (1945)

2. *"Garbo talks"*   ANNA CHRISTIE (1930)

3. *"Garbo laughs"*   NINOTCHKA (1939)

4. *"Just when you thought it was safe to go back in the water"* JAWS 2 (1978)

5. *"They're young, they're in love . . . they kill people"* BONNIE AND CLYDE (1967)

6. *"The most incredible thing that ever happened is about to happen to you"* TITANIC (1997)

7. *"Back in the days when you had to beat it before you could eat it"* CAVEMAN (1981)

. . . And the Least Imaginative Ad Line

"It's terrific!" CITIZEN KANE (1941)

The Best Ad Line That Was Never Used

Faced with the impossible challenge of marketing Monte Hellman's offbeat (to say the least) art film *Cockfighter* (1974), the staff at Roger Corman's New World Pictures became a little giddy, coming up with the following ad line:

"He came into town with his cock in his hand, and what he did with it was illegal in forty-nine states."

. . . And My Favorite Movie Ad (Since I Wrote It)

"In 1942, RKO premiered Orson Welles's The Magnificent Ambersons *on a double bill with* Mexican Spitfire Sees a Ghost.

"In 1977, New World Pictures continues in this tradition with Hollywood Boulevard, *a film by Joe Dante and Allan Arkush, plus on same bill* Cover Girl Models.*"*
—*New York Times*, April 24, 1977

Hitting the Jackpot
3 Movies That Won All 5 Major Academy Awards

It Happened One Night (COLUMBIA PICTURES, 1934)

> *Best Picture* (HARRY COHN)
> *Best Director* (FRANK CAPRA)
> *Best Screenplay* (ROBERT RISKIN)
> *Best Actor* (CLARK GABLE)
> *Best Actress* (CLAUDETTE COLBERT)

One Flew Over the Cuckoo's Nest (FANTASY FILMS, UNITED ARTISTS, 1975)

> *Best Picture* (SAUL ZAENTZ, MICHAEL DOUGLAS)
> *Best Director* (MILOS FORMAN)
> *Best Adapted Screenplay* (LAWRENCE HAUBEN, BO GOLDMAN)
> *Best Actor* (JACK NICHOLSON)
> *Best Actress* (LOUISE FLETCHER)

The Silence of the Lambs (STRONG HEART/DEMME, ORION, 1991)

> *Best Picture* (EDWARD SAXON, KENNETH UTT, RON BOZMAN)

Best Director (JONATHAN DEMME)
Best Adapted Screenplay (TED TALLY)
Best Actor (ANTHONY HOPKINS)
Best Actress (JODIE FOSTER)

My Academy Award "Rules"

While honored more in the breach than in the observance, these informal, uncodified rules (based on my observations from watching virtually every Oscarcast since 1958) can help viewers at home predict the unpredictable.

Nominations and Awards

1. The Best Picture winner must be a commercial hit. But it would be gauche to give the award automatically to the year's number-one hit (think: *E.T.*). So, a respectably good grosser usually will do just fine.

2. Technical awards are given on merit; "above-the-line" awards are given for political or sentimental reasons.

3. British people should be honored as often as possible, to emphasize how little regard Hollywood has for its own output.

4. Movies about physically or mentally handicapped people are virtually certain of being nominated. This allows Academy members to feel simultaneously virtuous and superior.

5. Oscars for Best Documentary cannot be given to films that are popular with the public or the critics.

6. The greatest movie actors are not honored with Oscars until they are old, ill, or retired, when they are given Oscars for making fun of themselves (e.g., Humphrey Bogart in *The African Queen*, John Wayne in *True Grit*), or are given honorary Oscars (e.g., Charlie Chaplin, Cary Grant, Henry Fonda).

7. Just as comedies are seldom considered worthy of Oscars, comedians are not given Oscars unless they are long retired, when they are given honorary awards.

8. The Best Supporting Actress winner must be grotesque or play a grotesque character.

9. Great directors have a hard time winning Oscars if they are too popular—for example, Steven Spielberg, who had to wait for his Oscars as director and producer until he made *Schindler's List*. Even more egregious is the strange case of Alfred Hitchcock, who never was voted an Oscar but had to settle instead for the Irving G. Thalberg Memorial Award (as a producer) in 1968. Some observers thought Hitchcock was sending the Academy a message when his entire acceptance speech consisted of only four words: "Thank you . . . very much."

10. Female directors cannot be nominated unless they are foreigners—the only two women ever nominated for Best Director are Italy's Lina Wertmuller, for *Seven Beauties* (1976), and Australia's Jane Campion, for *The Piano* (1993). Note: This rule particularly applies to Barbra Streisand, who might stand a chance of being nominated if she'd emigrate somewhere far away from Hollywood.

The Oscar Show

1. The script for the show must contain as many bad jokes and as much witless banter as possible. To obtain this result, it is advisable to keep bringing back Bruce Vilanch as one of the writers.

2. Young presenters should take pains to garble unusual names, especially the names of nominees from foreign countries. This means no one involved with the show should dare to correct them during the previous night's rehearsal.

3. Political comments by winners, hosts, and presenters are discouraged by the Academy, unless they are supportive of current U.S. government positions.

4. Although everyone in Hollywood wants to win an Academy Award, and the studios spend fortunes promoting their movies for Oscars, it would be vulgarian and antiegalitarian to refer to someone as a "winner," as in "And the winner is . . ." Instead these boringly hypocritical words must be used: "And the Oscar goes to . . ."

5. Both the Academy president and Motion Picture Association of America president Jack Valenti must be allowed to consume precious screen time to make pointless and clumsy speeches, while the winners of the Scientific and Technical Awards are relegated to a fast montage of clips from another evening's ceremony. This way the audience at home will never be educated about the industry's technical wizards.

6. Musical numbers on Oscar shows must be as ghastly as possible, with inappropriate singers, garish settings, and embarrassing choreography. Whenever possible, the person

who sang the nominated song in the film should not be allowed to sing it on the Oscar show. (See the following list.)

7. The best parts of the Oscar shows are the acceptance speeches, so they must be kept as short as possible, with the winners forced to rattle off their speeches at top speed while competing with play-off music by the pit orchestra. This way more time can be saved for those god-awful musical numbers.

8. Every winner of an honorary Oscar must be given a standing ovation, whether Hollywood really likes the SOB or not.

And the Oscar DOESN'T Go To
The 5 Most Excruciating Musical Numbers Ever Performed on Oscar Shows

1. *"Snow White"* (1989)   The mother of all bad musical numbers, producer Allan Carr's mind-boggling opening medley inspired a lawsuit from the Walt Disney Company for misappropriating the Snow White character. Eileen Bowman, as Snow White, giddily exchanged banter with official Oscar show greeter Army Archerd of *Daily Variety*, interacted with reluctant audience members in the auditorium, and sang "Proud Mary" with a mortified Rob Lowe. A nonstop parade of bad taste and unintentional hilarity, this supposed tribute to Hollywood tradition also included a re-creation of the Cocoanut Grove nightclub with (of all people) Merv Griffin singing "I've Got a Lovely Bunch of

Cocoanuts" to a venerable gathering including Roy Rogers and Dale Evans, Vincent Price, Dorothy Lamour, and Buddy Rogers. You'll never see this incredible number on television again, because the Academy had to promise Disney it would not reuse it—a promise the Academy probably would have made *without* the threat of legal action. (Note: If any film scholars want to study the "Snow White" number, I have it preserved on videotape.)

2. *"What's New, Pussycat?"* (1966)   Has television ever witnessed a more embarrassing display of sheer gaucherie and flop-sweat than the twenty-year-old Liza Minnelli desperately belting out this number? The fact that the song was performed with such panache by Tom Jones under the movie's opening credits only made Liza's rendition seem more awful by comparison.

3 & 4. *"Talk to the Animals"* and *"The Bare Necessities"* (1968)   A double dose of unconscious racial stereotyping was offered on this show (aired the day after the funeral of Martin Luther King Jr.) when Sammy Davis Jr. vamped it up to "Talk to the Animals" from *Doctor Dolittle* and Louis Armstrong cavorted with people-size Disney animal characters in "The Bare Necessities" from *The Jungle Book*. As Mason Wiley and Damien Bonda described the "Talk to the Animals" number in their hilarious book *The Real Oscar: The Unofficial History of the Academy Awards*, "Dressed in a Nehru jacket, beads, and high-heeled shoes, Davis tore into the song, punctuating it with the ad-libs 'Sock it to me, baby!' and 'Here come de judge, here come de judge!' "

5. *"There's No Business Like Show Business"* (1959) When cohost Jerry Lewis was informed by producer Jerry Wald that the show was finishing twenty minutes early, Lewis tried to fill the time by leading an array of embarrassed Hollywood stars in a seemingly interminable series of improvised comedy and musical routines. "My God, have we fallen to this?" Spencer Tracy asked later. NBC eventually pulled the plug and filled the remaining time with a short film about guns.

. . . And the 4 Best

1. *Stanley Donen accepting his honorary Oscar* (1998) The former hoofer who codirected *Singin' in the Rain* tap-danced with his Oscar while crooning Irving Berlin's "Cheek to Cheek." A sublime, magical moment.

2. *"It's Great Not To Be Nominated"* (1958) Kirk Douglas and Burt Lancaster showed dazzling panache as a pair of song-and-dance men performing this fondly remembered duet written by Sammy Cahn and Jimmy Van Heusen.

3 & 4. *Host Billy Crystal's satirical opening medleys* (1992 AND 1997) This tradition began in 1990 when Crystal asked the audience, in a pointed allusion to the previous year's "Snow White" debacle, "Where is that big, terrible number that usually opens the Oscars?" Crystal's wittiest tour-de-force routines have included the 1992 medley starting with him being wheeled out on a stretcher as a strait-jacketed Hannibal Lecter and the 1997 montage of the host appearing in film clips parodying nominated movies.

You Ain't Heard Nothin' Yet
Lists About Movie Genres

You Ain't Heard Nothin' Yet
10 Underrated Movie Musicals

Hallelujah (1929)   Many viewers have trouble seeing past this movie's antiquated portrayal of African Americans, which seems stereotypical and condescending by today's standards. But for its time, King Vidor's early MGM talkie was daring and innovative both thematically and technically. He liberated his cumbersome cameras by taking them on location in Tennessee to capture the authentic look and sound of Southern black culture.

Blonde Venus (1932)   This extravagant, almost surrealistic Josef von Sternberg movie is usually ridiculed as the least of his Marlene Dietrich cycle. But for those who can respond emotionally to his tortured take on mother love and romantic masochism, *Blonde Venus* offers an unceasing array of visual and aural astonishments, not least of which is the "Hot Voodoo" number in which nightclub chanteuse Dietrich strips down from a gorilla costume. The film's emotional ambience is captured in Dietrich's adoption of the cynical credo "Whether down to Gehenna or up to the throne, he travels fastest who travels alone."

Show Boat (1936)   Has there ever been a more astounding surfeit of riches in a musical than the passage in *Show Boat* in which three great numbers follow in succession: "Make Believe" (Irene Dunne, Allan Jones), "Ol' Man River" (Paul Robeson), and "Can't Help Lovin' Dat Man" (Helen Morgan, Hattie McDaniel, Robeson, and Dunne)? The rest of the movie is uneven, but James Whale's direction is replete with visual and dramatic frissons. This black-and-white version, which flopped on its original release by Universal and was missing from TV for many years, is easily the best of three films made from Edna Ferber's novel and the 1927 Jerome Kern–Oscar Hammerstein II stage musical, but it's been overshadowed by MGM's 1951 color version.

La Marseillaise (1938)   It may seem surprising to label this Jean Renoir movie a "musical," but Renoir's sweeping panorama of the French Revolution is constructed around the song that served as the people's political rallying cry and eventually became their national anthem. Throughout Renoir's masterful succession of vignettes depicting the convulsions on all levels of French society, we hear the song evolving until it is marched triumphantly by the people of Marseilles to the Parisian barricades. Those who claim music is apolitical by nature should watch *La Marseillaise*.

French Cancan (1955)   A good argument could be made that this, along with *Singin' in the Rain*, is one of the two best musicals ever made. On the most obvious level, *French Cancan* is simply a joyously choreographed, opulently colorful recreation of the birth of the cancan at Paris's celebrated Moulin Rouge nightclub in 1880 (and far more lyrical than John Huston's 1952 film *Moulin Rouge*). But Jean Renoir's meditation on performing and its effects on both participants and spectators is one of the cinema's most complex treatments of theatricality. Jean Gabin movingly plays the director's surrogate, the impresario Danglard, as a man obsessed with his art to the exclusion of all else.

Mary Poppins (1964)   Immensely popular, but not taken seriously by critics in its day, Disney's *Mary Poppins* is a highly sophisticated musical drama, with superb songs by Richard and Robert Sherman and a moving story line about parental neglect of children. Director Robert Stevenson's visual style marvelously blends fantasy and reality in this adaptation of P. L. Travers's book about an English nanny (Julie Andrews) who's "practically perfect in every way." No less a technical wizard than Stanley Kubrick watched *Mary Poppins* five times in its initial release.

At Long Last Love (1975)   Peter Bogdanovich's critically lambasted homage to Cole Porter whimsically cast two limited (to say the least) musical performers in the lead roles (Burt Reynolds and Cybill Shepherd), but this 1930s-set musical is cleverly constructed and visually graceful. Some charmingly virtuosic numbers involving supporting players Madeline Kahn, Duilio Del Prete, Eileen Brennan, and John Hillerman evoke memories of Ernst Lubitsch's *The Love Parade* (1929).

Pennies from Heaven (1981)   Actually far superior to the acclaimed British TV miniseries by Dennis Potter upon which it is based, Herbert Ross's film was rejected by movie audiences for its unrelenting grimness (including the audience with whom I saw it—at, appropriately enough, Milwaukee's Downer Theater). But there is profound emotion in the movie's ironic interplay between harrowing Depression-era reality and the pop songs intended to bring escape to ordinary people living lives of quiet desperation. *Pennies from Heaven* shows what Noël Coward meant when he wrote, "Extraordinary how potent cheap music is."

The Weavers: Wasn't That a Time! (1982)   This movie is only underrated in the sense that it isn't widely enough known—everyone who has seen it loves it. The pioneering folksinging group best known for their hit recording of Leadbelly's "Good Night, Irene"—Ronnie Gilbert, Lee Hays, Fred Hellerman, and Pete Seeger—were blacklisted in the 1950s because of their long-standing left-wing political views. While telling their story, Jim Brown's documentary chronicles the group's reunion for one last concert at New York's Carnegie Hall. Their radical idealism undimmed, their spirits unvanquished, their voices nearly as resonant as in their heyday, the Weavers had such a joyous time performing together again that this movie became a precious time capsule of American popular culture.

Everyone Says I Love You (1996)   Like *At Long Last Love*, Woody Allen's musical was an easy target for ridicule because of his commingling of nonsingers (including himself) with professionals, but *Everyone Says I Love You* is a dazzling postmodernist romp, perhaps most akin to Jean-Luc Godard's *Une Femme Est Une Femme* (1960). Both resurrecting and critically examining the much-maligned "burst-into-song" conventions of old musicals, *Everyone Says I Love You* includes one of the genre's most delirious fantasy sequences, in which music and dancing literally cause Goldie Hawn to become light on her feet.

The 25 Best Unexpected Musical Numbers in Movies

The Smiling Lieutenant (ERNST LUBITSCH, 1932)   Claudette Colbert sings "Jazz Up Your Lingerie" to Miriam Hopkins.

Bolero (WESLEY RUGGLES, 1934)   Carole Lombard and George Raft do a sexy dance together.

It Happened One Night (FRANK CAPRA, 1934)   Clark Gable, Claudette Colbert, and the other bus passengers sing "The Daring Young Man on the Flying Trapeze."

Ruggles of Red Gap (LEO MCCAREY, 1935)   Leila Hyams teaches Roland Young how to play drums.

Born To Dance (ROY DEL RUTH, 1936)   James Stewart sings "Easy to Love."

Modern Times (CHARLES CHAPLIN, 1936)   Chaplin finally breaks his silence by singing a nonsense song.

Suzy (GEORGE FITZMAURICE, 1936)   Cary Grant sings "Did I Remember?" to Jean Harlow.

La Grande Illusion (JEAN RENOIR, 1937)   The French prisoners (in drag) sing "La Marseillaise."

Idiot's Delight (CLARENCE BROWN, 1939)   Clark Gable sings and dances to "Puttin' on the Ritz."

Citizen Kane (ORSON WELLES, 1941)   Orson Welles and chorus girls dance as they and Charles Bennett sing "Charlie Kane."

Casablanca (MICHAEL CURTIZ, 1942)   Patrons at Rick's Café Americain sing "La Marseillaise" to drown out Nazis singing "Deutschland über Alles."

Thank Your Lucky Stars (DAVID BUTLER, 1943)   Bette Davis sings "They're Either Too Young or Too Old."

The Bells of St. Mary's (LEO MCCAREY, 1945)   Ingrid Bergman's Sister Mary Benedict sings a song about spring in Swedish to a captivated Father O'Malley (Bing Crosby).

Rio Grande (JOHN FORD, 1950)   Dick Foran sings "I'll Take You Home Again, Kathleen" to John Wayne and Maureen O'Hara.

The Quiet Man (JOHN FORD, 1952)   The men in Cohan's pub sing "The Wild Colonial Boy" to John Wayne; Ward Bond sings "The Humor Is On Me Now."

Rio Bravo (HOWARD HAWKS, 1959)   Ricky Nelson, Dean Martin, and Walter Brennan sing "Cindy."

Jules and Jim (FRANÇOIS TRUFFAUT, 1962)   Jeanne Moreau sings "Le Tourbillon."

Deliverance (JOHN BOORMAN, 1972)   Hoyt T. Pollard and Ronny Cox play "Dueling Banjos."

Blazing Saddles (MEL BROOKS, 1974)   Ordered by their foreman to "sing a nigger work song," Cleavon Little and other blacks on a chain gang respond with Cole Porter's "I Get a Kick Out of You."

Young Frankenstein (MEL BROOKS, 1974)   Dr. Frankenstein and his monster (Gene Wilder and Peter Boyle) sing and dance to "Puttin' on the Ritz."

Bound for Glory (HAL ASHBY, 1976)   Over the end credits, a medley of folksingers (including Woody Guthrie) sing Guthrie songs.

To Be or Not to Be (ALAN JOHNSON, 1983)   Anne Bancroft and Mel Brooks sing "Sweet Georgia Brown" in Polish.

Indiana Jones and the Temple of Doom (STEVEN SPIELBERG, 1984)   Kate Capshaw sings "Anything Goes" in Chinese.

Bob Roberts (TIM ROBBINS, 1992)   Woody Guthrie (in a previously unheard recording) sings "I Want to Know" over the end credits.

The Joshua Logan Memorial Award
For the 10 Worst Musicals Ever Made

High Society (CHARLES WALTERS, 1956)   This musical version of *The Philadelphia Story* has Cole Porter songs and a dream cast (Bing Crosby, Frank Sinatra, Grace Kelly, and Louis Armstrong), but the staging is so deadly dull that the director must have been comatose.

Invitation to the Dance (GENE KELLY, 1957)   Kelly's insufferably pretentious film telling three stories entirely through dance sat on the shelf at MGM for five years.

South Pacific (JOSHUA LOGAN, 1958) Using distracting color filters is only one of the many ways Logan finds to clumsily squander the beauty of this Rodgers and Hammerstein musical.

Girls! Girls! Girls! (NORMAN TAUROG, 1962) The Elvis Presley movie that made me stop going to Elvis movies includes "Song of the Shrimp" (and, to be fair, "Return to Sender").

Gypsy (MERVYN LEROY, 1962) One of the great works of the American musical theater is bungled through poor direction, inappropriate casting, and censorship restrictions.

Camelot (LOGAN, 1967) For one brief, shining moment this project looked promising as a movie. Then Joshua Logan was hired to direct it.

Paint Your Wagon (LOGAN, 1969) An unbelievably hammy and klutzy musical Western starring Lee Marvin and Clint Eastwood.

Man of La Mancha (ARTHUR HILLER, 1972) To quote *Leonard Maltin's Movie & Video Guide*, "Beautiful source material has been raped, murdered, and buried."

Lost Horizon (CHARLES JARROTT, 1973) Stupefyingly bad Burt Bacharach–Hal David musical version of the James Hilton fantasy features Liv Ullmann and John Gielgud (as Chang). Bette Midler used to regale her concert audiences by calling this movie *Lost Her Reason*, and declaring, "I never miss a Liv Ullmann musical."

Chatter-Box (TOM DESIMONE, 1977) Candice Rialson plays a young woman with a singing vagina.

The 10 Best Jazz Films

by Jonathan Rosenbaum

What follows is a personal list of neither the best films on jazz (e.g., *Jazz on a Summer's Day*) nor the best examples of jazz on film (such as the Fats Waller soundies or the 1981 *Johnny Griffin at the Village Vanguard*), but something more special and rarified: films in which the aesthetics of jazz and the aesthetics of film find some happy and mutually supportive meeting ground.

1. ***Black & Tan*** (DUDLEY MURPHY, 1929)   Remarkable not only as an experimental narrative by the (often uncredited) main author of *Ballet mécanique* and as a radical political statement about to whom jazz belongs, but also as a ravishing, poetic marriage between the music of Duke Ellington and the poetics of death and orgasm. Only twenty-one minutes long, but the aesthetics of jazz and film start here.

2. ***When It Rains*** (CHARLES BURNETT, 1995)   A twelve-minute miracle, and, alas, the only film on this list by a black filmmaker, this is a jazz parable about the discovery of common '60s roots via a John Handy album in contemporary L.A., with a wonderful offscreen commentary.

3. ***A Great Day in Harlem*** (JEAN BACH, 1994)   An hour-long documentary that offers a first-rate historical companion piece to the Burnett film, dissecting a 1958 group photograph of fifty-seven key jazz musicians,

durable both as oral history and as a capsule survey of the art.

4. *Thelonius Monk: Straight, No Chaser* (CHARLOTTE ZWERIN, 1988)   Sizzling music, in-depth portraiture.

5. *Bird* (CLINT EASTWOOD, 1988)   For all the legitimate quibbles that must be made—about substituting new accompanists, short-shrifting the issues of racism, and muddling certain musical and biographical facts—the man and his music almost get the canvas they deserve.

6. *Jammin' the Blues* (GJON MILI, 1950)   James Agee was right to call it arty, and as a documentary it's dated, but Lester Young achieves his apotheosis, on camera and in chiaroscuro.

7. *'Round Midnight* (BERTRAND TAVERNIER, 1986)   Though the music is never as good as it should be and sentimentality eventually takes over, Dexter Gordon's performance, Alexandre Trauner's sets, and the sheer love of the music prevail.

8. *To Have and Have Not* (HOWARD HAWKS, 1944)   Not because the jazz is especially distinctive, but because Hawks gives it a dramatic function in the interplay between characters that periodically makes the music and the story interchangeable.

9. *The Long Goodbye* (ROBERT ALTMAN, 1973)   What Hawks does for connection, Altman does for disconnection, with a comparable improvisational spirit and sense of play.

10. A tie between two flawed but fragrant blossoms of the '60s: Shirley Clarke's 1962 *The Connection* (even if it misconstrues the greatness of the original Living Theatre stage production, and mainly for Freddie Redd and Jackie McLean) and Thomas Reichman's 1968 *Mingus* (an incomplete portrait of a genius near the height of his powers).

BACK STAGE

JONATHAN ROSENBAUM is the film critic of *The Chicago Reader*. He is the author of *Moving Places, Placing Movies* and *Movies as Politics*; editor of *This Is Orson Welles* by Welles and Peter Bogdanovich; and a member of the New York Film Festival selection committee.

Jonathan Lethem's Favorite Science Fiction Movies

(in alphabetical order, and with annotations, disclaimers, and cheats)

First, the disclaimer. These are in no way the most *important* SF movies—such a list would have to include movies I admire from a chilly distance, such as *Metropolis*, others I really don't like at all, such as *E.T.*, and one that obsessed me at age thirteen and now makes me confused and glum—*Star Wars*. Instead these are the films that stir me, excite me, provide me with those thrilling epiphanies of disjunction, paradox, and alienation that I seek from both written *and* filmed SF. To give an example, I prefer mostly dreadful movies that provide even a handful of such moments—think *Zardoz*, or *Total Recall*, or *Dune*—to solid mediocrities such as *Outland*, *Silent Running*, or *Soylent Green*.

Thus:

Alphaville (JEAN-LUC GODARD, 1965)   I first saw *Alphaville* when I was fifteen, and I'm not objective about it at all. A ballad of love struggling to survive in a technological dystopia—for me the film equivalent of Orwell's *1984*, but funnier and more universal.

Blade Runner (RIDLEY SCOTT, 1982)   I mean the version without the mood-killing voice-over and the dumb happy ending, of course. Like only a handful of other films in my experience (*King of Comedy* and *Magnificent Ambersons* come to mind), it grows every time I see it. I'm always struck by how many different people—from Harrison Ford and Ridley Scott down to Rutger Hauer, Daryl Hannah, Sean Young, and Vangelis—seem to have achieved their career peaks, creatively, in the very same film. Sort of like the 1990 Cincinnati Reds, I guess.

Brazil (TERRY GILLIAM, 1985)   The first time I saw *Brazil*, I was disappointed. I don't know why, unless it was months of hype proclaiming it a brilliantly inventive, mordant, and funny dystopian movie, practically tailored for my taste. I focused on a couple of fantasy sequences featuring metallic wings that I didn't like, and Jonathan Pryce, who seemed miscast—too fussy and bureaucratic, not really Everyman enough, or adequately charming. (Imagine Peter Sellers, or Buster Keaton, or a young Dustin Hoffman even.) Then I saw it a second time, and ever since it's seemed brilliantly inventive, mordant, and funny—practically tailored for my taste.

Dark Star (JOHN CARPENTER, 1974)   Most people remember this for the pratfalls and drug jokes, but the film sets a solipsistic mood that's poignant, evocative, and strange, and is loaded with conceptually striking set pieces. Here's where space travel first got grunged up, well before *Star Wars* and *Alien*—unless you count Tarkovsky's refutation of the antiseptic *2001* (see *Solaris*, next page).

The Day the Earth Stood Still (ROBERT WISE, 1951) I've always thought *Day* uniquely captures the cerebral, portentous flavor of classic written SF from the '30s and '40s.

Forbidden Planet (FRED MCLEOD WILCOX, 1956)   What a conflagration of pleasures is *Forbidden Planet*. Leslie Nielsen, Robby the Robot, Walter Pidgeon, watered-down Shakespeare and bastardized Freud, all in the same movie. The direction is undistinguished, but the movie is chock-full of '50s production values anyway. From the amiable-but-square crew visiting the styrofoam-rock-planet-with-breathable-air to the lordly and mysterious Dr. Morbius (Pidgeon) and his scantily clad daughter (Anne Francis), this is really the link between the serials and *Star Trek*— some kind of golden mean of domesticated SF. And like the few good episodes of the original *Star Trek*, it can somehow be enjoyed for sincere and camp values simultaneously.

Invasion of the Body Snatchers (Don Siegel, 1956)/*The Incredible Shrinking Man* (Jack Arnold, 1957) These films go together for me as perfect distillations of the dark side of the '50s psyche—the Cold War and the incipient social revolutions of the '60s combining to inspire all-time highs in solipsism, paranoia, and male fear of shrinkage and engulfment. Pointing the way to *The Twilight Zone*, both are marked by their restraint, their suggestiveness, their open-ended poetry.

The Man Who Fell to Earth (Nicolas Roeg, 1976) Roeg mostly seems precious or overblown elsewhere, but this is a perfect match of style to subject. Perpetually underrated film—if it had been the director's only work it would seem classic. He should have done more SF.

Solaris/Stalker (Andrei Tarkovsky, 1972/1979) Tarkovsky's glacial, hypnotizing slowness divides the world into two camps, so I won't be losing anyone I haven't already lost by saying you need to be sure you see the *long* version of *Solaris*. *Stalker* is the greater film, but for me they both rival *2001*, and Tarkovsky rivals Kubrick as SF's greatest director. Surrender to these films for one of the great experiences in cinema. Just bring a snack.

The Terminator (James Cameron, 1984)/*Alien* (Ridley Scott, 1979) Another pair of twins. Wonderful, tightly constructed genre entertainments, each followed by vastly inferior sequels. And together these movies ruined the high-budget end of the genre for at least fifteen years. *Terminator* showed studios how to make gun movies in SF drag, and *Alien* showed them how to make monster movies in SF drag, and that's all they've done since. It's so much easier to make gun and monster movies. *Alien* is classier, richer, more dimensional—I love it as much for the death scene of Ian Holm's android character as for anything to do with the alien—but *Terminator*, more like a B picture, is simply one of the most undeniably thrilling movies I've seen.

Incidentally, Ian Holm is also in *Brazil*—the only performer with an interesting part in more than one of the movies on my list. He's also in *Time Bandits*, *Naked Lunch*, *Dreamchild*, *Kafka*, and *The Fifth Element*. What does this mean? Nothing.

The Thing from Another World (CHRISTIAN NYBY, BUT REALLY HOWARD HAWKS, 1951)   I was reading about the production history of *The Thing* recently and was struck by the fact that making science fiction or horror films was so déclassé in '50s Hollywood that even a director like Hawks, with a reputation as a maverick jack-of-all-genres, was made to feel bad about it. Then it struck me that nobody ever seems to take this into consideration in the controversy over attribution for the film. Why is it always assumed that Hawks threw his editor Christian Nyby the credit as an act of generosity? Couldn't it as easily have been Hawks's diffidence about the genre?

Certainly Hawks is the most important director between Lang and Kubrick to work in the field, however diffidently. And, paradoxically, the film is second-rank Hawks but top-drawer horror/SF.

2001: A Space Odyssey (STANLEY KUBRICK, 1968) When I was thirteen, I saw *Star Wars* twenty-one times in one summer. A few years later, at maybe fifteen or sixteen, I decided my obsession with *2001* was much cooler and worked to make Kubrick's film my answer to the question, "Which film have you seen the most times?" There was one day when I went alone to the Thalia on West 95th Street and watched it three times in succession, murmuring observations to my friend Eliot into a tape recorder throughout. During the third showing, I was discovered by two delighted hippies who promptly named me The Movie Kid.

Videodrome (DAVID CRONENBERG, 1983) Nowadays Cronenberg makes movies that coolly examine obsession, while he and his audience stand dispassionately to one side. But in his best earlier work, Cronenberg made films that *embodied* obsession, *were* obsessive, took you deep inside. Adaptations of actual Philip K. Dick novels notwithstanding, *Videodrome* is the closest cinematic equivalent to the disruptive experience of reading one of Dick's novels.

Finally, on another morning any of the following could have made the list: *A Clockwork Orange*, *RoboCop*, *Android*, THX 1138, *The City of Lost Children*, *The War of the Worlds*, *Sleeper*, *Phase IV*, *The Fly* (Cronenberg), *Quintet*.

JONATHAN LETHEM is author of the novels *Girl in Landscape*; *As She Climbed Across the Table*; *Amnesia Moon*; and *Gun, with Occasional Music*; and a collection of stories, *The Wall of the Sky, the Wall of the Eye*. He recently was listed as one of *Newsweek*'s "100 People for the New Century." He lives in Brooklyn, New York.

The 17 Most Memorable Movie Kisses

The Kiss (EDISON MANUFACTURING CO., 1896) Reenacting a scene from the stage farce *Widow Jones*, May Irwin and John Rice exchange kisses for the camera. Modern audiences may not find these two mature performers particularly sexy, but their brief love scene was the first of its kind in movies, and it scandalized audiences of its day. One of the first recorded pieces of film criticism was a review in the British publication *Chap Book* calling this movie "absolutely disgusting."

Flesh and the Devil (CLARENCE BROWN, 1927) Greta Garbo and John Gilbert fell in love while making this movie, and that's abundantly clear during their incandescent love scenes, ravishingly photographed by William Daniels. Daniels lit the big kiss with a tiny lamp held (as a flame) in Gilbert's palms. Two years later, Garbo made a movie entitled simply *The Kiss*, but it didn't attempt to rival the sexiness of *Flesh and the Devil*.

Gone with the Wind (VICTOR FLEMING, 1939) Never did a sky offer a more lurid romantic backdrop than when Clark Gable planted his lips so indelibly on Vivien Leigh's in *Gone with the Wind*. Silhouetted against a fiery orange studio sky, Gable's Rhett Butler holds Scarlett O'Hara's head in his hands as he murmurs with fierce tenderness, "Kiss me, Scarlett, kiss me . . . once . . ."

Regis Toomey and Jane Wyman in *You're in the Army Now* (LEWIS SEILER, 1941) Theirs is the longest kiss in screen history—three minutes and five seconds. But viewers may well prefer other kisses on this list, because (to quote the old cigarette commercial), "It's not how long you make it, it's how you make it long."

Lauren Bacall and Humphrey Bogart in *To Have and Have Not* (HOWARD HAWKS, 1944)   Perhaps stunned by his good fortune, Bogart remains virtually impassive when the sultry young Bacall comes over and plants a kiss on his lips, telling him, "It's even better when you help." But at the end of the scene, he does follow her advice to "just whistle. You know how to whistle, don't you, Steve? You just put your lips together and blow."

Notorious (ALFRED HITCHCOCK, 1946)   Before he breaks the bad news about her espionage assignment, Cary Grant and Ingrid Bergman are inseparable as they kiss in their Rio de Janeiro "love nest."

The Quiet Man (JOHN FORD, 1952)   Returning to his boyhood home on a stormy Irish night, John Wayne boldly pulls Maureen O'Hara to him and kisses her in the doorway. Then, as the camera moves in, she slaps him, demonstrating her Irish sexual ambivalence. (Steven Spielberg quoted from this shot in *E.T.*, when Henry Thomas kisses the adolescent Erika Eleniak.) The long take of Wayne kissing O'Hara in a graveyard during a rainstorm is, if anything, even sexier than the couple's first kiss.

From Here to Eternity (FRED ZINNEMANN, 1953) Deborah Kerr and Burt Lancaster's torrid embrace on the beach has been much quoted, much imitated.

To Catch a Thief (ALFRED HITCHCOCK, 1955) Although it's become the ultimate romantic cliché in movies, the fireworks exploding behind Cary Grant and Grace Kelly in the final scene still carry a potent erotic charge.

Pillow Talk (MICHAEL GORDON, 1959) As a seduction ploy, Rock Hudson teases Doris Day with the notion that he might be gay. When she finally challenges him to show whether he's interested in her romantically, his kiss knocks her socks off. The offscreen ironies, known to relatively few people at the time, now enhance the electricity of this enjoyable, much-maligned romantic comedy.

Some Like It Hot (BILLY WILDER, 1959) Tony Curtis pretends to be impotent in order to induce Marilyn Monroe to arouse him. And, boy, does she try. Although anyone watching this scene would find it hard to comprehend his displeasure, Curtis later made the famous comment that kissing Monroe was "like kissing Hitler."

Jules and Jim (FRANÇOIS TRUFFAUT, 1962) Jim (Henri Serre) returns from World War I to be reunited with Catherine (Jeanne Moreau). During a discreetly elliptical series of dissolving images of Moreau in bed, the narrator tells us—in one of the screen's most memorable romantic lines—"Their first kiss lasted all night."

Kiss (ANDY WARHOL, 1963) This fifty-minute picture deserves inclusion because of its single-mindedness—it consists entirely of Naomi Levine kissing three men: Rufus Collins, Gerald Malanga, and Ed Saunders.

Devil in Miss Jones (GERARD DAMIANO, 1973) The tongue-kissing (etc.) love scene between Georgina Spelvin and a snake is just one of several boundary-crossing sexual scenes in *Devil in Miss Jones*. A unique porno film featuring a genuinely powerful, three-dimensional performance, *Miss Jones* casts Spelvin as a middle-aged virgin who commits suicide and then is given one last chance for carnal pleasure before being returned to a sexless eternity in Hell. *Variety* reviewer Addison Verrill aptly observed that "her performance is so naked it seems a massive invasion of privacy."

Annie Hall (WOODY ALLEN, 1976) Walking to the deli on their first date, Woody Allen asks Diane Keaton to give him a kiss so they won't have to worry about it all through dinner and will be able to digest their food properly. In its off-hand way, this charming vignette is as romantic as any passionate movie clinch.

Catherine Deneuve and Susan Sarandon in *The Hunger* (TONY SCOTT, 1983) Seldom have two major stars of the same gender performed such an explicit love scene as these gorgeous women did in the vampire movie *The Hunger*.

Kevin Kline and Tom Selleck in *In & Out* (FRANK OZ, 1997) Demonstrating that same-sex kissing between men is no longer as shocking as it once would have seemed, *In & Out* has fun with this scene of Selleck's TV reporter surprising Kline's outed bisexual with a vigorous kiss. Selleck, a prominent Hollywood Republican, received points from critics and audiences for proving he was more hip than previously believed.

"Well, nobody's perfect"
The Screen's 10 Most Unlikely Romantic Couples

Katharine Hepburn and Bob Hope in *The Iron Petticoat* (RALPH THOMAS, 1956) One of the least-seen of Hepburn's movies, this *Ninotchka* knockoff suffered from a dearth (to put it mildly) of romantic chemistry. (See "Vy you are smilink?: Strange Ethnic Castings.")

Jack Lemmon and Joe E. Brown in *Some Like It Hot* (BILLY WILDER, 1959)   "Oh, you don't understand, Osgood. I'm a man!" "Well, nobody's perfect."

Richard Burton and Rex Harrison in *Staircase* (STANLEY DONEN, 1969)   It took some courage for two of the screen's great Lotharios to play a gay couple, but the audience didn't respond in kind.

Bud Cort and Ruth Gordon in *Harold and Maude* (HAL ASHBY, 1971)   An aghast U.S. Army psychiatrist in the movie tells Harold that it's normal for a boy to want to sleep with his mother but very abnormal to want to sleep with his grandmother.

Timothy Bottoms and Cloris Leachman in *The Last Picture Show* (PETER BOGDANOVICH, 1971)   One of the most poignant screen pairings of an older woman with a younger man.

Gene Wilder and the sheep in *Everything You Always Wanted to Know About Sex (But Were Afraid to Ask)* (WOODY ALLEN, 1972)   In the segment of this comedy sketch anthology entitled "What Is Bestiality?" Wilder's character tells his four-legged inamorata how wonderful it is that they found each other, "You, a girl from Armenia, and me, a boy from Jackson Heights."

Julie Christie and the computer in *Demon Seed* (DONALD CAMMELL, 1977)   This movie was jokingly referred to in Hollywood as *Semen Deed*.

Dustin Hoffman and Charles Durning in **Tootsie** (SYDNEY POLLACK, 1982) Perhaps inspired by Lemmon and Brown, Hoffman's cross-dresser and Durning's older man didn't seem entirely an implausible couple.

Luciano Pavarotti and Kathryn Harrold in **Yes, Giorgio** (FRANKLIN J. SCHAFFNER, 1982) The mind boggles at the image of a carnal pairing between the hefty opera singer and the svelte, sexy Harrold, playing his throat specialist. Although not without its quirky charms, the movie found no audience.

Stephen Rea and Jaye Davidson in **The Crying Game** (NEIL JORDAN, 1992) When the much-vaunted Big Secret of this movie is revealed—Davidson's character is actually a man in drag—Rea's IRA man isn't terribly fazed. Neil Jordan's *The Crying Game* shows that a subject once suited only for comedy can now be taken seriously. (However, this situation was spoofed when Sean Young dropped her shorts in the 1994 Jim Carrey comedy *Ace Ventura, Pet Detective*.)

Girl Friends
Female Buddy-Buddy Movies

Although the film industry has churned out male buddy-buddy movies ad nauseam, even stepping up its output during the 1970s in a backlash against the feminist movement, occasionally there have been some refreshing movies celebrating and exploring female friendship.

These Three (WILLIAM WYLER, 1936) with Miriam Hopkins and Merle Oberon, and its remake, **The Children's Hour**

(WYLER, 1962), with Audrey Hepburn and Shirley MacLaine (See " 'Include Me Out': The 12 Greatest Goldwynisms")

Old Acquaintance (VINCENT SHERMAN, 1943) with Bette Davis and Miriam Hopkins; and the 1981 remake, *Rich and Famous* (GEORGE CUKOR), with Jacqueline Bisset and Candice Bergen

Our Hearts Were Young and Gay (LEWIS ALLEN, 1944) with Gail Russell and Diana Lynn; and the 1946 sequel, *Our Hearts Were Growing Up* (WILLIAM D. RUSSELL)

Gentlemen Prefer Blondes (HOWARD HAWKS, 1953) with Marilyn Monroe and Jane Russell

How to Marry a Millionaire (JEAN NEGULESCO, 1953) with Marilyn Monroe, Lauren Bacall, and Betty Grable

Céline and Julie Go Boating (JACQUES RIVETTE, 1974) with Juliet Berto and Dominique Labourier

Julia (FRED ZINNEMANN, 1977) with Jane Fonda and Vanessa Redgrave

The Turning Point (HERBERT ROSS, 1977) with Shirley MacLaine and Anne Bancroft

Rock 'n' Roll High School (ALLAN ARKUSH, 1979) with P. J. Soles and Dey Young (See "Gabba Gabba Hey: *Rock 'n' Roll High School* Trivia")

Personal Best (ROBERT TOWNE, 1982) with Mariel Hemingway and Patrice Donnelly

The Witches of Eastwick (GEORGE MILLER, 1987) with Cher, Michelle Pfeiffer, and Susan Sarandon

Thelma & Louise (RIDLEY SCOTT, 1991) with Susan Sarandon and Geena Davis

Waiting to Exhale (FOREST WHITAKER, 1995) with Whitney Houston, Angela Bassett, Loretta Devine, and Lela Rochon

The First Wives Club (HUGH WILSON, 1996) with Bette Midler, Goldie Hawn, and Diane Keaton

Career Girls (MIKE LEIGH, 1997) with Katrin Cartlidge and Lynda Steadman

Love Is a Many Splendored Thing
20 Interracial Romances in Movies

Although society today is far more accepting of miscegenation than it once was, movies about the subject still are relatively rare and highly variable in quality.

Broken Blossoms (D. W. GRIFFITH, 1919) Lillian Gish and Richard Barthelmess (as a Chinese)

The Bitter Tea of General Yen (FRANK CAPRA, 1933) Barbara Stanwyck and Nils Asther (as the Chinese general)

Pinky (ELIA KAZAN, 1949) Jeanne Crain (as an African American passing for white) and William Lundigan

Japanese War Bride (KING VIDOR, 1952) Don Taylor and Shirley Yamaguchi

Love Is a Many Splendored Thing (HENRY KING, 1955) William Holden and Jennifer Jones (as a Eurasian)

The Crimson Kimono (Samuel Fuller, 1959)   Victoria Shaw and James Shigeta

Shadows (John Cassavetes, 1959)   Lelia Goldoni (as a light-skinned African American) and Anthony Ray

All Night Long (Basil Dearden, 1961)   Paul Harris and Marti Stevens as characters modeled after Shakespeare's Othello and Desdemona

A Patch of Blue (Guy Green, 1965)   Sidney Poitier and Elizabeth Hartman

Guess Who's Coming to Dinner (Stanley Kramer, 1967) Sidney Poitier and Katharine Houghton

Joanna (Michael Sarne, 1968)   Genevieve Waite and Calvin Lockhart

Ali—Fear Eats the Soul (Rainer Werner Fassbinder, 1974) Brigitte Mira and Eli Hedi Ben Salem

Jungle Fever (Spike Lee, 1991)   Wesley Snipes and Annabella Sciorra

The Bodyguard (Mick Jackson, 1992)   Kevin Costner and Whitney Houston

Love Field (Jonathan Kaplan, 1992)   Michelle Pfeiffer and Dennis Haysbert

Mississippi Masala (Mira Nair, 1992)   Denzel Washington and Sarita Choudhury

Othello (Oliver Parker, 1995)   Laurence Fishburne and Irène Jacob

Heaven & Earth (OLIVER STONE, 1993)   Tommy Lee Jones and Hiep Thi Le

Pocahontas (MIKE GABRIEL, ERIC GOLDBERG, 1995)   Disney animated movie about the romance between the Native American woman Pocahontas and British Captain John Smith (the voice of Pocahontas is supplied by Irene Bedard and singer Judy Kuhn; Mel Gibson is the voice of Captain Smith)

One Night Stand (MIKE FIGGIS, 1997)   Wesley Snipes with Nastassja Kinski and Ming-Na Wen

The Marrying Kind
Movies About Happy Marriages

From *The Private Life of Henry VIII* and *Gone with the Wind* through *Scenes from a Marriage*, *Bob & Carol & Ted & Alice*, *Husbands and Wives*, and *The Ice Storm*, there have been innumerable movies about troubled marriages, but relatively few good ones about happy marriages. Perhaps filmmakers are heeding the wisdom of Tolstoy's famous observation in *Anna Karenina*, "Happy families are all alike; every unhappy family is unhappy in its own way." But when a good marriage (or gay partnership, as in *La Cage aux Folles*) is plausibly portrayed on-screen, the results can be enchanting. I'm not referring to the bland and uninteresting representations of marriage common in Hollywood's Golden Age, but rather to movies that reflect the myriad tensions present in any marriage, yet still manage to show how, with some diplomatic accommodations, a couple can live together in mutually enriching harmony.

Private Lives (SIDNEY FRANKLIN, 1931)   This is essentially a filmed play, but what a play! Noël Coward's sparkling farce about a divorced couple who show up at a hotel with silly new partners and fall in love all over again is the epitome of *soigné* badinage, but with deeper emotions always present between the lines. As Coward once observed of his own work, *Private Lives* is "only superficially superficial." Robert Montgomery and Norma Shearer brought a deft mixture of lightness and underlying gravitas to this early talkie.

The Thin Man series   In six delightful movies, from *The Thin Man* (1934) through *Song of the Thin Man* (1947), William Powell and Myrna Loy sparkle as Nick and Nora Charles, the wealthy, bibulous couple who engage in detective work as an amusing avocation. The best thing about their work is that they can enjoy it together (along with their dog, Asta), trading sexy repartee and endearments.

The Awful Truth (LEO MCCAREY, 1937)   One of the most influential of all romantic comedies, *The Awful Truth* is the never-equaled prototype for the oft-used plot about an estranged couple coming to realize they're far more miserable apart than together. (This was actually the third screen version of the 1921 play by Arthur Richman, and there would be another, the 1953 musical *Let's Do It Again*, but McCarey's version, adapted by Viña Delmar, is the memorable one.) Underneath McCarey's slapstick antics was a strongly Catholic view of the sanctity of marriage, but the message goes down easily when it's carried by Cary Grant and Irene Dunne. The highlights include a courtroom hearing over custody rights to the couple's dog, Mr. Smith (played by Asta from *The Thin Man*), and Dunne's hilarious impersonation of Grant's airheaded Southern girlfriend.

Heaven Can Wait (ERNST LUBITSCH, 1943)   Despite his rakish habits, wealthy playboy Henry Van Cleve (Don Ameche) still manages to hold on to the most important treasure in his life, his wife Martha (Gene Tierney). This ravishing Technicolor romance, both nostalgic and brashly comedic, chronicles the ups and downs and the ultimate success of their long-enduring marriage. Shortly before his death in 1947, Lubitsch had this to say to his future biographer Herman G. Weinberg about *Heaven Can Wait*: "I consider it one of my major productions, because I tried to break away in several respects from the established moving picture formula. I encountered partly great resistance before I made this picture because it had no message and made no point whatsoever. The hero was a man only interested in good living with no aim of accomplishing anything, or of doing anything noble. . . . Besides, I showed the happy marriage in a truer light than it is usually done in moving pictures where a happy marriage is only too often portrayed as a very dull and unexciting by-the-fireplace affair."

The Best Years of Our Lives (WILLIAM WYLER, 1946) Myrna Loy became known as Hollywood's "perfect wife" because of her *Thin Man* series and dramatic roles like this one, in which she plays the loyal spouse of returning World War II serviceman Fredric March. The unusual depth of emotion the film brings to the awkward rekindling of their relationship is partly due to the fact that Wyler based it on his own long and happy marriage to former actress Margaret (Talli) Tallichet.

Adam's Rib (GEORGE CUKOR, 1949) Spencer Tracy and Katharine Hepburn spar off as opposing attorneys in a divorce case involving Judy Holliday. The brilliant screenplay by the married writing team of Ruth Gordon and Garson Kanin finds a refreshing balance by being both strongly feminist—Hepburn educates the still somewhat chauvinistic Tracy about women's rights—and staunchly in favor of the institution of marriage. A subsequent Tracy-Hepburn movie by the same writers and director, *Pat and Mike* (1952), also was a winning and positive portrait of a loving partnership, this one between two strongly opposite characters, a dese-and-dose sports manager and his classy star athlete, whose chemistry enables them to leap over any hurdle.

Cheaper by the Dozen (WALTER LANG, 1950) Clifton Webb and Myrna Loy raise twelve children. One of the most enjoyable family movies ever made, *Cheaper by the Dozen* was based on the popular memoir by Frank B. Gilbreth Jr. and Ernestine Gilbreth Carey. The comedy comes from an efficiency expert's attempt to run his large household by scientific principles, while his psychologist wife actually runs the show. The warmth comes from the family's cohesion despite the obvious danger of claustrophobia. By the time of the sequel, *Belles on Their Toes* (Henry Levin, 1952), Mrs. Gilbreth had been widowed and had to raise her children by her own independent devices.

The Marrying Kind (CUKOR, 1952) Sometimes, as was true with the novelist E. M. Forster, a gay artist can show far more understanding and empathy for the dynamics of heterosexual marriage than can most heterosexual artists. Another superb film on the subject by gay director George Cukor, *The Mar-*

rying Kind also was written by Gordon and Kanin. This bittersweet film deals movingly but unsentimentally with the troubles (including the death of a child) undergone by an ordinary young couple (Judy Holliday and Aldo Ray) in their precarious early years of marriage.

A Star Is Born (CUKOR, 1954)   Perhaps it's a bit of a stretch to include this tragic love story (the best of several versions of a classic Hollywood tale) in a list of movies about happy marriages, but there is so much that is joyous and mutually liberating about the union of actor Norman Maine (James Mason) and singer Esther Blodgett (Judy Garland). Before Maine's alcoholism destroys his career, it seems as if his love for Esther and his support for her rising career is what he needs to finally pull him through. Their bond endures beyond death in her famous ending line, "This is Mrs. Norman Maine."

La Cage aux Folles (EDOUARD MOLINARO, 1978)   The humor largely plays off gender stereotypes in this uproarious French comedy about a gay couple played by Ugo Tognazzi and Michel Serrault, with Serrault as the "feminine" half of the couple. The happily settled partners unfortunately have to disguise their true sexual inclinations to fool the visiting parents of Tognazzi's son's fiancée. Though the concept is somewhat retro, it was so jolly in execution that both straight and gay viewers throughout the world flocked to the movie. *La Cage aux Folles* spawned two sequels plus a mildly entertaining 1996 American remake, *The Birdcage*, directed by Mike Nichols and starring Robin Williams and Nathan Lane.

Family Values
My 14 Favorite Movies About Families

1. *The Magnificent Ambersons* (ORSON WELLES, 1942)   See "Flyover Movies: 13 Ways of Looking at the Midwest."

2. *Tokyo Story* (YASUJIRO OZU, 1953)   Near the end of this classic about an elderly Japanese couple (Chishu Ryu and Chieko Higashiyama) emotionally neglected by their children, a young girl asks the family's compassionate daughter-in-law (Setsuko Hara), "Isn't life disappointing?" She replies with a serenely accepting smile, "Yes. It is."

3. *Make Way for Tomorrow* (LEO MCCAREY, 1937)   *Tokyo Story* was directly influenced by this heartbreaking story of an old couple (Beulah Bondi and Victor Moore) forced to separate because of their children's ingratitude. The film is prefaced with a title reading simply, "Honor Thy Father and Thy Mother."

4. *The Godfather Part II* (FRANCIS FORD COPPOLA, 1974)   The movie that asks the question (in Italian), "When Pop had troubles, did he ever think that maybe by trying to be strong, and trying to protect his family, that he could lose it instead?"

5. *How Green Was My Valley* (JOHN FORD, 1941)   Huw (Roddy McDowall) draws lines across a map of the world showing where his older brothers and sister have scattered, telling his mother (Sara Allgood), "And you are the star shining on them from this house, all the way across the continents and the oceans."

6. *Psycho* (ALFRED HITCHCOCK, 1960) As Norman Bates (Anthony Perkins) succinctly puts it, "A boy's best friend is his mother." (See "Moviemakers' Favorite Lunatic: Ed Gein on Film.")

7. *Late Spring* (OZU, 1949) The pain of a child's departure from home has never been more deeply felt on-screen than in *Late Spring*. An aging father (Chishu Ryu) forces his devoted, spinsterish daughter (Setsuko Hara) to marry. Although he thinks he is doing so for her own good, his decision leaves them both emotionally devastated.

8. *The Grapes of Wrath* (FORD, 1940) While many viewers fondly remember Twentieth Century–Fox studio chief Darryl F. Zanuck's forced ending of Ma Joad (Jane Darwell) expressing indomitable optimism ("We're the people"), Ford's emphasis, simultaneously angry and elegiac, was on the inexorable breakup of the Joads after they are forced off their land. Ford compared their plight to that of his Irish forebears during the famine of the nineteenth century.

9. *Long Day's Journey into Night* (SIDNEY LUMET, 1962) Eugene O'Neill's monumental tragedy about an Irish family destroyed by avarice, drug addiction, and tuberculosis was brought to the screen with all its raw emotional power.

10. *I Remember Mama* (GEORGE STEVENS, 1948) Starring Irene Dunne and looking back with nostalgia to the director's own boyhood in San Francisco, this is a heartfelt tribute to the immigrant women who held their families together in America. (I haven't seen the horror-movie takeoff called *I Dismember Mama*.)

11. ***Mommie Dearest*** (FRANK PERRY, 1981) After Joan Crawford (Faye Dunaway) goes on one of her rampages, there's a fantastic moment when her young adopted daughter, Christina (Mara Hobel), is shown in close-up murmuring with precocious self-possession, "JE . . . sus *Christ*!"

12. ***Meet Me in St. Louis*** (VINCENTE MINNELLI, 1944) If (to quote Tolstoy) "Happy families are all alike," then this glorious Technicolor musical from MGM is the cinematic archetype of an essentially happy family.

13. ***The Texas Chain Saw Massacre*** (TOBE HOOPER, 1974) Contemporary psychology believes in treating the entire family's problems, not just their manifestation in one troubled individual. The collective psychosis of this Texas clan is an extreme case in point. (Also see "Moviemakers' Favorite Lunatic: Ed Gein on Film.")

14. ***Helter Skelter*** (TOM GRIES, 1976 TV MOVIE) Once America had Andy Hardy and *Father Knows Best*, but by the late 1960s we had the Manson Family. Orson Welles had an even more chilling ending in mind for this saga. He told me that if he had directed a film about Charles Manson, he would not have shown the killings. Instead he would have shown Sharon Tate and her friends casually sitting in the house when the patio doors suddenly fly open to reveal the murderers—with a quick fade to black. Just *typing* these words gives me the creeps.

Make Way for Tomorrow
The 15 Best Movies About Old Age

"Old age is a shipwreck."
> —Charles de Gaulle, quoted by Orson Welles on the last night of his life

1. *Tokyo Story* (YASUJIRO OZU, 1953) See previous list.

2. *Make Way for Tomorrow* (LEO MCCAREY, 1937) See previous list.

3. *Chimes at Midnight* (ORSON WELLES, 1966) The aging Sir John Falstaff (Welles) is banished by his former boon companion when Prince Hal (Keith Baxter) is crowned King Henry V.

4. *Ikiru* (AKIRA KUROSAWA, 1952) In the cinema's closest equivalent to Tolstoy's *The Death of Ivan Ilych*, a bureaucrat (Takashi Shimura) tries to make sense of his life as he dies of cancer.

5. *Late Spring* (OZU, 1949) See previous list.

6. *Lady for a Day* (FRANK CAPRA, 1933) To maintain the fiction she has created for the sake of her daughter, an old Broadway beggar (May Robson) is transformed into a society lady by her gangster cronies.

7. *El Dorado* (HOWARD HAWKS, 1967) An aging gunfighter (John Wayne), crippled by a bullet lodged against his spine, comes to the aid of a sheriff friend (Robert Mitchum) in a range war.

8. *Umberto D* (VITTORIO DE SICA, 1952)   A Roman pensioner (Carlo Battisti) living alone with his dog is faced with the threat of homelessness.

9. *Going My Way* (MCCAREY, 1944)   A doddering old priest (Barry Fitzgerald) is gently eased out of his pastorship by his young curate (Bing Crosby).

10. *The Grapes of Wrath* (JOHN FORD, 1940)   On the road to California, dispossessed tenant farmer Grandpa William James Joad (Charley Grapewin) dies clasping a handful of dirt, and Pa Joad (Russell Simpson) loses his traditional role as Ma (Jane Darwell) holds the family together.

11. *The Shootist* (DON SIEGEL, 1976)   A legendary gunfighter dying of cancer (John Wayne) vainly tries to find peace in his final days.

12. *Love Among the Ruins* (GEORGE CUKOR, 1975 TV MOVIE)   A barrister (Laurence Olivier) eloquently defends the honor of the actress (Katharine Hepburn) who initially does not remember jilting him long ago.

13. *Harold and Maude* (HAL ASHBY, 1972)   An eccentric concentration camp survivor (Ruth Gordon) teaches a repressed young man (Bud Cort) how to love life.

14. *The Immortal Story* (WELLES, 1968)   A wealthy and lonely Macao merchant (Welles) tries to play God by making a romantic fable come true in real life.

15. *King Lear* (GRIGORI KOZINTSEV, 1969)   No adaptation of Shakespeare's harrowing play about a king's "foolish,

fond" old age has captured the tale's rugged majesty as well as this Russian film starring Yuri Yarvet. Kozintsev's screenplay is based on Boris Pasternak's translation of *King Lear*.

...And a Booby Prize to

On Golden Pond (MARK RYDELL, 1981)   Sure, there are wonderfully moving scenes, especially the long take in which a distraught Henry Fonda, after becoming lost in the woods near his home, is comforted by his wife (Katharine Hepburn). But why does writer Ernest Thompson feel he has to rely so heavily on coarse humor to make his elderly characters accessible to the youth audience? Let's put it this way: Do you really want to hear Henry Fonda tell Katharine Hepburn he wants to "suck face"?

No More Blarney: Understanding the Irish Through Movies

by Ruth O'Hara

There has been an upsurge of interest in Irish history and culture in recent years, as evidenced by the numerous movies dealing with Irish themes, such as *My Left Foot*, *Michael Collins*, *The Crying Game*, *The Commitments*, *Far and Away*, *The Boxer*, and *Some Mother's Son*. The portrayal of the Irish in movies made both in

Ireland and abroad has been a major source of people's perceptions of Irish culture. Such representations often have been responsible for perpetuating the traditional stereotypical Irishman best described by G. K. Chesterton as "The Irishman of the English farce, with his brogue, his buoyancy, and his tender-hearted irresponsibility." Undeniably, these depictions of the Irish provide wonderful entertainment and comic relief in such movies as *The Quiet Man* and *The Rising of the Moon*. But they also have helped fuel the negative perception perhaps best summed up by the English poet and critic Matthew Arnold, who wrote that the Irish were "great fantasisers, great peddlers of ballads, mysteries and dreams, but ultimately incompetent when it came to translating dream into decision, when it came to responsibly ordering and organizing their boundless fancies."

Some of the movies I believe have been most guilty of shamelessly indulging in "stage-Irish" stereotypes are *Far and Away* (Ron Howard, 1992), *Flight of the Doves* (Ralph Nelson, 1971), *The Secret of Roan Inish* (John Sayles, 1994), *A Prayer for the Dying* (Mike Hodges, 1987), and *Darby O'Gill and the Little People* (Robert Stevenson, 1959). However, in the first list that follows, I have identified some of my favorite movies that help us understand the Irish. These, I believe, present a more realistic, if not always flattering, view. They are among many movies, particularly some of the more recent ones, that have represented Ireland in a much more complex, nuanced, and realistic way, seeing both its strengths and limitations more clearly. The result is a richer and less sentimental cinematic view of the Irish.

1. *A Man of No Importance* (SURI KRISHNAMMA, 1994) This highly entertaining and touching story of repressed homosexuality in 1960s Ireland captures many of the contradictions in the Irish attitudes toward friendship, love, and sex. Albert Finney plays a Dublin bus conductor obsessed with producing Oscar Wilde plays. The homage to Wilde underscores the hypocrisy of a culture that stakes its claim to the creativity of such literary figures while disassociating itself from the more controversial aspects of their personalities.

2. *The Snapper* (STEPHEN FREARS, 1993) Traditionally, the Irish are viewed as a rural people with a great connection to the land. But more than 50 percent reside in the cities and lead a distinctively urban lifestyle. Stephen Frears's movie portrays such a city family coming to terms with their unmarried daughter's pregnancy. Many Irish object to the Roddy Doyle–based script for what they consider its excessive use of vulgar language, setting themselves above this view of Ireland by claiming that it represents the earthier lower classes. However, in my opinion, this movie presents one of the most accurate depictions of everyday working-class and middle-class Dublin people. Scenes of family meals, sibling interactions, and a birthday celebration are nostalgic reminders of my youth in Dublin. I too remember having the ruse of being given a bicycle pump as a present while the bicycle waited in the next room. I guess me ma and da were only messin', too.

3. *The Plough and the Stars* (JOHN FORD, 1936)   Based on a play by Sean O'Casey, this dank, somber John Ford melodrama is more evocative of my grandmother's tales of the troubled years surrounding independence than is the more successful and critically acclaimed *Michael Collins* (Neil Jordan, 1996). Ford's depiction of this era captures more of the quiet desperation and futility surrounding the 1916 Rising than is conveyed by Jordan's flamboyant effort.

4. *The Ballroom of Romance* (PAT O'CONNOR, 1982 TV MOVIE)   This story of unmarried women in rural Ireland, based on the William Trevor novel, is almost terrifying in its starkness. The movie centers around a woman entering middle age (Brenda Fricker) who stays on the farm to care for her crippled father. Opportunities for romance have passed, and she attends the local Saturday night dance, where all that is left to her are the attentions of the more boorish, unsophisticated, and drunken older bachelors. With its portrayal of the women waiting anxiously for the men to arrive from the pub sufficiently drunk to have gained courage to deal with the opposite sex, the movie captures much of the lack of ease between the sexes that is all too common in Irish society.

On the morning following the first screening of *The Ballroom of Romance* on Eire's national television service, Radio Telefís Éireann (RTE), in 1982, my neighbor Kitty Fitzpatrick stated, as if to shock, that the dance scenes were exactly like those she had attended in the 1950s. "What are you talking about?" said her daughter Kate. "I was at a dance like that last night."

5. *My Left Foot* (JIM SHERIDAN, 1989)   For generations, the Irish have focused on education as the ultimate means to self-improvement and escape from poverty. Even when education was forbidden to the Irish, they learned their Latin and Greek in the hedges. For Christy Brown, just as for a whole nation, intellectual attainment guaranteed respect and freedom. This film about Brown's extraordinary triumph over his disability to achieve literary fame captures much of the Irish drive for education, which often invoked the efforts of all family members to ensure that someone could go to college. That cornerstone of so many aspects of Irish life and culture, the Irish mother—at once nurturing and fiercely determined and demanding—is played wonderfully by Brenda Fricker. Fricker and Daniel Day-Lewis, as Christy, won much-deserved Oscars for their performances.

. . . And the Worst Irish Accents in Movies

1. Victor McLaglen in *The Informer* (JOHN FORD, 1935) and *The Quiet Man* (FORD, 1952). Fond as I am of this terrific English actor, his broad Cockney accent makes him wholly unbelievable as either an Irish rebel or a squire.

2. Tom Cruise in *Far and Away* gives a performance rife with stage-Irish accent and mannerisms. Cruise's wife, Nicole Kidman, has a more than credible rural Irish accent in the movie; however, it's a totally inappropriate accent for the daughter of landed gentry.

3. Maureen O'Hara as the fiery Mary Kate Danaher in *The Quiet Man* lets her natural Dublin accent intrude into her characterization of a rural woman from Connemara.

. . . The Best Portrayals of the Irish by Non-Irish Actors

1. Albert Finney is the epitome of working-class Dublin wit, mannerisms, and eccentricities in *A Man of No Importance*.

2. The delectable Alan Rickman produces a flawless portrayal of the ascetic, starchy statesman Eamon de Valera in *Michael Collins*.

3. Maggie Smith is perfect as the soft-spoken, clandestinely alcoholic Dublin music teacher in Jack Clayton's film version of Brian Moore's *The Lonely Passion of Judith Hearne* (1987).

. . . And the Best Portrayals of Non-Irish Characters by Irish Actors

1. Liam Neeson conveys little of his Irish background in his wonderful characterization of the German businessman Oskar Schindler in Steven Spielberg's *Schindler's List* (1993).

2. Dan O'Herlihy makes a magnificent Macduff in Orson Welles's *Macbeth* (1948). With his rich burr and leonine beauty, O'Herlihy plays Shakespeare's noble Scottish warrior to perfection.

3. Cyril Cusack is distinctively Gallic in style as the villainous French ambassador during the Reign of Terror in *The Elusive Pimpernel* (MICHAEL POWELL AND EMERIC PRESSBURGER, 1950).

4. Gabriel Byrne is most convincing as the German Professor Bhaer, the scholarly but passionate mentor of Winona Ryder's Jo in *Little Women* (GILLIAN ARMSTRONG, 1994).

BACK
STAGE RUTH O'HARA, a native of Ireland, emigrated to the United States in 1984. She is a member of the adjunct faculty at New College, San Francisco, where she teaches courses on Irish culture. In addition, she is a research psychologist at the Stanford University School of Medicine. Dr. O'Hara received her undergraduate degree from University College, Dublin, and her Ph.D. in psychology from the University of Southern California.

In Glorious Black-and-White
The 20 Most Beautifully Photographed Black-and-White Movies

1. *They Were Expendable* (JOSEPH H. AUGUST; DIRECTOR, JOHN FORD, 1945)

2. *The Grapes of Wrath* (GREGG TOLAND; DIRECTOR, FORD, 1940)

3. *The Magnificent Ambersons* (STANLEY CORTEZ, HARRY J. WILD ET AL.; DIRECTOR, ORSON WELLES, 1942)

4. *Broken Blossoms* (BILLY BITZER; DIRECTOR, D. W. GRIFFITH, 1919)

5. *Sunrise* (CHARLES ROSHER, KARL STRUSS; DIRECTOR, F. W. MURNAU, 1927)

6. *Jules and Jim* (RAOUL COUTARD; DIRECTOR, FRANÇOIS TRUFFAUT, 1962)

7. *Schindler's List* (JANUSZ KAMINSKI; DIRECTOR, STEVEN SPIELBERG, 1993)

8. *Flesh and the Devil* (WILLIAM DANIELS; DIRECTOR, CLARENCE BROWN, 1927)

9. *The Scarlet Empress* (BERT GLENNON; DIRECTOR, JOSEF VON STERNBERG, 1934)

10. *A Day in the Country* (CLAUDE RENOIR; DIRECTOR, JEAN RENOIR, 1936)

11. *The Bitter Tea of General Yen* (JOSEPH WALKER; DIRECTOR, FRANK CAPRA, 1933)

12. *The Seven Samurai* (ASAKAZU NAKAI; DIRECTOR, AKIRA KUROSAWA, 1954)

13. *Wagon Master* (GLENNON; DIRECTOR, FORD, 1950)

14. *The Night of the Hunter* (CORTEZ; DIRECTOR, CHARLES LAUGHTON, 1955)

15. *The Best Years of Our Lives* (TOLAND; DIRECTOR, WILLIAM WYLER, 1946)

16. *Persona* (SVEN NYKVIST; DIRECTOR, INGMAR BERGMAN, 1966)

17. *How Green Was My Valley* (ARTHUR MILLER; DIRECTOR, FORD, 1941)

18. *The Last Picture Show* (ROBERT SURTEES; DIRECTOR, PETER BOGDANOVICH, 1971)

19. *8½* (GIANNI DI VENANZO; DIRECTOR, FEDERICO FELLINI, 1963)

20. *Raging Bull* (MICHAEL CHAPMAN; DIRECTOR, MARTIN SCORSESE, 1980)

. . . and the entire body of work of James Wong Howe.

10 Great Animated Feature Films That Have Nothing To Do with Disney

by Ray Greene

The Walt Disney Company's influence is absolutely pervasive in contemporary feature animation, but it wasn't always that way. Today, even Disney's competitors do everything they can to emulate the character designs and three-dimensional realism of the Disney house style. Audiences, meanwhile, have become conditioned to view any animated feature that isn't created according to the Disney organization's visual priorities as somehow inferior, cheap, not up to par.

In fact, animation is at least potentially as full of visual possibilities as any other graphics-based art form. Throughout the history of film, a whole range of animators have attempted to liberate the feature film format from the overwhelming commercial predominance of the Mouse House. Not all of these titles will be for every taste, but each demonstrates that, if Disney were to vanish tomorrow, there would still be unlimited possibilities available to artists working with the quicksilver magic of color and line.

1. **Yellow Submarine** (1968)   Undervalued as an animated film because of its tie-in to the Beatles phenomenon, *Yellow Submarine* is in fact a visually adventurous, delightfully whimsical animated reflection of "us-versus-them" counterculture themes from the era (the music-hating Blue Meanies as stand-ins for rock-hating parents). The visuals are equal parts pop art and psychedelic concert poster; the script, written in part by *Love Story* author Erich Segal, is fanciful, picaresque, and worthy in its best moments of A. A. Milne or Lewis Carroll. A whole generation of experimental animators cut their teeth on this one.

2. **Coonskin** (aka *Streetfight*, 1975)   Iconoclastic animation auteur Ralph Bakshi's best film is also his most neglected, owing to its controversial subject matter: an urban, blaxploitation-style retelling of the Uncle Remus

stories that inspired Disney's insipid *Song of the South*. The narrative approach is self-consciously Brechtian, with agitprop asides on race, poverty, and violence dropped into the narrative like hyped-up public service announcements. Insanely violent, insanely political, and visually audacious, *Coonskin* was suppressed in its day when the Congress of Racial Equality labeled it a racist film. It isn't, but it also doesn't offer false optimism in its view of some of American society's most intractable social problems. A reassessment of this one is *long* overdue.

3. *Akira* (1988) The wildest feature-length animation in the world is currently being created in Japan and exported under the genre heading "Japanimation" or "anime" (pronounced "AN-ih-may"), depending on the political correctness of those involved in the discussion. *Akira* is anime's masterpiece: a complex rumination on modern Japan's lingering atomic malaise and its quest for spiritual meanings in a technologically overwhelming modern world. Wrapped up in a bizarre but fascinating science-fiction plotline that is as impossible to describe as it is engrossing, *Akira* blends the hallucinatory sheen of a John Woo action movie with the philosophical complexity of *Hiroshima, Mon Amour*. Adapted and directed by Katushiro Otomo from his graphic novel of the same name.

4. *Mad Monster Party?* (1967) Rankin-Bass, the company that produced such object-animation classics as *Rudolph the Red-Nosed Reindeer* and *Santa Claus Is*

Coming to Town for television, took a stab at theatrical features with this uneven but goofily enjoyable film. A Jimmy Stewart soundalike is the unknowing nephew of a mad scientist (voiced by horror great Boris Karloff) who is summoned to a remote castle to take over the family business. Characters based on the Lugosi *Dracula*, the Lon Chaney Jr. *Wolf Man*, King Kong, and Karloff's own immortal monster from *Frankenstein* appear for the titular bash. Partial screenplay credit belongs to the great Harvey Kurtzman, who wrote virtually all the classic material contained in the original '50s version of *Mad* magazine, with *Mad* artist Jack Davis responsible for the character designs. Not great, but far superior to *The Nightmare Before Christmas*, if nothing else; less deserving oddities have attained "cult" status.

5 & 6. *Gulliver's Travels* (1939) and **Mr. Bug Goes to Town** (aka *Hoppity Goes to Town*, 1941) Disney's only serious rival for "king of the animation producers" during the 1930s was Max Fleischer, creator of Betty Boop and Koko the Clown, and the popularizer of the King Features Syndicate's Popeye the Sailor. Fleischer's career actually predated Disney's, and his influence on Disney was immense; Disney's first successful venture into animated short subjects, which put a live-action Alice into a cartoon Wonderland, was based on a simple inversion of Fleischer's *Out of the Inkwell* shorts, which loosed the cartoon Koko in a live-action world.

The technical innovations for which the Fleischer Studio was responsible are too immense to list here, though it's worth noting that Max Fleischer invented the rotoscoping process by which Disney animated "realistic" human beings for decades, and was shooting workable "3-D" animation landscapes *years* before Disney's supposed pioneering of that effect in *Snow White and the Seven Dwarfs*. After *Snow White* set box-office records, Fleischer was pressured into feature-length animation by his backers at Paramount, in a move that ultimately proved financially ruinous. Fleischer's shortcomings as a story editor are apparent in both his adaptation of Jonathan Swift's *Gulliver's Travels* and his Capraesque *Mr. Deeds* of the insect world, *Mr. Bug Goes to Town*. But both films are full of gorgeous animation, stunning visual set pieces, and a charming, off-the-cuff sense of improvised whimsy, which was something of the Fleischer Studio's specialty of the house.

7. *Heavy Traffic* (1973)   Another animated milestone from maverick director Ralph Bakshi, *Heavy Traffic* is also something virtually unique in the annals of feature-length animation: a gritty, imaginary autobiography from an animation auteur. Pioneering themes that later would be revisited in his bloated, wobbly, and studio-financed *Cool World*, Bakshi's shoestring production tells the story of an aspiring alternative comic-book artist who seeks to capture themes worthy of a latter-day Zola in his critically reviled pop art form. The ambition alone is staggering, but Bakshi pulls off nearly everything he attempts. Violent, sensual, abrasive, and indispensable, *Heavy Traffic* is a must-see for adventurous animation fans.

8. *Fantastic Planet* (1973)   A "head" film in the best sense, this French-made effort creates a dreamlike science-fiction landscape with many of the social contours of Fritz Lang's *Metropolis*. A humanoid race is kept as slaves and house pets by a bizarre, blue-skinned species of giants on a faraway planet. When an automated tutoring device is stolen by a humanoid renegade, the oppressed learn of their true station in life, and revolution as well as a series of surreal visual revelations is the result. Based on a popular French newspaper serial, *Fantastic Planet* received a special jury prize when it debuted at Cannes.

9. *The Adventures of Mark Twain* (1985)   Before he hit pay dirt with the California Raisins, "Claymation" maestro Will Vinton created this picaresque, fanciful spiritual "biography" of the great American humorist. The framing plotline is derived from Twain's little-known Huck Finn sequel *Tom Sawyer Abroad*, which launched Tom and Huck in a hot-air balloon into a series of transcontinental adventures. Here, the master of the journey is Twain himself, and every door opens onto an imaginative short-film adaptation based on one of his works. The *Mysterious Stranger* segment alone is a near masterpiece.

10. *Watership Down* (1978)   Conceived as a feature-length vehicle for legendary animator John Hubley, *Watership Down* ultimately was completed by its producer Martin Rosen when Hubley left the project. The resulting film is a stunning and serious-minded animation epic which remains remarkably faithful to the ecological underpinnings of Richard Adams's

bestselling novel. A warren of rabbits is driven from its communal hole by human developers and must embark on a desperate journey for a place to call home. The film failed in its original release; by exploiting animation's ability to anthropomorphize animals to unusually dramatic effect, Rosen created a fable that is far too disturbing for children, but which appeared on the surface to be too juvenile for adults. Grown-ups who pass up this one are missing out on one of the finest and most challenging animated features of its type.

Honorable Mentions

1. *Heavy Metal* (1981) Anthology film based on stories from the protocyberpunk comics magazine. Wildly uneven and determinedly adolescent, but the best passages are very good indeed.

2. *Wicked City* (1987) More prime Japanese "anime," marred only by excessive violence even by genre standards and a troubling streak of misogyny.

3. *Who Framed Roger Rabbit* (1988) Sure, it was released by Disney's Touchstone arm. But Steven Spielberg's Amblin produced it and, more important, *Back to the Future*'s Robert Zemeckis directed it (with Richard Williams backstopping him on the animation side). Zemeckis is clearly more attuned to the slapstick sass of prime *Looney Tunes* animation than he is to the Disney house style, and that is all to the good.

4. ***Gay Purr-ee*** (1962)   A last gasp of glory from innovative '50s animation house UPA. Script and character designs by the great Chuck Jones; voices include Judy Garland and Robert Goulet; original songs by *Wizard of Oz* duo Harold Arlen and E. Y. (Yip) Harburg. The graphic style reflects UPA's preference for caricature over three-dimensional Disney clutter, making this agreeable *Lady and the Tramp* knockoff look positively prescient in the age of *Ren and Stimpy* and *King of the Hill.*

Non-Disney Titles to Avoid

Anything directed by Don Bluth; anything produced by a major American studio after the record-breaking release of Disney's *Beauty and the Beast.*

RAY GREENE is editor-at-large for *Boxoffice* magazine, for which he was editor-in-chief from 1994 through 1997. He was a contributing editor and essayist for *L.A. View* from 1992 to 1996, and he is a regular contributor to the on-line magazine *Mr. Showbiz* and ABCNEWS.com. Greene is also the founding editor of *Boxoffice Online* (www.box office.com), which was selected by *The Net* magazine as the best film information site on the Internet in 1997. He is currently at work as writer and director of a feature-length documentary about exploitation movies.

Showstoppers
The 12 Best Movies About the Theater

Footlight Parade (LLOYD BACON/BUSBY BERKELEY, 1933)
Never were Berkeley's musical fantasies more grandiose than
in this delirious backstage saga about a director-hoofer (James
Cagney) whose indefatigable spirit encapsulates the can-do
attitude of the New Deal. When the curtain rises on the "By
a Waterfall" number, the sheer impossibility of the number
becomes its eye-popping raison d'être.

Twentieth Century (HOWARD HAWKS, 1934) Every arro-
gant, megalomaniacal stage producer who ever tore his hair
and screamed at his actors is encapsulated in John Barrymore's
all-stops-out comic performance as Oscar Jaffe ("I close the
iron door on you!"). Hawks's uproarious screwball comedy,
written by Ben Hecht and Charles MacArthur from their own
play, also boasts a career-making performance by Carole Lombard, whose dizzy antics keep Barrymore in peak form.

Yankee Doodle Dandy (MICHAEL CURTIZ, 1942) James
Cagney's heartfelt tribute to George M. Cohan and his Irish-
American acting family (Walter Huston, Rosemary DeCamp,
and Jeanne Cagney): "My mother thanks you, my father
thanks you, my sister thanks you, and I thank you." An ener-
getic valentine to the good old days of vaudeville and
musical theater in the late nineteenth and early
twentieth centuries. My great-uncle Eddie Foy Jr.
plays his own vaudevillian father.

To Be or Not to Be (ERNST LUBITSCH, 1942)
Lubitsch was pilloried for daring to find humor
in the life-or-death drama of a Polish acting

troupe outwitting the Nazis. As "that great, great actor Joseph Tura," Jack Benny found the endearingly hammy role of a lifetime, but the most electrifying scene is Felix Bressart's impassioned recitation of Shylock's "Hath not a Jew eyes?" speech. Never has playacting seemed more urgent than at this moment, the Jewish filmmaker's cri de coeur in the face of the Nazi Holocaust.

Children of Paradise (MARCEL CARNÉ, 1945)   One of the greatest movies of any era, *Children of Paradise* was the last film made by Frenchmen during the Nazi occupation, and the filmmakers poured into it their impassioned belief in the ability of entertainment to give meaning to people's daily lives. Jean-Louis Barrault (as the mime Baptiste) and Arletty give performances of timeless majesty in this grand spectacle written by Jacques Prévert about a nineteenth-century acting troupe.

All About Eve (JOSEPH L. MANKIEWICZ, 1950)   The mother of all backstage dramas. Director Mankiewicz's dazzling screenplay is an encyclopedic compendium of hard-won theatrical wisdom, demonstrating how ambitious fan Eve Harrington (Anne Baxter) craftily usurps the stardom of the legendary Margo Channing (Bette Davis). "Fasten your seatbelts—it's going to be a bumpy night," snaps Bette, giving impersonators enough material to last a lifetime.

The Golden Coach (JEAN RENOIR, 1953)   Renoir always proclaimed his belief in the primacy of actors in film and the importance of theatrical artifice in shaping our perceptions of reality. His sheer delight in theatricality was given its fullest, freest rein in this ravishing color film, a comedy-melodrama about an Italian acting troupe on tour through South America in the eighteenth century. As Camilla, the flamboyant Anna Magnani has perhaps her richest screen role.

The Producers (MEL BROOKS, 1967) Two small-time producers (Zero Mostel and Gene Wilder) stage what they're certain is the world's worst play—a musical by a neo-Nazi (Kenneth Mars), titled *Springtime for Hitler*. Much to their shock, the oversubscribed monstrosity becomes a camp sensation, and they wind up going to jail. Mel Brooks's outrageous directing debut is a scream from start to finish.

Theatre of Blood (DOUGLAS HICKOX, 1973) Perhaps it's perverse for critics to love this movie, for it's a black comedy about a hammy Shakespearean actor (the perfectly cast Vincent Price) taking revenge on all the London theater critics who have failed to appreciate his genius. The way he does it is to kill them one by one, using methods employed by villains in Shakespearean plays. Delicious.

The Last Metro (FRANÇOIS TRUFFAUT, 1980) Suffused with a cineaste's echoes of *To Be or Not to Be*, *Children of Paradise*, and *The Golden Coach*, Truffaut's movie about a Paris theater company during the Nazi occupation carries a somber urgency all its own. The director pays tribute to the daring and professionalism of actors in this suspenseful tale of an actress (Catherine Deneuve) sustaining her husband's theater as a refuge from the nightmarish world outside.

Those Lips, Those Eyes (MICHAEL PRESSMAN, 1980) Not all theater is Broadway opening nights and backstage intrigue among the stars; more often it's far-fetched backwater dreams and bittersweet disillusionment. This likably modest comedy-drama written by David Shaber revolves around a starry-eyed local *putz* (Tom Hulce) carrying on a misguided love affair with a fetching New York actress (Glynnis O'Connor) during a summer-stock season in Cleveland.

Noises Off (PETER BOGDANOVICH, 1992) Although it hardly made an impact with the paying public, Bogdanovich's virtuosic staging of Michael Frayn's backstage farce is a delightful send-up of the vanity and insecurity of actors. With breathtaking panache and graceful visual wit, Bogdanovich smoothly interweaves events on- and offstage as the boundaries between life and theater become utterly indistinguishable.

Say It Ain't So
10 Truly Terrible Biopix

1. *The Babe Ruth Story* (ROY DEL RUTH, 1948) Mawkish to a ludicrous extreme, especially when the Babe hits a ball that seriously injures a cute little boy's dog, then rushes the mutt to the hospital. In my book *High and Inside: An A-to-Z Guide to the Language of Baseball*, I report what happened when Ruth came to Hollywood shortly before his death to help Allied Artists promote the upcoming movie: "Studio publicist Dave Kaufman arranged a photo opportunity at which the Babe met the actor who played him on-screen, William Bendix, and joined the press in watching Bendix take batting practice, resplendent in a Yankees uniform. Proving a better actor than hitter, Bendix took mighty swings but, much to the Bambino's disgust, could barely hit the ball out of the infield. After one puny Bendix effort rolled weakly toward the pitcher's mound, Ruth turned to the members of the press and growled, 'Hell, I can *piss* farther than he can hit!' "

2. *Up Close & Personal* (JON AVNET, 1996)   With Michelle Pfeiffer as the airheaded character derived from the self-destructive TV anchorwoman Jessica Savitch. This treacly, sexist film is perhaps the most sanitized biopic ever made in Hollywood. John Gregory Dunne, who wrote the screenplay with his wife, Joan Didion, offered an extended alibi for their dreadful hackwork in his 1997 book *Monster: Living Off the Big Screen.*

3. *W. C. Fields and Me* (ARTHUR HILLER, 1976)   With Rod Steiger as W. C. Fields and Valerie Perrine as his mistress Carlotta Monti. Steiger is an absolute horror with his putty nose and his morose rendition of the great comedian. Perrine plays Monti as an empty pneumatic container.

4. *Gable and Lombard* (SIDNEY J. FURIE, 1976)   With James Brolin as Clark Gable and Jill Clayburgh as Carole Lombard. This pathetic mismatch of actors and roles proves how difficult it is for modern actors to incarnate bygone stars. It probably shouldn't even be tried.

5. *Gypsy* (MERVYN LEROY, 1962)   With Natalie Wood as Gypsy Rose Lee. This clumsy transcription of the great stage musical squanders most of its charm, energy, and sex appeal. Bette Midler's 1993 TV-movie remake was much better but still not worthy of the source.

6. *Lisztomania* (KEN RUSSELL, 1975)   With Roger Daltrey as Franz Liszt. Not for lovers of classical music—to say the least—this is Russell at his most floridly out of control. But it does have Daltrey kissing Fiona Lewis's breasts to the beat of a metronome.

7. *Mrs. Parker and the Vicious Circle* (ALAN RUDOLPH, 1994)   With Jennifer Jason Leigh as Dorothy Parker. Leigh gives one of the all-time worst performances, slurring her dialogue because Parker was an alcoholic (much of the part had to be redubbed to make it marginally intelligible), and generally setting a new standard for "mannered" acting.

8. *Wilson* (HENRY KING, 1944)   With Alexander Knox as one of America's most overrated presidents, Woodrow Wilson, who narrowly won reelection in 1916 by promising to keep the country out of war, then led it into World War I a few months later. An interminable patriotic snoozathon, *Wilson* was a pet project of Twentieth Century–Fox production chief Darryl F. Zanuck, and it's strictly the waxworks.

9. *The Greatest Story Ever Told* (GEORGE STEVENS, 1965) With Max von Sydow as Jesus. Max actually is splendid, if rather gloomily Scandinavian, as the Man from Nazareth. But Stevens turned this otherwise reverential movie into a sacrilegious send-up by giving cameo roles to a host of glaringly inappropriate Hollywood actors, including Shelley Winters (as The Woman of No Name), Ed Wynn (Old Aram, a Blind Man), Donald Pleasence (The Dark Hermit), Sal Mineo (Uriah), Pat Boone (Young Man at the Tomb), and, of course, John Wayne as The Centurion ("Truly this man was . . . the son of *God*"). Von Sydow told me how funny he thought it was to see Wayne decked out in his helmet and short skirt, looking "like an old lady." (See "The 10 Most Profound Hollywood Jokes" and "Ye Gods!: The 15 Least Appropriate Castings in Historical Roles.")

10. *Night and Day* (MICHAEL CURTIZ, 1946)   With Cary Grant as a strictly heterosexual Cole Porter. As screenwriter William Bowers recalled, "Cary Grant had me brought in. They had been working on the script for two years. They were due to start shooting the next week, and they decide they can't use anything in the script. Now, there is a marvelous Hungarian by the name of Mike Curtiz directing it, and I go in for the first meeting with him and he says, 'You know this Cole Porter?' I say, 'No, I don't know him, but I know who he is.' 'I'm going to tell you about him,' he says. 'When he was born he was given $6 million for being born. And when he was twelve years old he was given $10 million just for being twelve years old. He goes to Yale University. He meets this girl, they get married, and she is worth $20 million. He goes out and he writes all these goddamn songs and makes another $8 million. I figure what we've got in this story is a case of struggle, struggle, struggle.' It was a ghastly picture, too."

The Crowd Roars
My Favorite Sports Movies

All-around sports—*Pat and Mike* (GEORGE CUKOR, 1952), with Katharine Hepburn playing a multitalented athlete based on the legendary Babe Didrikson Zaharias (who appears briefly as herself)

Baseball—*Fear Strikes Out* (ROBERT MULLIGAN, 1957), *Bull Durham* (RON SHELTON, 1988), *Field of Dreams* (PHIL

ALDEN ROBINSON, 1989), *Cobb* (SHELTON, 1994), *The Bingo Long Traveling All-Stars & Motor Kings* (JOHN BADHAM, 1976)

Basketball—*Hoop Dreams* (STEVE JAMES, 1994), *He Got Game* (SPIKE LEE, 1998)

Bowling—*The Big Lebowski* (JOEL COEN, 1998)

Boxing—*The Harder They Fall* (MARK ROBSON, 1956), *Gentleman Jim* (RAOUL WALSH, 1942), *Raging Bull* (MARTIN SCORSESE, 1980, for the ring sequences only)

Car Racing—*The Crowd Roars* (HOWARD HAWKS, 1932)

Football—*School Daze* (LEE, 1988). I stopped being a football fan when Richard Nixon began using football metaphors to describe the Vietnam War—appropriately enough, since football is violent, territorial, and involves a group of eleven men ganging up on a single ballcarrier. So I list *School Daze*, which depicts a college football game entirely through the reactions of the audience, without showing any of the action on the field.

Golf—*Tin Cup* (SHELTON, 1996)

Horse Racing—*Kentucky Pride* (JOHN FORD, 1925), *Broadway Bill* (FRANK CAPRA, 1934)

Hunting (violent)—*Moby Dick* (JOHN HUSTON, 1956), *White Hunter, Black Heart* (CLINT EASTWOOD, 1990)

Hunting (nonviolent)—*Hatari!* (HAWKS, 1962)

Rugby—*This Sporting Life* (LINDSAY ANDERSON, 1963)

Soccer—*Victory* (HUSTON, 1981, for Pele's bicycle kicks)

Track and Field—*College* (JAMES W. HORNE/BUSTER KEATON, 1927), *Personal Best* (ROBERT TOWNE, 1982), *Tokyo Olympiad* (KON ICHIKAWA, 1966)

Wrestling—*Blood and Guts** (PAUL LYNCH, 1978), *Flesh* (FORD, 1932)

My 15 Favorite Westerns

When I was growing up in Milwaukee during the 1950s, I used to come home every afternoon to watch a Western on television, on a show called *Foreman Tom's Jamboree*. I remember that after a while, I grew awfully darn tired of seeing the Indians always get beaten. Since I've rooted for the underdog ever since I can remember (I was a little guy then and was beaten up a lot myself), I began to long for the day when I would see a Western in which the Indians won. Finally there came the great day when, to my intense pleasure, I saw one. I can't remember what it was, but I'd like to think it might have been one of the movies on this list, *Fort Apache*. There haven't been many others.

1. *Shane* (GEORGE STEVENS, 1953)

2. *The Searchers* (JOHN FORD, 1956)

3. *Wagon Master* (FORD, 1950)

4. *Fort Apache* (FORD, 1948)

---

*I cannot tell a lie—I wrote the original story and collaborated on the screenplay of this movie, which actually wasn't all that good. But I couldn't resist the opportunity to list it in the same category as a John Ford movie.

5. *Rio Bravo* (HOWARD HAWKS, 1959)

6. *El Dorado* (HAWKS, 1967)

7. *Tell Them Willie Boy Is Here* (ABRAHAM POLONSKY, 1969)

8. *The Wild Bunch* (SAM PECKINPAH, 1969)

9. *The Gunfighter* (HENRY KING, 1950)

10. *She Wore a Yellow Ribbon* (FORD, 1949)

11. *Unforgiven* (CLINT EASTWOOD, 1992)

12. *My Darling Clementine* (FORD, 1946)

13. *Red River* (HAWKS, 1948)

14. *The Battle at Elderbush Gulch* (D. W. GRIFFITH, 1913)

15. *Support Your Local Sheriff!* (BURT KENNEDY, 1969)

Scarred for Life
The Seminal Influence of The Searchers

As Stuart Byron wrote in his 1979 *New York* magazine article "*The Searchers*: Cult Movie of the New Hollywood," "You could construct half the syllabus for a course on contemporary American cinema just from films that, consciously or not, have been influenced by [John Ford's 1956 Western] *The Searchers*. 'All modern American literature comes from one book by Mark Twain called *Huckleberry Finn*,' said Ernest Hemingway, and I think that in the same broad sense it can be said that all recent American cinema derives from John Ford's *The Searchers*."

Here are some of the movies that have been partly inspired by *The Searchers* or have included references to it—among them are several landmark modern movies that, in turn, have spawned many imitators of their own. (In addition, "That'll Be the Day," the 1957 hit song written by Buddy Holly and Jerry Allison for the Crickets, was inspired by John Wayne's catchphrase in *The Searchers*.) Also see what Byron calls the "seminal" chapter on *The Searchers* in my book *John Ford* (with Michael Wilmington, 1974), first published in the Autumn 1971 issue of *Sight and Sound* as "Prisoner of the Desert" (our nod to the French title of *The Searchers*, *La Prisonnière du Désert*).

Weekend (JEAN-LUC GODARD, 1967; contains a reference to *Prisoner of the Desert*, which the English subtitler didn't realize actually was *The Searchers*)

Once Upon a Time in the West (SERGIO LEONE, 1968)

Who's That Knocking at My Door? (MARTIN SCORSESE, 1968)

Big Jake (GEORGE SHERMAN, 1971)

Ulzana's Raid (ROBERT ALDRICH, 1972)

Dillinger (JOHN MILIUS, 1973)

Mean Streets (SCORSESE, 1973)

The Wind and the Lion (MILIUS, 1975)

Winterhawk (CHARLES B. PIERCE, 1975)

The Quest (TV MOVIE, LEE H. KATZIN, 1976; followed that year by a TV series spin-off)

Taxi Driver (SCORSESE, 1976)

Close Encounters of the Third Kind (STEVEN SPIELBERG, 1977)

Star Wars (GEORGE LUCAS, 1977)

Big Wednesday (MILIUS, 1978)

The Deer Hunter (MICHAEL CIMINO, 1978)

Hardcore (PAUL SCHRADER, 1979)

Windwalker (KIETH MERRILL, 1980)

Year of the Dragon (CIMINO, 1985)

 # Jessica McBride's Favorite Movies About Native Americans

1. *Windwalker* (KIETH MERRILL, 1980) A lyrical, touching film about a Cheyenne man's search for his lost twin son. Particularly noteworthy because it's a movie about Native Americans that has no Great White Hope, in fact no white characters at all. The Indian dialect is beautiful to hear. The inspiring Indian view of death and family holds lessons for all. I will never forget the old man's comment after he finds his lost son, "It's a good day to die," and his complete lack of fear about death now that the last missing piece in his life story has been found.

2. *Thunderheart* (MICHAEL APTED, 1992) Indian spirituality and mysticism pulses through this film about a part-Indian man's search for his identity. I enjoyed the

fact that this is one of the few films that show Indians in the present, not the past tense. It is set against the backdrop of the American Indian Movement, an often-forgotten moment in history that boasted warriors as grand and noteworthy as those of the past. Graham Greene is excellent as an Indian policeman who reveals a unique Indian sense of humor that is not often seen in movies. There is a powerful ending that shows the strong Indian sense of community and spirituality.

3. *Incident at Oglala* (APTED, 1991) A well-crafted, intricate documentary that serves as a companion piece to *Thunderheart*, Apted's *Incident at Oglala* establishes without a doubt that a great injustice was done to Leonard Peltier. Any viewer of this film will be outraged that Peltier remains in prison for the murder of FBI agents he clearly never killed. The movie illustrates the government's continuing goal to destroy Indian resistance well into the twentieth century. A very important film.

4. *Little Big Man* (ARTHUR PENN, 1970) Doses of comedy allow the viewer to stomach the extraordinary atrocities the white man committed against the Indian in the nineteenth century. Yet those atrocities resonate deeply with the viewer, perhaps because the Indian characters are so likable. *Little Big Man* is a fine satire that skewers those who deserve it (such as Custer) without adopting an air of pomposity. Dustin Hoffman is excellent as the 121-year-old Jack Crabb, the narrator of the story, but Chief Dan George runs away with the

movie in a majestic performance as his grandfather, Old Lodge Skins.

5. *Geronimo: An American Legend* (WALTER HILL, 1993)   Indian actor Wes Studi is a searing presence as the Apache warrior driven by a love for his culture and by anger over the massacre of his family. *Geronimo* is a sensitive portrait of a tortured, driven, and legendary man once stereotyped as being a person solely motivated by blood lust.

6. *Black Robe* (BRUCE BERESFORD, 1991)   *Black Robe* is a serious film that shows the destructive influence the well-meaning Jesuit missionaries had on the Huron in Quebec. This movie is unusual for its depiction of woodland Indians; the majority of movies about Indians focus on the tribes of the plains and the deserts. Breathtakingly filmed, *Black Robe* also showcases a time period that is little explored in movies about Indians, the 1600s, examining the first contacts between the French and the tribes. One of its strengths is that it does not glorify either side, the Indians or the whites. Many modern-day movies about Indians tend to glamorize them; *Black Robe* avoids this pitfall, at times revealing in stark detail the bleak and brutal lives led by the Indians of that time period.

7. *Dances with Wolves* (KEVIN COSTNER, 1990)   Beautiful vistas make this three-hours-plus movie a dream to watch. *Dances with Wolves* captures the lost grandeur of the Sioux. Indians are shown as people, and the viewer comes to care about each individual character, as well as about a vanishing moment in history that

can never be recaptured. Like *Windwalker*, *Dances with Wolves* strives for authenticity, allowing the Indian characters to speak in their own traditional language. Both as director and actor, Kevin Costner conveys a genuine appreciation for the culture he encounters.

 JESSICA MCBRIDE, the author's daughter, is a police reporter with the *Milwaukee Journal Sentinel*. She grew up near an Ojibwa reservation and has traveled within many of the Indian communities of Wisconsin while studying woodland Indian culture. She is currently at work on a novel set in Wisconsin.

John McBride's Favorite "Bond, James Bond" Movies

Dr. No (TERENCE YOUNG, 1962)   In the first James Bond film, you learn of the many future characters and rituals to come in the following Bond movies.

Goldfinger (GUY HAMILTON, 1964)   From suffocating paint to guillotinelike hats, this film is filled with off-the-wall weapons and villains.

The Man with the Golden Gun (HAMILTON, 1974)   This island paradise is no paradise at all. An evil man with three nipples is after Bond.

Moonraker (LEWIS GILBERT, 1979)   This movie has terrific scenes of outer-space adventure and suspense. Roger Moore is at his best.

Tomorrow Never Dies (ROGER SPOTTISWOODE, 1997) The most recent Bond picture is full of high-tech action, but it still incorporates Bond's classic wit.

. . . And His Least Favorite

On Her Majesty's Secret Service (PETER R. HUNT, 1969) George Lazenby was at fault in this movie. The poor guy just didn't have what it takes to be 007.

Live and Let Die (HAMILTON, 1973)   The flaw in *Live and Let Die* was that Roger Moore hadn't discovered his best talent—his wit. But perhaps it was the writers' doing.

[BACK STAGE]   JOHN MCBRIDE, the author's son, is a seventh-grade student in Palo Alto, California. Although he was his father's research assistant on *Steven Spielberg: A Biography*, John doesn't want to be a writer when he grows up—he plans to become a computer engineer.

My 20 Favorite War Movies

The Big Parade (KING VIDOR, 1925)

The General (BUSTER KEATON AND CLYDE BRUCKMAN, 1927)

The Battle of Midway (DOCUMENTARY; JOHN FORD, 1942)

San Pietro (DOCUMENTARY; JOHN HUSTON, 1943)

They Were Expendable (FORD, 1945)

Fort Apache (FORD, 1948)

The Red Badge of Courage (HUSTON, 1951)

The Saga of Anatahan (JOSEF VON STERNBERG, 1953)

The Seven Samurai (AKIRA KUROSAWA, 1954)

Paths of Glory (STANLEY KUBRICK, 1957)

Spartacus (KUBRICK, 1960)

Merrill's Marauders (SAMUEL FULLER, 1962)

The Sorrow and the Pity (DOCUMENTARY; MARCEL OPHULS, 1970)

Apocalypse Now (FRANCIS FORD COPPOLA, 1979)

The Big Red One (FULLER, 1980)

Shoah (DOCUMENTARY; CLAUDE LANZMANN, 1985)

Full Metal Jacket (KUBRICK, 1987)

Glory (EDWARD ZWICK, 1989)

Heaven & Earth (OLIVER STONE, 1993)

Schindler's List (STEVEN SPIELBERG, 1993)

High Anxiety
The 12 Best Mental Hospital Movies

1. *Shock Corridor* (SAMUEL FULLER, 1963)   A luridly expressionistic yarn about a reporter (Peter Breck) who goes insane while solving a crime in a mental institution, *Shock Corridor* is Fuller's corrosive allegory of the psychological

ills of American society in that tumultuous period. (See "My 25 Favorite Movies" and "The Greatest Bad Line in the History of Movies.")

2. *Let There Be Light* (JOHN HUSTON, 1945) Long banned by the U.S. Army (it was not cleared for release until 1980), this deeply compassionate study of soldiers being treated for shell shock contains some of the most moving scenes ever filmed. (See "My 25 Favorite Movies.")

3. *Titicut Follies* (FREDERICK WISEMAN, 1967) A shocking, totally unflinching documentary filmed in a Massachusetts state prison hospital for the mentally ill.

4. *Lilith* (ROBERT ROSSEN, 1964) The insidious romantic lure of mental illness is captured in the web a seductive inmate (Jean Seberg) spins toward an orderly (Warren Beatty).

5. *High Anxiety* (MEL BROOKS, 1977) An uneven but often uproarious satire of Hitchcock movies (including the corny mental hospital thriller *Spellbound*), *High Anxiety* is set in the Psycho Neurotic Institute for the Very, *Very* Nervous.

6. *Bedlam* (MARK ROBSON, 1946) Producer Val Lewton's ghastly, customarily stylish look at the way the mad were treated in eighteenth-century London.

7. *The Persecution and Assassination of Jean-Paul Marat, as performed by the inmates of the Asylum of Charenton, under the direction of the Marquis de Sade* (aka *Marat/Sade*) (PETER BROOK, 1966) This riveting film version of the celebrated play by Peter Weiss explores the theatricality and the cruelty of madness.

8, 9, & 10. *Frances* (GRAEME CLIFFORD, 1982)/*Committed* (SHEILA MCLAUGHLIN AND LYNNE TILLMAN, 1983)/*Will There Really Be a Morning?* (FIELDER COOK, 1983 TV MOVIE) Fittingly, it took no fewer than three movies (respectively starring Jessica Lange, McLaughlin, and Susan Blakely) to deal with the shattered life of Hollywood actress Frances Farmer, who was incarcerated and ultimately lobotomized for her unconventional behavior and politics. One was based on Farmer's posthumously published autobiography, *Will There Really Be a Morning?* (1972), written largely by her best friend of later years, Jean Ratcliffe. Most enlightening of all, however, are William Arnold's 1978 biography, *Shadowland*, and the haunting Frances Farmer installment of Ralph Edwards's *This Is Your Life* (1958).

11. *The Snake Pit* (ANATOLE LITVAK, 1948) Although melodramatic and stagey, this film deserves a place of honor as the first major cinematic exposé of mental hospital conditions.

12. *Mr. Deeds Goes to Town* (FRANK CAPRA, 1936) When *Mr. Deeds* was released in the Soviet Union, it was retitled *Grip of the Dollar* and ended when multimillionaire Gary Cooper is committed to an insane asylum for wanting to give his money to the poor. Even though the scene in the asylum is brief, it resonates deeply because of Deeds's disturbing, near-catatonic surrender to the forces of darkness. The roller-coaster mood swings of *Mr. Deeds* reflect Capra's own manic-depressive tendencies as a man, an artist, and a social commentator.

...And the Worst Mental Hospital Movies

1. *One Flew Over the Cuckoo's Nest* (MILOS FORMAN, 1976)   For its condescending attitude toward the mentally ill—only our hero (Jack Nicholson) is truly sane, while most of the other inmates are smugly ridiculed by the director. When I expressed my views to Milos Forman in 1976, he replied, "I am not going to apologize for making a commercial movie."

2. *David and Lisa* (FRANK PERRY, 1962)   For its unbearably treacly sentimentalization of mental illness in teenagers.

3. *King of Hearts* (PHILIPPE DE BROCA, 1966)   For its self-congratulating message (which found great favor among American college students in that period) that the insane are the only sane people in society. A dangerously foolish notion.

4. *Spellbound* (ALFRED HITCHCOCK, 1945)   For not capturing madness as memorably as Hitchcock's *Vertigo* (which includes James Stewart's chilling scene of catatonia) and *The Wrong Man* (chronicling the mental disintegration of Vera Miles, the wife of a man falsely accused).

Moviemakers' Favorite Lunatic
Ed Gein on Film

Ed Gein (as in *fiend*), a quiet, seemingly gentle farmer from Plainfield, Wisconsin, was unmasked in 1957 as one of the most bizarre murderers of modern times. Not only a grave robber and a cannibal, Gein also was fond of dancing in the moonlight wearing the preserved skin of dead women who resembled his mother. He was so far out in his ghoulishness that he single-handedly ripped the tranquil facade from 1950s conformity. No wonder this mild-mannered fiend who literally lived in a rural charnel house fascinated us children growing up in a state still dominated by the specter of Joe McCarthy (another kind of monster), and inspired a wealth of sick "Ed Gein jokes." Sample: "Why does Ed Gein cover his chairs before he goes to bed? So they won't get goose pimples."

Although not as well remembered today as fellow Cheesehead Jeffrey Dahmer (what *is* it about the milk in my home state?), Gein was the subject of *Deviant*, a superb 1989 biography by Harold Schechter, and he has served as a constant inspiration to filmmakers. From Alfred Hitchcock's seminal *Psycho* (1960), based on a novel by Milwaukee's Robert Bloch, to Werner Herzog's *Stroszek* (1977), filmed in Plainfield with the help of Errol Morris (who conducted a still-unpublished Gein oral history, *American Gothic*), Gein's story has been approached in more or less oblique fashion, as if the real facts are still too horrific to let loose. The following are the movies comprising the Ed Gein subgenre (not including the host of otherwise unrelated "slasher" movies that followed in the wake of *Psycho*).

Psycho (ALFRED HITCHCOCK, 1960)

Three on a Meathook (WILLIAM GIRDLER, 1972)

Deranged (BOB CLARK, 1974)

The Texas Chain Saw Massacre (TOBE HOOPER, 1974)

Stroszek (WERNER HERZOG, 1977)

Psycho II (RICHARD FRANKLIN, 1983)

The Texas Chainsaw Massacre 2 (TOBE HOOPER, 1986)

Manhunter (MICHAEL MANN, 1986)

Psycho III (ANTHONY PERKINS, 1986)

Bates Motel (RICHARD ROTHSTEIN, 1987 TV MOVIE)

The Texas Chainsaw Massacre: A Family Portrait (BRAD SHELLADY, 1988 DOCUMENTARY)

Leatherface: Texas Chainsaw Massacre III (JEFF BURR, 1989)

Psycho IV: The Beginning (MICK GARRIS, 1990 TV MOVIE)

The Silence of the Lambs (JONATHAN DEMME, 1991)

Texas Chainsaw Massacre: The Next Generation (KIM HENKEL, 1997; a reedited version of the 1995 movie *The Return of the Texas Chainsaw Massacre*)

Flyover Movies
13 Ways of Looking at the Midwest

People in Hollywood contemptuously refer to Middle America as "flyover" country—that is, the part of America they fly over while shuttling between L.A. and New York. But film-makers who know where to look have given us some powerful stories about the Midwestern region of this country, where I grew up.

True Heart Susie (D. W. GRIFFITH, 1919)   The small-town sensibility has never been portrayed more positively and touchingly than in Griffith's engagingly modest pastoral romance, starring Lillian Gish in one of her most luminous performances. Billy Bitzer's cinematography is as delicate as Gish's portrayal of the title character from Indiana, whose sweetness and strength transcend life's disappointments and betrayals.

Scarface (HOWARD HAWKS, 1932)   Hawks, who spent his early years in the Midwest, used Chicago crime lord Al Capone as the model for this audacious black comedy about a gangster named Tony Camonte (Paul Muni). Screenwriter Ben Hecht, a former Chicago newsman, had the Borgias in mind when he introduced an incestuous subplot involving Tony's sister Cesca (Ann Dvorak). In the hyperviolent Brian De Palma/Oliver Stone remake (1983), the setting was transferred to Miami's Cuban-American underworld.

Alice Adams (GEORGE STEVENS, 1935)   A sparkling film version of Booth Tarkington's novel about a social-climbing young Indiana woman trying desperately to escape her stultifying family. Expertly satirizing the cloying dullness that surrounds her, *Alice Adams* features a performance by Katharine Hepburn that is simultaneously amusing and heartbreaking.

Young Mr. Lincoln (JOHN FORD, 1939)   Ford's justly celebrated portrait of Lincoln's early days in New Salem and

Springfield is so intimate and vivid that it seems to transport the viewer back in time. Henry Fonda's uncanny incarnation of the "young jack-leg lawyer" has been viewed by American audiences as heartwarming, but by French critics as chilling and inhuman. The film is rich enough to support both interpretations.

Abe Lincoln in Illinois (JOHN CROMWELL, 1940) Less poetic than Ford's version but more comprehensive, this sturdy biopic was based on Robert Sherwood's Pulitzer Prize–winning play. Raymond Massey makes a rather sepulchral but still convincing Lincoln in an episodic story ending with his departure from Springfield in 1861. Ruth Gordon makes the much-maligned Mary Todd Lincoln both understandable and admirable.

The Magnificent Ambersons (ORSON WELLES, 1942) Welles, a Wisconsin native, claimed that his father was one of the models for automobile inventor Eugene Morgan in Booth Tarkington's Pulitzer Prize–winning 1919 novel about the tragic decline of a family of Midwestern gentry. With Joseph Cotten playing Eugene in Welles's adaptation, the end of a way of life is conveyed with Chekhovian grace as the Ambersons' comfortable insularity is gradually destroyed by the polluting force of the automobile. Despite its mutilation by RKO, *Ambersons* remains one of the greatest American films.

Kings Row (SAM WOOD, 1942) Buried scandals and gossip, incest and suicide, sexual punishment by amputation—has there ever been a film that more chillingly captured what Michael Lesy called the "death trip" aspect of small-town Midwestern life? Illinois native Ronald ("Where's the rest of

me?") Reagan gave his best performance in this overly elliptical but still haunting version of the lurid novel by Harry
Bellamann.

Meet Me in St. Louis (VINCENTE MINNELLI, 1944)   As an
idealized tribute to the warmth and vigor of Midwestern family life, this ravishing Technicolor musical can't be beat. Minnelli's joyous and kinetic MGM movie, starring his then-wife
Judy Garland, is set around the time of the 1904 St. Louis
Exposition.

All I Desire (DOUGLAS SIRK, 1953)   Anyone who has ever
been stigmatized for rebelling against a repressive Midwestern
background will identify with Barbara Stanwyck in this corrosive Sirk melodrama. After leaving her family to pursue a
stage career in New York, the disillusioned Stanwyck finds a
cruelly condemnatory and gloating reception on her return
home.

Some Like It Hot (BILLY WILDER, 1959)   Set partly in Chicago during the Roaring Twenties, this greatest of all American sound comedies starts off, incredibly enough, with a
re-creation of the Saint Valentine's Day Massacre. Only *Scarface* captures the insanity of that period as colorfully as this
uproarious classic of bullets, jazz, and transvestism, which
Wilder wrote with I. A. L. Diamond.

Medium Cool (HASKELL WEXLER, 1969)   Director and cinematographer Wexler's powerful blend of documentary and fiction set during the 1968 Democratic convention in Chicago,
when the police riot against antiwar demonstrators destroyed
the Democrats' chances for reelection and capped the most
violent year in American politics since the Civil War.

The Emigrants (JAN TROELL, 1971) and *The New Land* (TROELL, 1972)   Companion pieces by the Swedish director-cinematographer, beautifully filmed in Wisconsin and Minnesota, about a Swedish immigrant family headed by Max von Sydow and Liv Ullmann. Based on four novels by Wilhelm Moberg, this epic saga captures the courage and travail the land exacted from those who sought to become Americans.

The War at Home (GLENN SILBER AND BARRY ALEXANDER BROWN, 1979)   A thorough and fascinating, if sometimes politically simplistic, documentary about the antiwar movement at the University of Wisconsin, Madison. Silber and Brown intercut retrospective interviews with news footage shot by local TV crews to depict a heartland town thrown into turmoil during the Vietnam War.

Lessons Learned from Movies About Teachers: 7 Movies Chosen by Steven Spielberg's Grade School Teacher Patricia Scott Rodney

Goodbye, Mr. Chips (SAM WOOD, 1939)   Chips (Robert Donat) said, "As long as you believe in yourself, you can go as far as you can dream!" I believe that axiom is particularly true for Steven Spielberg. When Steven was in seventh and eighth grades in Arizona, I was one of his teachers. As part of my curriculum, each student was to choose a career field to investigate. In addition to reading about a particular career, each student was required to learn about the necessary skills and education levels, interview people in the particular field, and, finally, generate a product. Steven chose to write, produce, and direct a movie. He involved his family and his classmates in the making of a Western filmed in the desert outside Scottsdale. He used students for his cast and spent his allowance for props, fake blood being a particular favorite. When his movie debuted in our classroom, his classmates and I believed that Steven had produced a timeless epic. We ran the film backward and forward many, many times, sometimes providing additional dialogue and sound. Steven became a hero and was invited to film class plays and other school events. Incidentally, one of the "extras" and a member of the film crew is also a producer-director in Hollywood. His name is Randy Wright, and I'm told he calls himself "the poor man's Spielberg."

Dangerous Minds (JOHN N. SMITH, 1995)   In this movie, Michelle Pfeiffer experienced the "first-day trauma" that often sends tyros fleeing. On the very first day of my professional teaching career, a little boy threw up on me (twice). Even after I cleaned the floor, the boy, and my clothes, the rest of the class held their noses and screamed, "Peeee-U, you stink!" One little guy bolted for the window, threw it open and screamed, "Help me! They're torturing me!" The priest from the neighboring church called to report possible child abuse. The principal questioned my competence. I questioned my sanity for choosing to teach junior high. Sometimes, even after twenty-five years in the classroom, I remember that terrible beginning and wonder what motivated me to return for Day Two.

The Cowboys (MARK RYDELL, 1972)   In *The Cowboys*, John Wayne's character is a trail boss, teacher, and mentor to eleven boys on a cattle drive. In the language of "eduspeak," he provided scared, gutsy little kids with the opportunity for learning by doing. He was a team builder who drew on the students' prior knowledge, providing active participation in a climate that was challenging and rewarding.

While working as a school administrator on the Tohono O'odham Reservation in Arizona, I came to know a man named Phil Woolever. Phil is a poet, a playwright, and the best handicapper of boxing matches in the United States. He is also one of the most interesting and dedicated educators I have ever known. Although he is not a teacher, earns far less than a teacher, and sometimes receives less respect, Phil comes to school daily with a positive attitude, a creative style, and a professional spirit. Not unlike John Wayne's character, he helps kids live up to their potential by providing experiences that are spirit-enhancing, skill-developing, and rewarding in every sense of the word. Although Phil's special-needs students have yet to be on a cattle drive as in *The Cowboys*, he provides educational opportunities not included in any school curriculum. He makes sure that every kid can drive a car whether or not he or she will ever be able to pass a driver's test. He finds jobs for the students and supervises them while they are on the job. Phil takes them on trips and helps them learn to order from a menu, ask for directions, and negotiate the Tucson bus routes. He provides information on health, sex, and contraception (when asked). He knows all of their parents, brothers, sisters, and boy/girlfriends. He lives the axiom from *The Cowboys*, "It's not how you're buried, it is how you're remembered." Phil will be remembered.

To Sir, with Love (JAMES CLAVELL, 1967)   "Sir" (Sidney Poitier) told the students that his classroom rules were acceptable deportment and cleanliness. Although good conduct allows for a good teaching climate, the "cleanliness" part also cannot be overlooked. In my years in the classroom, I have had scores of students in junior high who believed that "clean" was a dirty word. I was frequently faced with the dilemma of freeing the classroom from the potentially toxic effects of students who had spent days and nights sleeping and playing with the dog, rolling around in the dirt, sweating, and adroitly avoiding the bath or shower. My strategy for rescuing the hapless bathless kids was to take them aside at a moment when the whole world was not looking on and tell them that it was not acceptable to smell that bad, explain a bit of basic hygiene, and end with the question, "When you are grown up and have your name in *Who's Who* or your face on *Time* magazine, do you want your old classmates to remember you as 'Smelly (insert last name)'?" I would always report the conversation to the parents so they could be standing by with the proper cleaning supplies and emotional support. It must have worked at least once, since I have never heard anyone call my most well known former student "Smelly Spielberg."

Dead Poets Society (PETER WEIR, 1989)   What a wonderful teacher (played by Robin Williams) and what talented students! I was so inspired that I actually considered giving up retirement and seeking a job so I could have another shot at motivating and helping students acquire the love of learning. In retrospect, I believe that all too often I chose to reduce the curriculum to the level of the greatest number, leaving the gifted to fend for themselves. Imagine what I and they missed.

Lean on Me (JOHN G. AVILDSEN, 1989)   In the middle '60s there were no classrooms set up for children with average or better IQ who could not learn in the traditional manner. Today these children are considered eligible for special-education services under the labels of "learning disabled" or "attention deficit disordered." So, when faced with a growing number of students who would not shut up, sit down, and learn, Scottsdale answered the problem by collecting problem kids ages ten through sixteen (grades six through eight) in one large room. For this hazardous duty, the district recruited me and an extraordinarily talented woman named Phyllis Schoolitz. Together we took the fifty-two kids nobody wanted because of learning or behavior problems and created the best possible educational experience for them. Because the system expected little from us, we were not compelled to design our teaching to achieve test results or fulfill parents' expectations. Instead, we could teach to the kids' individual strengths and help them compensate for the holes in their information or skills.

The baseball bat–toting Joe Clark, the high school principal played in *Lean on Me* by Morgan Freeman, was successful with the hard-core behavior problems by removing many students and raising standards. We, on the other hand, created a program that turned the kids (lowest in terms of personal resources and school social structure) into the caretakers of the most sought-after school programs. Our class ran intramurals, produced the school plays, and provided lunchtime and after-school diversions. Our students did all the important jobs of managing the programs, and some also participated on an equal footing with mainstream students. Our students were the timers, prompters, actors, and cooks. From these experiences they learned how to read, compute, and succeed. So, while I cheer for the success of students treated with "tough love" in *Lean on Me*, I also know that the "Mom" approach can be successful too.

Up the Down Staircase (ROBERT MULLIGAN, 1967)   The new teacher played by Sandy Dennis is sweet, naive, and totally unprepared for the task of teaching uninterested and disenfranchised students. In the ed-biz vernacular, the teacher learned quickly and well what is meant by the "teachable moment." The principal was portrayed as a jerk who hid in the hideous environment he helped to maintain. In my personal experience, few administrators are as ugly as that fellow. I have had the great good fortune to work with (I insist on "with," not "for") wonderful, caring, and talented administrators who support valuable programs and cut programs that might be in vogue but are not in step with student needs. Watching the school-dance sequence in the movie was uncomfortable for me. In the '60s and '70s, junior high teachers were expected to chaperone and participate in school dances.

Although I considered the duty to be part of my job, I enjoyed watching and dancing, sometimes with other teachers and frequently with the kids. Today, dancing with students would be risky at best.

BACKSTAGE

PATRICIA SCOTT RODNEY holds a bachelor of arts degree from Duchesne College in Omaha and a master's degree from Chapman College in California. She views herself as a lifetime educator. Ms. Rodney began her career in Omaha and has taught in Scottsdale and Benson, Arizona, and on the Tohono O'odham Reservation. She has been a classroom teacher, a special-education teacher, and a public-school administrator. Today she lives in Tucson, where she volunteers as the Granny Nanny of the perfect child and as a docent at the Desert Museum.

Gabba Gabba Hey
Rock 'n' Roll High School Trivia

I'm proud to have been one of the screenwriters of *Rock 'n' Roll High School*, the 1979 punk-rock musical starring the Ramones. This $280,000 Roger Corman production for New World Pictures has gone on to become a cult classic. In fact, I keep running into people who tell me it's their favorite movie. Although it was unavailable for years except in TV syndication, *Rock 'n' Roll High School* was reissued in 1997 on videotape and DVD, and on laserdisc with commentary by director Allan Arkush and others who worked on it. But I've never written about the movie before, and there is much about its making that, until now, has never been revealed.

1. The project originally was called *Girls' Gym*, the title of a sixty-page treatment dictated into a tape recorder over a two-day period in 1977 by the director, Allan Arkush, and his partner in the New World editing department, Joe Dante. The treatment had no plot, only a series of scenes in which high school kids goof off around the school. In the climax, a chimpanzee drinks a drug concocted by the students, turns into a King Kong–size behemoth, and breaks through the roof of the school. There was no political dimension to the treatment; the students were simply having some reckless fun. Charles B. Griffith, screenwriter of such Corman classics as *A Bucket of Blood* and *The Little Shop of Horrors*, was the first writer hired for the project, but I was told that Arkush found his work unsatisfactory. Griffith did not receive screen credit.

2. I was called in because New World production chief Jon Davison had optioned a screenplay of mine about teenagers in the 1950s, *Rock City*, loosely based on Dick Clark and *American Bandstand* (that project fell through after Corman showed the script to Clark, who didn't appreciate its satirical take). I was handed the *Girls' Gym* treatment on a Friday afternoon and told that if I could come up with a plotline over the weekend, I could write the script.

3. Since I had attended a strict Jesuit high school, Marquette University High School in Milwaukee, where the school disciplinarian whipped our asses with a sawed-off golf club, I naturally thought of making the story revolve around a repressive administration's attempt to control rebellious students. I based the plot on the experiences of

my father, Raymond E. McBride, when he led a student strike as student body president at Superior (Wis.) Central High School in 1927, to protest the firing of one of their favorite teachers. I combined that real-life event with some anarchic elements from the 1933 Jean Vigo classic *Zéro de Conduite*, about students at a boarding school who rebel against their tyrannical headmaster. My father was excited when I told him about *Rock 'n' Roll High School* but deeply disappointed when he saw it and realized it wasn't a docudrama about his 1927 school strike.

4. I based the character of the brainy and alluring Kate Rambeau (Dey Young) on my former girlfriend Laurel Gilbert; in her large glasses, Dey Young looked remarkably like Laurel. Wanting to slip a subtle double entendre into the name of this deceptively demure character, I dubbed her "Rambeau" after the town of Ramsdale in Vladimir Nabokov's *Lolita*. Arkush modeled the rock 'n' roll fanaticism of Riff Randell (P. J. Soles) on three girls he knew while working as an usher at New York's Fillmore East and borrowed her first name from a character in *West Side Story*. I drew Riff's bold, rebellious traits from my first girlfriend, the late Margaret Keshena. I named school quarterback Tom Roberts (Vincent Van Patten) after the star athlete at my high school, Tom Fox (coincidentally, Kate refers to Tom as a "fox"). Arkush named the sympathetic teacher Mr. McGree (Paul Bartel) after the Belgian painter René Magritte. The principal, Miss Togar (Mary Woronov), was named by one of the other writers, Russ Dvonch, after his high school principal (in my script, Woronov was the girls' gym teacher, Miss McQueen). Arkush named the school *macher*, Eaglebauer (Clint

Howard), after the character played by Edward Everett Horton in Ernst Lubitsch's *Design for Living*.

5. I named the school Ronald Reagan High School (Reagan was still three years away from being elected president). The ending was to include a shot of the students blowing up a statue of Reagan. Corman, however, did not want to offend Reagan, who lived near him in Pacific Palisades. So I came up with Vince Lombardi High School, after the Green Bay Packers' football coach, whom I used to watch in action during his glory days in the early 1960s, when I was selling hot dogs at Milwaukee County Stadium. Lombardi's gung-ho approach and famous saying "Winning isn't everything—it's the only thing" made him a perfect symbol of the militaristic discipline the students disdain. Ironically, in the sequel, *Rock 'n' Roll High School Forever* (1991), the school was called Ronald Reagan High School, but by that time, Reagan had come and gone as president of the United States and was safer to satirize.

6. I decided to politicize the ending of *Rock 'n' Roll High School*, in keeping with its newfound radicalism. The idea of having the students blow up their school was suggested to me by the 1970 Sterling Hall bombing at the University of Wisconsin, Madison. Four radicals blew up the building, which housed the Army Mathematics Research Center, killing a graduate student. I covered the bombing while working as a reporter on *The Wisconsin State Journal*, assigned to the student antiwar protest movement. The Sterling Hall bombing was the subject of Tom Bates's 1992 book *Rads*, which has been purchased for filming.

7. In his 1997 laserdisc commentary, Arkush claimed that blowing up a high school "had been a fantasy of mine since I was in high school." If that was the case, he didn't mention it to me at the time, nor did he show me a treatment he claimed to have written containing such a scene. In fact, Arkush was nervous about my ending, telling me he was afraid that blowing up the school would make the kids "unsympathetic." However, "As far as Roger was concerned, [blowing up the school] was the whole reason for making the movie," Arkush recalled. Corman felt that what made *Rock 'n' Roll High School* successful was "the anarchy of the film, the fact that it is so wild and the fact that the students act out every teenager's ultimate dream—they take over the high school, and finally they blow it up in the last scene." The way I managed to talk Arkush into going along with my ending was by passing him the information (gleaned from a fellow journalist) that director Jonathan Kaplan was planning to end his then-filming *Over the Edge* with kids setting fire to a community center. As I correctly guessed, that whetted our director's desire to outdo a more expensive movie directed by a fellow Corman protégé. In his 1981 book *Cult Movies*, Danny Peary writes of *Rock 'n' Roll High School*, "This may be a silly comedy but there is no other commercial American film in which an American institution is destroyed and no one is punished for the deed."

8. After I had written five drafts of the script, Arkush, at Paul Bartel's urging, decided to take the movie in an even zanier direction, handing it over for a rewrite to Richard Whitley and Russ Dvonch, who had written for the TV series

National Lampoon's Animal House. On the laserdisc, Whitley explained their approach to *Rock 'n' Roll High School*: "Allan was talking about, you know, political and social values, and Russ and I just wanted to get into, like, Three Stooges and Bob Hope jokes." They rewrote the dialogue and added the characters of Eaglebauer and the fascistic hall monitors (Loren Lester and Daniel Davies), among other changes, but kept the other characters and much of the story line, including the anarchic final sequences. Among the discarded elements were a track competition and war games conducted on the school athletic field against students dressed as Arabs ("We may have to fight those Arabs for that oil some day," explains a jingoistic teacher). Whitley and Dvonch added more scenes for the rock group—I had been told we could afford only three songs, but Arkush somehow managed forty-five!—and the amusing sex education lessons Eaglebauer gives to Tom and Kate.

9. Announcements shortly before filming began in November 1978 gave the title as *Disco High*. Corman "was under the influence of the grosses of *Saturday Night Fever*," Arkush recalled, but the aghast director was able to change the executive producer's mind about the title by pointing out that the Ramones were not a disco band and that, anyway, "you couldn't blow up a high school to disco music."

10. I was told to think of the Tubes for the rock group while working on the script. Before the Ramones were signed, offers were made to other rockers, including Todd Rundgren, who passed because he thought the script should have been more serious in tone, like Lindsay Anderson's

If . . ., which was similarly inspired by *Zéro de Conduite*. Cheap Trick asked for too much money; Devo and Van Halen also were considered. The Ramones proved a perfect choice, because their punk-rock style was a satirical throwback to the early days of rock 'n' roll in the 1950s, and we were satirizing '50s movies about teenage rebellion, such as *The Blackboard Jungle* and *Rock Around the Clock* (filmed at the same school as our movie).

11. Corman once referred to the Ramones as the "Ramonies." As a result, that mispronunciation was put in the mouth of Mr. McGree as he reads the group's name from a poster. Corman didn't understand the appeal of the Ramones, but Arkush explained that they were popular precisely because older people found them repulsive. Once Corman gave the green light, he "didn't stop us once," Arkush gratefully remembered.

12. Dick Miller, the Corman regular who plays the police chief, improvised his funny line "They're ugly, ugly, ugly people" after the director said to him, "Tell us what you think of the Ramones."

13. The romantic theme song heard under the credits, "Did We Meet Somewhere Before?," is sung by Paul McCartney and Wings. McCartney wrote it as the theme song for Warren Beatty's *Heaven Can Wait*, but Beatty decided not to use it. The Ramones' manager swung a deal whereby Arkush was able to use the song for only $500, provided McCartney did not receive screen credit.

14. Originally, Arkush planned to blow up the school by using a miniature, but Corman said it would be too expensive and wouldn't look believable. So the director

was forced to blow up a building for real. The production rented a Catholic school that had been condemned because it wasn't earthquake-safe, Mount Carmel High School in the Watts section of Los Angeles. On the first of two chilly December nights scheduled for shooting the ending, the veteran special effects man (who had a large burn scar across his face) rigged a naphthalene explosion, with powder charges in mortars and propane flame pots arrayed from the ground to the roof. The preparations looked so hairy to me that I decided to play it safe and watch the filming from across the street. Sure enough, there was a huge explosion, sending out a large fireball and showering glass over the crowd of extras. Arkush said the explosion "was about five times bigger than it was supposed to be." Along with trees and bushes, the American flag caught fire and tumbled spectacularly from its pole, making an impressive shot in slow motion, but one that Arkush decided not to use because it would have seemed "too symbolic." When the explosion took place at three in the morning, dazed and angry neighborhood residents streamed out of their homes in bathrobes, wondering what was happening—no one had warned them. Fortunately, there were no serious injuries, but the explosion gave some people minor burns and also broke windows and left scorch marks on the building.

15. Parts of *Rock 'n' Roll High School* were directed by Joe Dante (including the title number in the girls' gym, the students trashing the cafeteria, the elegantly shot long take in the girls' bathroom, and Riff winning a radio ticket contest), Jerry Zucker (scenes of the students running wild in the hallway), and Jon Davison (who rigged the

ingenious paper-airplane gimmick with Zucker). Dante took over the first unit for the last few days of shooting after Arkush collapsed in the Van Nuys High School gym and was taken away in an ambulance, brought down by the stress of the twenty-day schedule. Still, *Rock 'n' Roll High School* is a genuinely auteurist work, reflecting Arkush's distinctive vision in every frame.

16. The cinematographer of *Rock 'n' Roll High School*, Dean Cundey, later shot Steven Spielberg's *Jurassic Park*. Arkush notes, "*One shot* in *Jurassic Park* cost more than this movie."

17. None of us was paid much for our work on *Rock 'n' Roll High School*. Under the opening credits, when the name of New World Pictures appears on screen, you can dimly hear bird sounds mixed in during postproduction. The birds are going, "Cheep, cheep, cheep." Corman didn't notice the dig at his legendary cheapness.

18. *Rock 'n' Roll High School* opened poorly in Texas in April 1979 because it was marketed as a formulaic teen exploitation movie, playing in drive-ins and so forth. Among the opening venues was the Texas Theater in the Oak Cliff section of Dallas, the theater where Lee Harvey Oswald was captured. Fortunately, *Rock 'n' Roll High School* was tested as a midnight attraction in Chicago, where it began to catch on thanks to a favorable review by Gene Siskel and Roger Ebert, whom Arkush credits with having "saved the movie." It played for many months around the country as a midnight movie, later becoming the first feature ever shown on MTV.

19. Some people were upset about the school insurrection scenes, including Jack Valenti, president of the Motion Picture Association of America. After attacking the movie on a Los Angeles radio station, reviewer Gary Franklin encountered Valenti the next day at an industry function and told him about it. Valenti obliged with a radio interview describing *Rock 'n' Roll High School* as "swill." I told people that what Valenti *really* meant was that the movie was "swell," but with his Texas accent it just sounded like "swill."

20. Hey, don't blame us for the sequel. The writers, director, and producer (Michael Finnell) who worked on the original *Rock 'n' Roll High School* were not involved with the dismal *Rock 'n' Roll High School Forever*, written and directed by Deborah Brock for Corman's Concorde Pictures (Mary Woronov did play the dominatrix principal, albeit renamed Dr. Vadar, but the star was Corey Feldman). Corman admitted that "it didn't come together with the energy of the original *Rock 'n' Roll High School*." Arkush, P. J. Soles, and Dey Young are still hoping to do their own sequel, although if they wait much longer it might have to be called *Rock 'n' Roll Retirement Home*.

Sister Superior
The 10 Sexiest Nuns in Movies

My credentials for composing this list are impeccable. They include twelve years of

Catholic school, eight of them with Dominican nuns. I also directed an amateur movie called *The Missionary Position* (1972), about a nun who's impregnated by a priest. And I have an aunt who is a nun, Sister M. Jean Raymond McBride of the School Sisters of Notre Dame. My Aunt Margie's kindness, tolerance, and loyalty is so exemplary that she went to a Milwaukee theater full of screaming teenagers to see *Rock 'n' Roll High School* . . . and told me she liked it! So, I have no doubt she even will forgive me for making out this list. But just to be sure—*three Our Fathers and three Hail Marys* . . .

1. *Ingrid Bergman* in *The Bells of St. Mary's* (LEO MCCAREY, 1945)   The radio ads for this movie—a tension-filled, unconsummated romance between Bing Crosby's Father O'Malley and Bergman's Sister Mary Benedict—brought the sexual undertones right out into the open: "Ingrid Bergman has never been lovelier, hubba, hubba, hubba!"

2. *Audrey Hepburn* in *The Nun's Story* (FRED ZINNEMANN, 1959)   When this lovely young nun takes off her habit at the end and goes out into the world, it's every Catholic boy's wish come true.

3. *Deborah Kerr* in *Heaven Knows, Mr. Allison* (JOHN HUSTON, 1957)   At age ten, I was scandalized by this movie about a nun and a Marine stranded on a desert island during World War II. But when I saw it again years later, I was moved by the discretion with which Huston and his actors handle what could have degenerated into a dirty joke. The most touching scene is Mitchum's shy proposal of marriage and Kerr's kind and tactful way of saying, "No, Mr. Allison."

4. *Deborah Kerr* in *Black Narcissus* (MICHAEL POWELL AND EMERIC PRESSBURGER, 1946)   This ravishing color movie about British nuns in a Himalayan convent has all the overheated passion for which Powell and Pressburger were famous. Kerr's recollections of her life before taking the veil were censored when the film was first released in the United States.

5. *Catherine Lacey* in *The Lady Vanishes* (ALFRED HITCHCOCK, 1938)   In this comedy-thriller set on a train, Lacey is the false nun in high heels, an image that stirs all kinds of lurid fantasies.

6. *Shirley MacLaine* in *Two Mules for Sister Sara* (DON SIEGEL, 1970)   OK, Shirley's not really a nun, she's a hooker disguised as a nun in this Western, based on a story by Budd Boetticher. But who am I to quibble?

7. *Lillian Gish* in *The White Sister* (HENRY KING, 1923) Wordsworth's phrase "quiet as a nun / Breathless with adoration" could have been written to describe Gish's performance in this silent movie. Her sublime beauty demonstrates the close link between religious and sexual ecstacy.

8. *Silvia Pinal* in *Viridiana* (LUIS BUÑUEL, 1961)   Buñuel celebrated his return to Spain by packing as much blasphemy and anticlerical humor as possible into *Viridiana*. Silvia is deliciously risqué as a novice whose last taste of worldly pleasures escalates into an orgy with beggars and cripples, audaciously climaxed by Buñuel's parody of Leonardo da Vinci's *The Last Supper*.

9. *Susan Sarandon* in *Dead Man Walking* (TIM ROBBINS, 1995)   As Sister Helen Prejean, who ministers to a death-row inmate (Sean Penn), Sarandon wears civilian clothes and behaves impeccably. But it's her mature womanliness that enables Sarandon's worldly nun to understand a sinning man.

10. *Mary Tyler Moore* in *Change of Habit* (WILLIAM GRAHAM, 1969)   Mary's so adorable anyway, it's not hard to see why Elvis Presley would go for her, even without the added attraction of the habit. But she's got a tough choice to make—Elvis or God. Hardcore Elvis fans would say it's no choice at all, because they're one and the same.

. . . A Borderline Case

Julie Andrews in *The Sound of Music* (ROBERT WISE, 1966) I debated whether Julie can truly be described as "sexy" in this monumentally sweet musical concoction, and I couldn't really decide. But if you're into the crisp-and-starchy, British-nanny kind of nun fantasy, she is the epitome. Especially if you close your eyes and mentally superimpose Julie's bare-breasted scene in *S.O.B.* over the sisters singing "How Do You Solve a Problem Like Maria?"

. . . From Here to Eternity Award
To the Actress Who Became a Real-Life Nun

Dolores Hart, the comely starlet who appeared with Elvis Presley in *Loving You* (1956) and *King Creole* (1958), made a few more movies, including George Cukor's *Wild Is the Wind* (1957) and Philip Dunne's *Lisa* (1962). But after playing a stewardess trying to find a husband in *Come Fly with Me* (1963), Hart astonished Hollywood by entering a convent. She remains in the sisterhood today, by all accounts very happily so, as Mother Dolores of the Benedictine Order.

Schmucks with Underwoods
Lists About Writers

The Devil's Dictionary of Hollywood

"action"—Means "violence." Few filmmakers or makers of TV programs will admit that their stock-in-trade is violence, so they usually resort to this nonthreatening euphemism, especially when pressure groups are trying to crack down on screen mayhem.

"all-time"—Means "in the last ten or twenty years." When used in reference to box-office figures, the phrase "an all-time record" is more than slightly absurd, because the practice of routinely releasing complete box-office figures was not put into effect by studios until the early 1980s. Furthermore, inflation has rendered meaningless any direct comparisons between box-office grosses of modern movies and those of movies from previous eras.

"amicable"—Means "acrimonious." When a studio and a filmmaker announce they have reached an "amicable" parting, almost invariably the opposite is true. Otherwise why would they feel the need to describe it as "amicable"?

"the auteur theory"—Means "the director is God." After the elastic and largely illusory term "net profits," the most contentious concept in Hollywood—especially when the Directors Guild and the Writers Guild are feuding over credit issues—is the auteur theory. Originally known as *la politique des auteurs*, or "the policy of authors," it was developed by French critics in the 1950s largely to account for the situation of Hollywood filmmaking during the Golden Age, in which a great director such as Howard Hawks was able to impose his style and worldview on a film without having written the screenplay. When popularized in the United States by critic Andrew Sarris in the early 1960s, the *politique des auteurs* became known as "the auteur theory."

By the time it penetrated Hollywood a few years later, the auteur theory had been broadened and vulgarized, implying in its extreme that *every* director, whether or not he or she has a personal style, should be considered an auteur. Hollywood opponents of the auteur theory took the equally extreme position that only a writer-director should be considered an auteur. Along the way, the director became virtually omnipotent within the industry, leading to some ridiculous and even dangerous excesses, and the original French rationale for the *politique des auteurs* was forgotten.

"creative differences"—Means "We won't tell you why we can't work together anymore, because it's none of your damn business." Nobody wants to discuss the ugly facts surrounding a firing, a resignation, or even a mutual decision to part company. In the same vein, hardly anyone in Hollywood sees any upside in admitting his or her true age or income.

"denial"—Means "confirmation." According to McBride's First Law of Reporting on Hollywood, a story coming out of Hollywood should not be believed until it is officially denied. While this law of course has some exceptions, if a story is untrue there usually is no point in a studio's denying it, because to do so would only call more attention to the story. If Hollywood doesn't want the public to believe an unflattering truth, the usual strategy is an indignant denial. The truth, in such cases, will come out a few years later in an interview or a memoir, when it's no longer risky to admit it.

"flick"—Pejorative expression for "movie." In the early days of movies, snobs, such as people from the so-called legitimate theater, liked to mock silent pictures as "flickers." The word was considered so insulting that D. W. Griffith would throw people off his set for using it, or its variant "flick." Even today, its use has a condescending ring, such as in the phrase "horror flick."

"gross"—Does *not* mean "rentals" . . . and vice versa. Box-office gross refers to the amount of money taken in by theaters when a film is played. Film rentals (also not to be confused with "profit" or "earnings") are the amount returned to the distributor after the theaters take their shares. These terms are often confused in the press, and even within the film industry.

"a handshake deal"—Means "You're screwed." As Samuel Goldwyn so sagaciously put it, "A verbal contract isn't worth the paper it's written on."

"high concept"—Means low concept. This vile phrase, which has governed Hollywood filmmaking for the past twenty-plus years, implies that every movie should be capable of being reduced to a simple formula, preferably no more than a sentence in length. Reflecting Hollywood's condescension toward its audience, the "high concept" mentality allows marketing to control content and results in predictably shallow moviemaking designed to appeal to the widest possible market.

"I'll get back to you about it"—Means "I won't." Nobody in Hollywood ever likes to say no, although for most people, that is their job. Instead of an actual turndown, a project is given what is known as "a slow no." In the meantime, its status is described with that poetic phrase "a definite maybe."

"I loved it"—Means "If you think I'll tell you what I actually thought of your movie, you're crazy." This all-purpose euphemism is for use after studio screenings, especially when the filmmaker is standing in the doorway as the captive audience members exit. Billy Wilder was confronted with a similar problem as he left a Paramount screening room where Cecil B. DeMille had just screened his execrable 1952 circus movie *The Greatest Show on Earth*. Clasping DeMille's hand, Wilder told him earnestly, "Cecil, you have made *The Greatest Show on Earth*."

"Let's do lunch"—Means "I'm pretending to want to see you again so you don't think I'm brushing you off." If the person hearing the phrase "Let's do lunch" responds by actually trying to set a date for lunch, the person making the offer will hastily find an excuse to get off the phone.

"schmucks with Underwoods"—An old derogatory expression for screenwriters, the Rodney Dangerfields of the writing profession. This phrase is still used even though hardly any screenwriters use typewriters anymore. They even have software programs now that tell them how to build clichés into their scripts.

"Trust me"—Means "You'd better count your fingers after we shake hands."

The Pantheon of Screenwriters

In alphabetical order, with three of their best screenplays listed. Some of these scripts were written with collaborators.

Woody Allen: Manhattan, Annie Hall, Crimes and Misdemeanors

Ingmar Bergman: Winter Light, Persona, Wild Strawberries

Robert Bolt: Lawrence of Arabia, A Man for All Seasons, Ryan's Daughter

Sidney Buchman: Mr. Smith Goes to Washington, The Talk of the Town, Theodora Goes Wild

Jean-Claude Carrière: The Discreet Charm of the Bourgeoisie, Belle de Jour, The Milky Way

Francis Ford Coppola: The Godfather Part II, The Godfather, The Conversation

Philip Dunne: How Green Was My Valley, The Ghost and Mrs. Muir, Stanley and Livingstone

Samuel Fuller: Shock Corridor, Merrill's Marauders, Park Row

Jules Furthman: The Big Sleep, Shanghai Express, To Have and Have Not

Ruth Gordon and *Garson Kanin:* Adam's Rib, The Marrying Kind, Pat and Mike

Ben Hecht and *Charles MacArthur:* The Front Page, Twentieth Century, His Girl Friday

John Huston: The Man Who Would Be King; The Treasure of the Sierra Madre; Heaven Knows, Mr. Allison

Ring Lardner Jr.: Woman of the Year, M*A*S*H, The Cross of Lorraine

Herman J. Mankiewicz: Citizen Kane, Citizen Kane, Citizen Kane

Frances Marion: The Wind, The Champ, Dinner at Eight

Dudley Nichols: Stagecoach, The Informer, Air Force

Kogo Noda: Tokyo Story, Late Spring, An Autumn Afternoon

Frank S. Nugent: The Searchers, Fort Apache, The Quiet Man

Abraham Polonsky: Tell Them Willie Boy Is Here, Force of Evil, Body and Soul

Jacques Prévert: Children of Paradise, A Day in the Country, The Crime of Monsieur Lange

Samson Raphaelson: Trouble in Paradise, Heaven Can Wait, The Shop Around the Corner

Jean Renoir: The Rules of the Game, La Grande Illusion, Boudu Saved from Drowning

Robert Riskin: *Mr. Deeds Goes to Town, It Happened One Night, Lady for a Day*

Preston Sturges: *The Miracle of Morgan's Creek, Sullivan's Travels, The Palm Beach Story*

Robert Towne: *Chinatown, Shampoo, The Last Detail*

François Truffaut and **Suzanne Schiffman:** *Day for Night, The Story of Adele H., Small Change*

Billy Wilder: *Some Like It Hot, The Apartment, Sunset Boulevard*

Michael Wilson: *Lawrence of Arabia, The Bridge on the River Kwai, Salt of the Earth*

Steven Zaillian: *Schindler's List, Amistad* (uncredited), *Searching for Bobby Fischer*

My Favorite Line in Movies

In John Ford's classic Western *My Darling Clementine* (1946), the nurse from back East, Clementine (Cathy Downs), assists in an operation performed in a saloon on the fatally wounded Chihuahua (Linda Darnell). Following the operation, Wyatt Earp (Henry Fonda) looks admiringly at Clementine standing in the distance at the saloon door. When she leaves, Earp turns to the elderly bartender, Mac (Ford regular J. Farrell Mac-Donald), and asks, "Mac—you ever been in love?" Mac replies:

"No-o, I been a bartender all me life."

The Greatest Bad Line in the History of Movies

In Samuel Fuller's *Shock Corridor* (1963), a reporter (Peter Breck) has himself committed to a mental hospital to investigate a murder. He cracks the story but in the process goes truly mad and turns catatonic. At the end, his psychiatrist, Dr. Cristo (John Matthews), says sadly:

"What a tragedy—an insane mute will win the Pulitzer Prize."

The Most Beautiful Title in the History of the Cinema

Somewhere in Sonora

An otherwise routine John Wayne B Western directed by Mack V. Wright for Warner Bros. in 1933. The sonorous location named in the alliterative title is the Mexican state adjoining most of Arizona's southern border.

The Marquee de Sade
12 Movies Hurt by Bad Titles

"So many pictures are ruined by a bad title," says former Universal publicist Orin Borsten, who vainly tried to promote Steven Spielberg's *The Sugarland Express*. As for the title of this list, it is borrowed from a feature that once ran in the *National Lampoon*, suggesting double bills featuring the 1965 Natalie Wood movie *Inside Daisy Clover*. Among the marquee listings offered for theater managers were *"Thunderball/ Inside Daisy Clover," "Saturday Night and Sunday Morning/ Inside Daisy Clover,"* and *"8½/Inside Daisy Clover."*

1. *Closed Mondays* (WILL VINTON AND BOB GARDINER, 1974)   This Claymation short about a drunk having hallucinations in an art museum after hours is the hands-down winner for the all-time worst movie title. The reason? Some theater owners were willing to play *Closed Mondays* after it won an Academy Award in 1975 for best animated short subject. But when the title appeared in advertisements and on the lower half of marquees, nobody showed up for Monday performances. Theaters realized what was wrong and stopped playing, or at least promoting, the picture.

2. *The Sugarland Express* (STEVEN SPIELBERG, 1974)   This early Spielberg feature was not a fluffy Goldie Hawn comedy, as its title seemed to imply, but a somber drama with Hawn as a distraught mother trying to reclaim her infant son from a foster home. Partly because audiences were misled by the title, *The Sugarland Express* was one of Spielberg's few commercial failures.

3. *I Walked with a Zombie* (JACQUES TOURNEUR, 1943) Producer Val Lewton's haunting melodrama about voodooism in Haiti, beautifully directed by Tourneur, was loosely based on Charlotte Brontë's *Jane Eyre*. But the title, like those of other Lewton films, suggested a penny dreadful. Many shortsighted reviewers were slow to appreciate Lewton's low-budget masterpieces as a result.

4. *The Curse of the Cat People* (GUNTHER VON FRITSCH AND ROBERT WISE, 1944)   Another Lewton picture, this

one was billed as a sequel to *Cat People* but bore little resemblance to that classic shocker. Actually, it's a sensitive drama about a lonely little girl who lives in a fantasy world.

5. ***Dying Young*** (JOEL SCHUMACHER, 1991)   This Julia Roberts vehicle had the quintessential "downer" title. To borrow a phrase from Sam Goldwyn, her fans stayed away in droves.

6. ***The Fearless Vampire Killers or: Pardon Me, But Your Teeth Are in My Neck*** (ROMAN POLANSKI, 1967)   Polanski's stylish black comedy about vampirism, which starred his soon-to-be-murdered wife Sharon Tate, eventually was renamed with the director's intended title, *Dance of the Vampires*. The unsuccessful American release had not only a hokey title grafted onto it by producer Martin Ransohoff, but also a cornball animated prologue.

7. ***Liebestraum*** (MIKE FIGGIS, 1991)   This little-seen movie about a writer visiting his dying mother used for its title a German word that means "love dream" but has unfortunate echoes of *Lebensraum* ("living space"), the concept Adolf Hitler used to justify the expansionist, land-grabbing philosophy of the Third Reich. As *Leonard Maltin's Movie & Video Guide* puts it, *Liebestraum* is burdened with "a truly insane title."

8. ***Gorillas in the Mist*** (MICHAEL APTED, 1988)   The title of Apted's film about gorilla researcher Dian Fossey (Sigourney Weaver) was unappealing enough before it acquired racist notoriety when an L.A. cop used those four words as code for a call involving African Americans.

9. *Lolly Madonna xxx* (RICHARD C. SARAFIAN, 1973) This gibberish title violated one of the basic rules of movie titles: they must be easy for viewers to say and remember. Dealing with a backwoods feud, the film stars Jeff Bridges, Rod Steiger, and Robert Ryan and is also known as *The Lolly-Madonna War*.

10. *Flesh* (JOHN FORD, 1932) This is not a stag movie, but rather an MGM melodrama about a German wrestler played by Wallace Beery. The writers of this Ford oddity included Moss Hart and (uncredited) William Faulkner.

11. *Girls Demand Excitement* (SEYMOUR FELIX, 1931) One of John Wayne's early talkies, this campus comedy for Fox about male students trying to oust women from their college had a title that seemed to go out of its way to invite derision. Considering *Girls Demand Excitement* "the silliest picture of his career," according to biographers Randy Roberts and James S. Olson, Wayne later remarked, "It was just so goddam ridiculous that I was hanging my head."

12. *Human Desire* (FRITZ LANG, 1954) Discussing his film version of Emile Zola's novel *La Bête Humaine*, Lang dryly remarked to Peter Bogdanovich, "Ya. Have you ever seen any other kind of desire?"

Gavin Lambert's Favorite Hollywood Novels

In Horace McCoy's *I Should Have Stayed Home* (1938), a naive young man from the heartland arrives in Hollywood with hopes of becoming a movie star. After trying the hard honest way, he tries the easier corrupt way. Laconic and melancholy, this novel leaves him still marginalized as an extra, but still vaguely hopeful, in "the most terrifying town in the world."

In John O'Hara's *The Big Laugh* (1962), a sophisticated, ambitious young theater actor from the East becomes a Hollywood star, less on account of his acting talent than his skill at manipulation, blackmail, and sexual politics. An acid success story, as authentic in its impressions of top-echelon Hollywood as McCoy's account of the underside.

Although Scott Fitzgerald left *The Last Tycoon* incomplete when he died in 1941, it remains the most complete portrait of a breed of Hollywood producer who no longer exists. Monroe Stahr, wrote Fitzgerald, was one of the very few men who "have ever been able to keep the whole equation of pictures in their heads." Today, unfortunately, he seems like a character in a historical novel.

Raymond Chandler invented Los Angeles noir, but in *The Little Sister* (1949), Hollywood casts an alarming spell over most of its characters. They live out archetypal movie fantasies of rags to riches, irresistibly dangerous gangsters, or B-picture femmes fatales. "I must have men, amigo," says actress Dolores Gonzales. "But the man I

loved is dead. I killed him. That man I would not share."
This sardonic novel reflects a Los Angeles and a Hollywood strikingly close to modern times with its teenage
junkie, its agent who tapes every conversation in his office,
its brutal and brutalized cops who see only "the dirt, the
dregs, the aberrations and the disgust" of the world
around them.

You Play the Black and the Red Comes Up was written in 1937 by "Richard Hallas," an Englishman who used
his real name of Eric Knight when he published *Lassie
Come Home* a few years later. The earlier novel, "hard-
boiled" in the style of James M. Cain, could not be more
different. It's another fable of the young man from the
heartland who arrives in Los Angeles and lives on the margins of Hollywood until its unreality finally overwhelms
him. Then he decides that the whole place *doesn't exist.*
Everything, including the mountains and the Pacific
Ocean, is a mirage created by "back projection."

Finally, a brilliant and ruthless fiction of contemporary Los Angeles, with Hollywood as its haunting presence. In *The Informers* (1994), Bret Easton Ellis describes
the beautiful and tanned, the lost and the corrupt, in a
world of Valium, Walkmans, anorexia, bisexuality, MTV,
murder—and the movies. "Just read this fabulous screenplay. A remake of Camus's *The Stranger* with Meursault
as a bi break-dancing punk rocker."

GAVIN LAMBERT's books include the Hollywood novel
Inside Daisy Clover; an acclaimed collection of short
stories about Los Angeles, *The Slide Area*; the George
Cukor interview book *On Cukor*; and biographies of
Norma Shearer and Alla Nazimova. A former editor of

Sight and Sound, he has written the screenplays of such movies as *Sons and Lovers* and *I Never Promised You a Rose Garden*.

From Poe to Chandler:
The Shamus in Hollywood

by Noel O'Hara

Why was the Irish imagination so important in the creation of the detective genre in literature? Edgar Allan Poe, whose people came from County Cavan, created the detective genre in 1841 with his first story of C. Auguste Dupin, "The Murders in the Rue Morgue." The Doyles came to Scotland from Ireland, and Arthur Conan Doyle gave us the most famous of all detectives in Sherlock Holmes. Raymond Chandler, Irish on both sides, produced the most polished private eye in the American tradition, Philip Marlowe. James M. Cain, who was disappointed when he at last visited the land of his ancestors, inherited the native gift for tale bending, and Keyes, the head of the claims department in his novel *Double Indemnity*, is one of the more memorable detectives in popular fiction.

History made the Irish a secretive people, and so their curiosity about each other is sharp, to say the least. A loose tongue could be equally dangerous for the oppressed and the ruling class, who had lived side by side in mutual suspicion for hundreds of years. Eyes and ears had to become very sensitive to clues that would make for plausible tales about neighbors. Small wonder informers are significant in Irish literature, or that "Shamus," the Gaelic name for James and still very common in Ireland, became a synonym for *detective* in the United States. Some of Hollywood's most memorable classics have been adapted from detective fiction in that Irish tradition started by Poe and kept alive today by writers such as John Gregory Dunne and George V. Higgins. Even Gore Vidal, of the Irish Gores, has written detective stories, under the pseudonym of Edgar Box.

Murders in the Rue Morgue (ROBERT FLOREY, 1932)
Poe showed his Irish penchant for the gothic, as well as for detection, in this bizarre story. Always short of money, he came too early to enjoy the Hollywood money that did so much to sustain the best of twentieth-century American writers, such as Fitzgerald and Faulkner. Since the early part of the century, Poe's works have inspired many movies in different parts of the world. "The Murders in the Rue Morgue" has been adapted for the screen numerous times, and the one that survives best is the 1932 version, whose screenwriters included Irish-American John Huston.

The Hound of the Baskervilles (SIDNEY LANFIELD, 1939)
Basil Rathbone's portrayal of Sherlock Holmes, first seen in this movie based on Conan Doyle's tallest and most famous tale, is the definitive characterization of one of the most eccentric Englishmen in popular fiction. The Doyles were talented artists, and two of them, Conan's grandfa-

ther John and his uncle Dick, worked for *Punch*. John Doyle—who signed himself "H. B."—resigned because of the notoriously anti-Irish nature of its caricatures. Perhaps the eccentricity of Holmes sprang from the Irish Doyles' getting a bit of their own back!

Double Indemnity (BILLY WILDER, 1944) To Raymond Chandler, James M. Cain was "a Proust in greasy overalls, a dirty little boy with a piece of chalk and a board fence and nobody looking." But when it came to earning good money for adapting *Double Indemnity* for the screen, he didn't mind getting his hands dirty, it seems. Cain's gift for plot and Chandler's way with words added up to one of the most successful collaborations of two Irishmen in the history of motion pictures. Of course, there also were Edward G. Robinson as Keyes and Fred MacMurray at his best as Walter Neff, and Billy Wilder holding it all together.

The Big Sleep (HOWARD HAWKS, 1946) Chandler blessed Philip Marlowe with the pithy wit of the Irish—those memorable one-liners! His novels envisaged Marlowe as someone like Cary Grant in appearance, but he thought Bogart's portrayal in *The Big Sleep* the genuine article. Memorable, too, for the sulky sensuality of Bacall as the older Sternwood sister, a *provocateur* of some of Marlowe's best lines.

True Confessions (ULU GROSBARD, 1981) John Gregory Dunne, author of *Harp*, a memoir of what it was like to be Irish in the United States, used a brutal murder mystery as a focus on the society of his novel *True Confessions*. He had to shed most of the earthy Irish wit in adapting it for the screen in collaboration with his wife, Joan Didion. His story survives, however, as a memorable and unique depiction of Irish society in Los Angeles. A central strength of the novel, the ironic interplay of good and evil between the two brothers, one a priest and the other a homicide detective, is wonderfully preserved in the playing of Robert De Niro and Robert Duvall.

NOEL O'HARA is a freelance writer, an Irishman who lives for half of each year in the San Francisco Bay Area. His major area of interest is American writers with Irish ancestry, and he has written widely on the topic for newspapers such as the *Los Angeles Times* and national newspapers in Ireland. He also has published essays in *The Recorder: A Journal of the American Irish Historical Society* on such subjects as Raymond Chandler, Gore Vidal, Flannery O'Connor, Margaret Mitchell, and Eugene O'Neill. O'Hara is completing a book on Irish-American writers, which he calls a literary travelogue for anyone interested in the United States and its writers.

15 Famous Books That Have Never Been Filmed

Paradise Lost (1667), by John Milton Orson Welles could have made a great movie out of Milton's epic poem about Satan's defiance of his creator. Could anyone else?

Narrative of the Life of Frederick Douglass, an American Slave (1845), by Douglass This landmark in American autobiography cries out to be filmed, now that African-American history is being retrieved from cinematic oblivion in such films as *Rosewood* and *Amistad*. A former slave who secretly taught himself to read and write with rare eloquence, Douglass chronicles his rise to prominence as a leader of the abolitionist movement. Douglass was portrayed by Raymond St. Jacques in Edward Zwick's magnificent Civil War movie *Glory* (1989), but unfortunately the role allowed him to speak only one line (see Ben Burtt's 1991 documentary *The True Story of "Glory" Continues*, available with *Glory* on laserdisc, for an outtake featuring Douglass's celebrated speech "Men of Color to Arms").

Walden (1854), by Henry David Thoreau   A film version of Thoreau's philosophical book about life in the woods would need a similarly idiosyncratic narrative style. The filmmaker would have to approach it as a personal essay, perhaps combining Thoreau's observations with contextual information on the author's life, such as the help he received from his mother, who did his laundry and served him meals at her home near Walden Pond.

Family Happiness (1859), by Leo Tolstoy   Tolstoy's novella about a young woman's disillusioned perspective on marriage would seem easily adaptable to film. Unlike *War and Peace* or *Anna Karenina*, *Family Happiness* would not have to be pruned heavily for a dramatic adaptation, and its themes speak equally vividly to modern readers.

The Death of Ivan Ilych (1886), by Leo Tolstoy   Perhaps the most profound meditation on mortality in all of literature, this Tolstoy novella would make a powerful film, although one that probably would be so depressing it would drive people out of the theaters.

Maggie: A Girl of the Streets (1893), by Stephen Crane
Crane's gritty novella about an ill-fated young woman living
in the Bowery set a new standard for realism in American fiction, greatly influencing Hemingway, among others.

The Financier (1912), by Theodore Dreiser   Dreiser's sprawling saga of a ruthless American capitalist is packed with
socially conscious drama and would seem a natural for movies
(or a TV miniseries).

Look Homeward, Angel (1929), by Thomas Wolfe   Liberty
Films, the short-lived post–World War II partnership of Frank
Capra, William Wyler, George Stevens, and Sam Briskin,
acquired the rights to Wolfe's first novel and hired Michael
Wilson to write a script. The project collapsed along with Liberty in the aftermath of the commercial failure of Capra's *It's
a Wonderful Life*. The rights to the novel, like other Liberty
properties, were acquired by Paramount Pictures.

The Catcher in the Rye (1951), by J. D. Salinger   Perhaps
the most celebrated case of a book whose author adamantly
refuses to allow it to be filmed. That's not surprising, for on
the very first page of the book, Salinger's teenaged protagonist, Holden Caulfield, declares, "If there's one thing I hate, it's
the movies. Don't ever mention them to me." Jerry Lewis, who
strongly identified with Holden's alienation and his pride in
being able to spot "phonies," is one of the filmmakers who
have pursued the rights to the book, but Salinger's agent never
even responded to Lewis's queries.

Invisible Man (1952), by Ralph Ellison   One of the great
American novels, this multilayered look at African-American
identity, seen through the figure of a chameleon man who fills

many different social roles, may be too daunting a challenge for filmmakers. But wouldn't it make a perfect project for Spike Lee?

A Burnt-Out Case (1961), by Graham Greene   Despite the author's background as a film critic and screenwriter, most of his novels have not been transferred successfully to film. This story about a disillusioned Catholic architect who finds refuge in an African leprosarium presents unusual challenges for a filmmaker.

The Painted Bird (1965), by Jerzy Kosinski   Kosinski's harrowing, almost surreal novel about the Holocaust centers on a young boy (presumably a Gypsy or a Jew) who wanders on his own through the hostile countryside of occupied Eastern Europe. Although Kosinski claimed it was based on his own experiences, *The Painted Bird* seems much closer to the childhood experiences of his longtime acquaintance, Polish émigré filmmaker Roman Polanski. Polanski would be the perfect director to tackle a film version of this novel, but he might be unlikely to do so, since he passed up an offer from Steven Spielberg to direct *Schindler's List*, not wanting to relive his childhood traumas. With Kosinski's blessing, I tried to interest Hollywood studios in a film version of *The Painted Bird* in the early 1980s, but to no avail; before Spielberg brought *Schindler's List* to the screen, most people in Hollywood refused to consider the Holocaust as commercially viable subject matter.

Thy Neighbor's Wife (1980), by Gay Talese   This highly personal, even obsessive, exploration of the sexual freedom movement of the 1970s was purchased for filming, but the problems involved in actually depicting such activities in a mainstream movie may have helped scuttle the project. Now this period piece could be filmed with the same kind of critical perspective that has brought us such movies about '70s sexuality as *The Ice Storm* and *Boogie Nights*.

Libra (1988), by Don DeLillo   DeLillo's fascinating attempt to project himself into the consciousness of Lee Harvey Oswald was being developed as a film around the same time Oliver Stone was developing *JFK*. The *Libra* project collapsed, but this imaginative look at one of the most enigmatic personalities in modern American history still would make good film material, and a corrective to the glaringly inadequate TV movies about Oswald and his wife, Marina.

The Satanic Verses (1988), by Salman Rushdie   Given the notoriety of the novel, which forced Rushdie underground to avoid the *fatwa* (death sentence) pronounced on him by Iran's Ayatollah Khomeini, is it any wonder that filmmakers have not wanted to risk the same fate? Even Rushdie's gradual reemergence into public view hasn't led to a film adaptation of a book that, in any case, doesn't fit into any standard commercial niche.

The All-Time Best Story Pitch

Ken Russell convinced United Artists to let him make a biopic of Tchaikovsky, *The Music Lovers* (1971), by pitching it as a "story of a homosexual who falls in love with a nymphomaniac."

Breaking the Back of the Book
35 Brilliant Literary Adaptations

In Hollywood, the process of adapting literary material to the screen is charmingly referred to as "breaking the back of the book." Some of these movies are listed because they intelligently transformed great literary material into cinema (a much harder task than is usually realized), and some are listed because they so vastly improved over their sources. You guess which are which.

Way Down East (D. W. GRIFFITH, 1920)   Screenplay by Anthony Paul Kelly and Griffith, based on the play by Lottie Blair Parker, Joseph R. Grismer, and William Brady.

Greed (ERICH VON STROHEIM, 1925)   Screenplay by June Mathis and Stroheim, based on the novel *McTeague* by Frank Norris.

Trouble in Paradise (ERNST LUBITSCH, 1932)   Screenplay by Grover Jones and Samson Raphaelson, based on the play *The Honest Finder* by Laszlo Aladar.

Design for Living (LUBITSCH, 1933)   Screenplay by Ben Hecht, based on the play by Noël Coward.

Madame Bovary (JEAN RENOIR, 1934)   Screenplay by Renoir, based on the novel by Gustave Flaubert.

David Copperfield (GEORGE CUKOR, 1935)   Screenplay by Howard Estabrook, adaptation by Hugh Walpole, from the novel by Charles Dickens. (John Huston called *David Copperfield* "the only great film made from a great novel." See "The 10 Most Profound Hollywood Jokes.")

Mr. Deeds Goes to Town (Frank Capra, 1936)   Screenplay by Robert Riskin, based on the novella *Opera Hat* by Clarence Budington Kelland.

Gone with the Wind (Victor Fleming, 1939)   Screenplay by Sidney Howard (and Ben Hecht, John Lee Mahin, Oliver H. P. Garrett, et al., uncredited), based on the novel by Margaret Mitchell.

How Green Was My Valley (John Ford, 1941) Screenplay by Philip Dunne, based on the novel by Richard Llewellyn.

Casablanca (Michael Curtiz, 1942)   Screenplay by Julius J. Epstein, Philip G. Epstein, and Howard Koch, based on the play *Everybody Comes to Rick's* by Murray Burnett and Joan Alison.

Double Indemnity (Billy Wilder, 1944)   Screenplay by Wilder and Raymond Chandler, based on the novel by James M. Cain.

To Have and Have Not (Howard Hawks, 1944)   Screenplay by Jules Furthman and William Faulkner, based on the novel by Ernest Hemingway. (The only movie whose writing pedigree includes two winners of the Nobel Prize for literature. Hawks told Hemingway, "I can make a movie out of the worst thing you ever wrote," and Hemingway helped on the treatment, without credit.)

Great Expectations (David Lean, 1946)   Screenplay by Lean, Ronald Neame, and Anthony Havelock-Allan, based on the novel by Charles Dickens.

Force of Evil (ABRAHAM POLONSKY, 1948)   Screenplay by Polonsky and Ira Wolfert, based on Wolfert's novel *Tucker's People*.

The Third Man (CAROL REED, 1949)   Screenplay by Graham Greene, based on his own novella.

All About Eve (JOSEPH L. MANKIEWICZ, 1950)   Screenplay by Mankiewicz, based on the short story "The Wisdom of Eve" by Mary Orr.

Rashomon (AKIRA KUROSAWA, 1951)   Screenplay by Kurosawa and Shinobu Hashimoto, based on two short stories by Ryunosuke Akutagawa, "In a Grove" and "Rashomon."

The Red Badge of Courage (JOHN HUSTON, 1951)   Screenplay by Huston, based on the novel by Stephen Crane.

The River (RENOIR, 1951)   Screenplay by Rumer Godden and Renoir, based on Godden's novel.

The Searchers (FORD, 1956)   Screenplay by Frank S. Nugent, based on the novel by Alan LeMay.

The Tarnished Angels (DOUGLAS SIRK, 1957)   Screenplay by George Zuckerman, based on the novel *Pylon* by William Faulkner.

Jules and Jim (FRANÇOIS TRUFFAUT, 1962)   Screenplay by Truffaut and Jean Gruault, based on the novel by Henri-Pierre Roché.

The Manchurian Candidate (JOHN FRANKENHEIMER, 1962)   Screenplay by George Axelrod, based on the novel by Richard Condon.

Tom Jones (TONY RICHARDSON, 1963)   Screenplay by John Osborne, based on the novel by Henry Fielding.

Dr. Strangelove or: How I Learned to Stop Worrying and Love the Bomb (STANLEY KUBRICK, 1964)   Screenplay by Kubrick, Terry Southern, and Peter George, based on George's novel *Red Alert*.

Chimes at Midnight (ORSON WELLES, 1966)   Screenplay by Welles, based on the plays *Richard II*, *Henry IV Parts I and II*, *Henry V*, and *The Merry Wives of Windsor* by William Shakespeare, and (for the commentary) *The Chronicles of England* by Raphael Holinshed.

War and Peace (SERGEI BONDARCHUK, 1968)   Screenplay by Bondarchuk and Vasily Solovyov, based on the novel by Leo Tolstoy.

The Godfather (FRANCIS FORD COPPOLA, 1972)   Screenplay by Mario Puzo and Coppola (and Robert Towne, uncredited), based on Puzo's novel.

The Godfather Part II (COPPOLA, 1974)   Screenplay by Coppola and Puzo, based on Puzo's novel *The Godfather*.

The Man Who Would Be King (HUSTON, 1975)   Screenplay by Huston and Gladys Hill, based on the short story by Rudyard Kipling.

The Dead (HUSTON, 1987)   Screenplay by Tony Huston, based on the short story by James Joyce.

Howards End (JAMES IVORY, 1992)   Screenplay by Ruth Prawer Jhabvala, based on the novel by E. M. Forster.

Schindler's List (STEVEN SPIELBERG, 1993)   Screenplay by Steven Zaillian, based on the novel by Thomas Keneally.

The Bridges of Madison County (CLINT EASTWOOD, 1995) Screenplay by Richard LaGravenese, based on the novel by Robert James Waller.

L.A. Confidential (CURTIS HANSON, 1997)   Screenplay by Brian Helgeland and Hanson, based on the novel by James Ellroy.

"Additional Dialogue by Sam Taylor"
10 Ridiculous Literary Adaptations for the Screen

Love (EDMUND GOULDING, 1927)   For this silent version of Tolstoy's tragic novel *Anna Karenina*, starring real-life lovers Greta Garbo and John Gilbert, MGM not only changed the story to a modern setting and gave it an insipid new title, but also supplied theaters with a choice of two endings—one tragic, one happy. The movie originally was to have been titled *Heat*, before screenwriter Frances Marion pointed out that marquees would read, "Garbo and Gilbert in *Heat*." But "Garbo and Gilbert in *Love*" failed to enchant moviegoers.

Show Boat (HARRY POLLARD, 1929)   The first screen version of the great stage musical by Jerome Kern and Oscar Hammerstein II had one major flaw—it was a silent movie. Although made during the changeover from silents to talkies, this strange hybrid utilized the show's music only as an accompaniment. Why didn't they simply wait a few months?

The Taming of the Shrew (SAM TAYLOR, 1929)   This early-talkie Shakespeare adaptation starring Douglas Fairbanks and

Mary Pickford brought down ridicule upon itself by including the credit line "Additional Dialogue by Sam Taylor" (nobody remembers that Taylor also directed the movie).

The Magnificent Ambersons (ORSON WELLES, 1942)   When RKO took the cutting of *Ambersons* away from Welles and reshot parts of it, the studio added what reviewer Manny Farber called a "hearts-and-flowers finish," reuniting Joseph Cotten and Agnes Moorehead and thus making nonsense of everything that came before in Welles's profoundly moving adaptation of Booth Tarkington's novel. Fortunately, the ending is so awful it's easy for audiences to recognize that Welles had nothing to do with it.

The Fugitive (JOHN FORD, 1947)   Faced with the censorship difficulties involved in portraying Graham Greene's "whiskey priest" in this adaptation of his novel *The Power and the Glory*, Ford and screenwriter Dudley Nichols gave the Mexican priest (incongruously played by Henry Fonda) a mild fondness for altar wine and excised his womanizing tendencies.

Cat on a Hot Tin Roof (RICHARD BROOKS, 1958)   George Cukor sensibly refused to direct MGM's film version of the Tennessee Williams play about a closeted homosexual, because the studio refused to let the character of Brick (played by Paul Newman) have any homosexual inclinations. In so doing, the movie was left with the difficult task of explaining why the virile young Newman didn't have any sexual interest in his wife, played by Elizabeth Taylor at her most lusciously ripe.

Myra Breckenridge (MICHAEL SARNE, 1970)   This incoherent mess, which made mincemeat of Gore Vidal's satirical novel about transsexualism, may be the worst movie ever released by a major Hollywood studio.

The Scarlet Letter (ROLAND JOFFÉ, 1995) Once Demi Moore was cast as Hester Prynne in this rewrite of Nathaniel Hawthorne's great novel about Puritan New England, it perhaps was inevitable that Hester would be shown caressing herself in a bath, watching Gary Oldman's Reverend Dimmesdale as he bathes outdoors, and getting it on with him atop a pile of grain (the movie also includes an attempted rape, a masturbation scene involving Hester's servant girl, and a happy ending). But after assaulting the book so shamelessly, couldn't they at least have had the decency to change the title?

The Portrait of a Lady (JANE CAMPION, 1996) From the bizarrely inappropriate opening sequence, which resembles a TV fashion commercial, I knew this Nicole Kidman vehicle wasn't going to be a faithful adaptation of the great Henry James novel. But still, it was a bit of a surprise to see Isabel Archer's vacillation over two lovers depicted by showing all three of them in bed together.

Great Expectations (ALFONSO CUARÓN, 1998) If Charles Dickens were alive today, he'd sue to have his name removed from this wacky adaptation of his novel, which transplants the story from England to the Florida Gulf Coast and the contemporary New York art world. That gives Estella (Gwyneth Paltrow) an extended opportunity to pose nude for Ethan Hawke's dreary young protagonist, albeit with remarkable coyness given the circumstances. Dickens's poignantly mad Miss Havisham is reduced to a figure of camp, played by Anne Bancroft at her most floridly grotesque. As the escaped convict, Robert De Niro veers between reprising his chilling Max

Cady from Martin Scorsese's *Cape Fear* and stalking around like a road-company George C. Scott with bushy whiskers and putty nose.

23 Books That Should Be Filmed Again

François Truffaut told me there are only two justifications for remakes—when the original material has been filmed badly, or when it was compromised by censorship. In most of the instances below, great books were turned into mediocre or downright bad movies; in some cases, as with *Kings Row* and *The Diary of Anne Frank*, censorship of one kind or another resulted in serious evasions. And in other cases, including *Alice Adams* and *Dodsworth*, the first movie was excellent, but there's still room for another version. Some classic novels, such as *Adventures of Huckleberry Finn* and *Of Human Bondage*, are perennials for fresh adaptation.

Adventures of Huckleberry Finn, by Mark Twain (filmed in 1931, 1939, 1960, 1974, 1975 and 1981 for TV, 1985, and 1993; oddly, only the 1985 version has used the exact title of the book)

Alice Adams, by Booth Tarkington (filmed in 1923 and by George Stevens in 1935)

Babbitt, by Sinclair Lewis (filmed in 1924 and 1934)

The Bible, by various authors (among the many film adaptations is John Huston's 1966 *The Bible . . . in the Beginning*, about which *Leonard Maltin's Movie & Video Guide* comments, "Definitely one time you should read the Book instead.")

The Brothers Karamazov, by Fyodor Dostoyevsky (filmed by Richard Brooks in 1958)

The Dark Page, by Samuel Fuller (filmed as *Scandal Sheet* by Phil Karlson in 1952)

The Day of the Locust, by Nathanael West (filmed by John Schlesinger in 1975)

The Diary of Anne Frank (unexpurgated version; the 1955 stage adaptation of the originally published version of the book was filmed by George Stevens in 1959)

Dodsworth, by Sinclair Lewis (filmed by William Wyler in 1936)

The Great Gatsby, by F. Scott Fitzgerald (filmed in 1926, 1949, and 1974; the middle version, with Alan Ladd, is not bad)

Kings Row, by Harry Bellamann (filmed by Sam Wood in 1942)

Laughing Boy, by Oliver La Farge (filmed by W. S. Van Dyke in 1933)

Lord Jim, by Joseph Conrad (filmed in 1925 and 1965)

Main Street, by Sinclair Lewis (filmed by Archie Mayo in 1936 as *I Married a Doctor*)

Miss Lonelyhearts, by Nathanael West (filmed in 1933 as *Advice to the Lovelorn*, in 1958 as *Lonelyhearts*, and as a TV movie in 1983)

Of Human Bondage, by W. Somerset Maugham (filmed in 1934, 1946, and 1964)

The Portrait of a Lady, by Henry James (filmed by Jane Campion in 1996)

Resurrection, by Leo Tolstoy (filmed by Samuel Goldwyn in 1934 as *We Live Again*)

Show Boat, by Edna Ferber (filmed in 1929, 1936, and 1951)

The Sun Also Rises, by Ernest Hemingway (awkwardly filmed by Henry King in 1957 and remade for TV in 1984, with many foolish changes)

Tender Is the Night, by F. Scott Fitzgerald (filmed by Henry King in 1962)

Ulysses and *A Portrait of the Artist as a Young Man*, by James Joyce (filmed by Joseph Strick in 1967 and 1979, respectively; after seeing Strick's *Ulysses*, Truffaut observed that it would be hard to name the world's worst director, except that Strick made it easy to do so by making terrible movies based on some of the world's greatest literary masterpieces)

10 Movie Clichés of the 1920s

1. "That it is possible to get a telephone number within a few seconds after lifting the receiver."

2. "That all dissolute young men from the East always make good after they have been sent out West to 'the great open spaces where a man's a man.'"

3. "That under the bright lights of Broadway is the only place where a girl can go wrong."

4. "That it is possible to actually see through a keyhole what is transpiring in the next room."

5. "That women always stand helplessly by in a fight and never make any attempt to offer aid to their defender."

6. "That there are really honest and kindhearted police-men."

7. "That there are no ordinary men in the Sahara desert, all Arabs being sheiks."

8. "That persons always fall violently to the ground no matter in which part of the anatomy they are shot."

9. "That guns are capable of perpetual firing without reloading."

10. "That all country maidens are innocent."

> —from "Dogmas of the Movies" in *What's Wrong with the Movies* by Tamar Lane (1923)

 # Frankly, My Dear, I Give a Damn
by Bob Thomas

Exit lines must be a worrisome thing for movie writers: how to end a scene or a film with a line that will become a national catchphrase. A precious few in each generation achieve it.

Note: By all rights, the authors of classic exit lines should be credited. That is hard to do, since many scripts have multiple writers, some without on-screen credit.

Some lines are taken intact from plays or novels. With regret, I am unable to list the authors in this compilation.

Here are a few favorites:

"Mother of Mercy, is this the end of Rico?"
> Edward G. Robinson's dying words in *Little Caesar* (1931)

"I steal."
> Paul Muni, disappearing into the shadows at the end of *I Am a Fugitive from a Chain Gang* (1932)

"Oh, no, it wasn't the airplanes. It was beauty killed the beast."
> Robert Armstrong explaining what killed King Kong (1933)

"It's a far, far better thing I do than I have ever done. It's a far, far better rest I go to than I have ever known."
> Ronald Colman at the guillotine in *A Tale of Two Cities* (1937)

"Frankly, my dear, I don't give a damn."
> Clark Gable walking out on Vivien Leigh in *Gone with the Wind* (1939) despite her plaint of what would happen to her

"I'll be all around in the dark. I'll be everywhere—wherever you can look. Wherever there's a fight so hungry people can eat, I'll be there. Wherever there's a cop beatin' up a guy, I'll be there. . . ."
> Henry Fonda saying goodbye to Jane Darwell in *The Grapes of Wrath* (1940)

"Louis, I think this is the beginning of a beautiful friendship."

> Humphrey Bogart to Claude Rains at the fade-out of *Casablanca* (1942)

"You know how to whistle, don't you, Steve? You just put your lips together and blow."

> Lauren Bacall in her seductive departure from Humphrey Bogart in *To Have and Have Not* (1944)

"Made it, Ma! Top of the world!"

> James Cagney just before the oil refinery tank explodes in *White Heat* (1949)

"Captain, it is I, Ensign Pulver, and I just threw your stinkin' palm tree overboard. Now what's all this crud about no movie tonight?"

> Jack Lemmon finally finding the guts to confront his captain, James Cagney, in *Mister Roberts* (1955)

"Well, nobody's perfect."

> Joe E. Brown responding to the confession of his "fiancée," Jack Lemmon, that he is really a man in *Some Like It Hot* (1959)

"The son of a bitch stole my watch!"

> Walter Matthau as managing editor Walter Burns in *The Front Page* (1974), ensuring that reporter Hildy Johnson (Jack Lemmon) would be arrested and returned to his newspaper job—the same line spoken (but somewhat slurred) by Adolphe Menjou in the original 1931 version.

Perhaps the film world's most famous exit line, spoken by Orson Welles as the dying Charles Foster Kane in *Citizen Kane* (1941):

"Rosebud."

And no list of exit lines would be complete without the words of the immortal Porky Pig (Mel Blanc):

"B-b-b-that's all, folks."

BOB THOMAS has been reporting on Hollywood for the Associated Press since 1943. Among his thirty books are *Disney's Art of Animation* and several groundbreaking biographies of studio executives and producers, including Harry Cohn, Jack L. Warner, Irving Thalberg, David O. Selznick, and Walt Disney. His latest biography is *Building a Company: Roy O. Disney and the Creation of an Entertainment Empire.*

"Include me out"
The 12 Greatest Goldwynisms

The Polish-born producer Samuel Goldwyn (1879–1974) was legendary for his creative twisting of the English language. His utterances became widely known as "Goldwynisms." One of his former writers, Billy Wilder, succinctly defined a Goldwynism for me as a saying that has "an idiotic sort of illiteracy and yet it makes some sense." Goldwyn biographer A. Scott Berg points out, "With so many gag writers working for him, hardly a lunch in Hollywood went by without somebody's concocting a malapropism and passing it off as something Sam

Goldwyn had just said to him." But even if some Goldwynisms were created by writers or press agents playing up his comical image, several have achieved linguistic immortality.

"A verbal contract isn't worth the paper it's written on."

"Anyone who goes to a psychiatrist should have his head examined."

"I can answer you in two words. Im possible." (Berg reports that Charlie Chaplin "took credit for sticking [this] old music hall gag on Goldwyn.")

"That atom bomb is dynamite!"

When Sergei Eisenstein, director of the 1925 Russian silent classic *Potemkin*, came to Hollywood in 1930, he was invited to meet with Goldwyn, who was known for his interest in prestigious screen material. Eisenstein's associate Ivor Montagu recalled that after the introductions were made, "Sam addressed us—he spoke to me, seeming to be under the misapprehension that Eisenstein needed an interpreter." "Please tell Mr. Eisenstein," said Goldwyn, "that I have seen his film *Potemkin* and admire it very much. What we should like would be for him to do something of the same kind, but cheaper, for Ronald Colman."

When Goldwyn told his staff that he wanted to buy the film rights to Lillian Hellman's play *The Children's Hour*, one of them objected, "But, Sam, you can't make that. It's about lesbians!" Goldwyn replied, "All right, we'll make 'em Americans." *These Three*, Goldwyn's 1936 film version of the play, replaced the lesbian relationship with a heterosexual love triangle. (This story also has been told, with variations, about

Goldwyn considering film versions of the 1926 Arthur Horn-blow Jr.–Edouard Bourdet play *The Captive* and Radclyffe Hall's 1928 novel *The Well of Loneliness*.)

When Goldwyn decided he wanted to buy the film rights to Hellman's *The Little Foxes*, one of his staff objected, "But, Sam, it's so caustic." Goldwyn replied, "I don't care what it costs. Get it!"

"Let's bring it up to date with some snappy nineteenth-century dialogue."

"Tell me, how did you love the picture?"

"I don't care if it doesn't make a nickel. I just want every man, woman, and child in America to see it!" (Goldwyn said this of his acclaimed 1946 production *The Best Years of Our Lives*, which became a huge box-office hit.)

"In life you have to take the bitter with the sour."

"Gentlemen—include me out."

My 16 Favorite Film Books

The Day of the Locust, by Nathanael West (1939)   The greatest novel about Hollywood, an apocalyptic vision of American society as seen through the eyes of people on the fringes of the movie industry.

Picture, by Lillian Ross (1952)   An extraordinarily vivid account of the making of a film—John Huston's 1951 MGM version of *The Red Badge of Courage*—even if the film is actually much better than she makes it sound.

A Child of the Century, by Ben Hecht (1954)   The autobiography of Hollywood's greatest screenwriter, also a great reporter and playwright.

The American Cinema: Directors and Directions 1929–68, by Andrew Sarris (1968)   For my generation of film critics, this was the bible.

The Lubitsch Touch, by Herman G. Weinberg (1968)   A delightfully idiosyncratic study of the life and work of Ernst Lubitsch, the master of sophisticated comedy.

The Parade's Gone By . . ., by Kevin Brownlow (1968)   A monumental oral history of silent film.

Allan Dwan: The Last Pioneer, by Peter Bogdanovich (1970)   A fascinating oral history of a director who was there at the beginning. Included as part of Bogdanovich's massive 1997 collection of his interviews with directors, *Who the Devil Made It*.

From Reverence to Rape: The Treatment of Women in the Movies, by Molly Haskell (1973)   A brilliant analysis of why women's roles in movies have declined since Hollywood's Golden Age.

My Life and My Films, by Jean Renoir (1974)   The autobiography of the wisest man ever to make movies. A companion volume to Renoir's masterful biography *Renoir, My Father*.

Ozu, by Donald Richie (1974)   A thorough and lucid critical study of the Japanese master and his themes by the foremost English-language interpreter of Japanese cinema.

Hitchcock/Truffaut, by François Truffaut (1983 revised edition)   The best interview book about movies—and the best textbook about directing. Originally published in 1966 as *Le Cinéma selon Hitchcock*.

Outrageous Conduct: Art, Ego, and the Twilight Zone *Case*, by Stephen Farber and Marc Green (1988)   An incisive, revealing, and unflinching history of one of Hollywood's most appalling events.

Hitchcock's Films Revisited, by Robin Wood (1989)   Wood's latest revised version of his influential 1965 critical study is a model of erudition, eloquence, and humanism.

This Is Orson Welles, by Orson Welles and Peter Bogdanovich, edited by Jonathan Rosenbaum (1992)   Reading this wide-ranging interview book is the equivalent of spending several hours in the company of the cinema's greatest conversationalist.

Company of Heroes: My Life as an Actor in the John Ford Stock Company, by Harry Carey Jr. (1994)   I devoured in one sitting this marvelous memoir by one of Hollywood's most entertaining and insightful raconteurs. No other book has captured Ford's enigmatic personality as well as Carey's.

The Graham Greene Film Reader: Reviews, Essays, Scripts, & Letters, by Graham Greene, edited by David Parkinson (1994)   A collection by the most distinguished man of letters ever to devote himself wholeheartedly to writing about film.

12 Important Early Books on Cinema

W. K. L. Dickson and Antonia Dickson, *The History of the Kinetograph, Kinetoscope and Kineto-Phonograph* (1895)

Cecil M. Hepworth, *Animated Photography* (1898)

Vachel Lindsay, *The Art of the Moving Picture* (1915)

Hugo Münsterberg, *The Photoplay: A Psychological Study* (1916)

D. W. Griffith, *The Rise and Fall of Free Speech in America* (1916)

Rob Wagner, *Film Folk: "Close-Ups" of the Men, Women, and Children Who Make the "Movies"* (1918)

Terry Ramsaye, *A Million and One Nights: A History of the Motion Picture* (1926)

Joseph P. Kennedy (editor), *The Story of the Films* (1927)

Benjamin B. Hampton, *A History of the Movies* (1931, reprinted in 1971 as *History of the American Film Industry*)

Albert Bigelow Paine, *Life and Lillian Gish* (1932)

Gene Fowler, *Father Goose: The Story of Mack Sennett* (1934)

Lewis Jacobs, *The Rise of the American Film: A Critical History* (1939)

13 Memorable Movie Memoirs

Lauren Bacall, *By Myself* (1979)

Fred J. Balshofer and Arthur C. Miller, *One Reel a Week* (1967)

Ingmar Bergman, *The Magic Lantern* (1988), *Images: My Life in Film* (1994)

Karl Brown, *Adventures with D. W. Griffith* (1973)

Kirk Douglas, *The Ragman's Son* (1988), *Climbing the Mountain: My Search for Meaning* (1997)

Lillian Gish (and Ann Pinchot), *The Movies, Mr. Griffith and Me* (1969)

Elia Kazan, *A Life* (1988)

David Niven, *The Moon's a Balloon* (1972), *Bring on the Empty Horses* (1975)

Don Siegel, *A Siegel Film: An Autobiography* (1993)

François Truffaut, *Les Films de Ma Vie* (1975, English publication in 1978 as *The Films of My Life*)

10 Movie Actresses' Memoirs That Make YOUR Life Seem Wonderful

I'll Cry Tomorrow, by Lillian Roth (with Mike Connolly and Gerold Frank, 1954)

A Portrait of Joan: The Autobiography of Joan Crawford, by Joan Crawford (with Jane Kesner Ardmore, 1962)

The Lonely Life: An Autobiography, by Bette Davis (1962)

Ecstacy and Me: My Life as a Woman, by Hedy Lamarr (1966) (See "The 10 Least Reliable Movie Autobiographies")

Will There Really Be a Morning?, by Frances Farmer (with Jean Ratcliffe, 1972)

No Bed of Roses, by Joan Fontaine (1978)

Self Portrait, by Gene Tierney (with Mickey Herskowitz, 1979)

Ordeal, by Linda Lovelace (with Mike McGrady, 1980)

Lana, The Lady, The Legend, The Truth, by Lana Turner (1982)

No Bells on Sunday: The Rachel Roberts Journals, by Rachel Roberts (edited by Alexander Walker, 1984)

The 10 Least Reliable Movie Autobiographies

Steps in Time, by Fred Astaire (1959)   Astaire's longtime collaborator and alter ego, Hermes Pan, described this book to me as "perhaps the least informative autobiography ever written."

My Autobiography, by Charles Chaplin (1964)   This pretentious extravaganza of name-dropping and pseudo-philosophizing glosses over much that's truly fascinating about

Chaplin's life and work. See David Robinson's 1985 biography *Chaplin* for a fuller and more accurate portrait.

Fun in a Chinese Laundry, by Josef von Sternberg (1965) Anyone reading this woolly book of ramblings will learn precious little about Sternberg or his movies. He seemed to delight in mystifying and antagonizing his readership.

Where's the Rest of Me? by Ronald Reagan (1965; with Richard G. Hubler) Bizarrely, Reagan chose as the title of his first autobiography his famous line in the 1942 movie *Kings Row*, when his character looks down below his waist and realizes in horror that his legs have been amputated. Although Reagan has never been celebrated for his candor or his capacity for self-scrutiny, was he subconsciously trying to tell us something by making that line a Freudian metaphor for his life's story? From his more august perch as ex-president, Reagan chose a far more conventional title for his second memoir, *An American Life* (with Robert Lindsey, 1990).

Ecstacy and Me: My Life as a Woman, by Hedy Lamarr (1966) This book was so outrageously juicy that Hedy sued her own ghostwriters for misrepresentation!

The Name Above the Title, by Frank Capra (1971) Capra's largely fictitious exercise in what reviewer Elliott Stein aptly labeled "autohagiography."

I Am Not Spock, by Leonard Nimoy (1975) and ***I Am Spock***, by Nimoy (1995) OK, which one do you want to believe? In his second book of memoirs, Nimoy called the title of his first book "an enormous mistake." He blamed it on his need to explore and insist upon the differences between himself and his most famous character. Assuring angry fans, "I don't hate the Vulcan," Nimoy wrote in volume two, "I've made a lot of mistakes in my lifetime, but this one was a biggie and right out there in public. Perhaps it wasn't quite as bad as Roseanne Arnold singing the 'Star-Spangled Banner' off-key, grabbing her crotch, and spitting in a stadium full of baseball fans, but mine did start a firestorm that lasted several years and caused a lot of hard feelings."

Memoiren, by Leni Riefenstahl (1987)   Riefenstahl is still trying to convince people that she was an apolitical believer in art for art's sake and a political naïf when she made her notorious 1935 Nazi propaganda film *Triumph of the Will*. What's just as tragic is that many people who should know better continue to swallow her mendacious excuses.

Me, by Katharine Hepburn (1991)   As the title indicates, this is not only a maddeningly egotistical volume, but one whose writing style irritatingly consists mostly of short, stacatto phrases that make genuine communication between author and reader difficult, if not impossible.

Well, It's Easier Than Writing
Writers Acting in Movies

Some of these writers have acted in other movies as well.

Maya Angelou   *How to Make an American Quilt* (1995)

Saul Bellow and Susan Sontag   *Zelig* (1983)

Peter Benchley   *Jaws* (1975)

Truman Capote *Murder by Death* (1976)

G. K. Chesterton and George Bernard Shaw *Rosy Rapture—The Pride of the Beauty Chorus* (1914)

Sir Arthur Conan Doyle *The $5,000,000 Counterfeiting Plot* (1914)

Elinor Glyn *It* (1927)

Graham Greene *Day for Night* (1973, under the pseudonym "Henry Graham"—the director, François Truffaut, did not recognize him)

Zane Grey *White Death* (1936)

Thomas Keneally *The Devil's Playground* (1976)

Jerzy Kosinski *Reds* (1981)

Norman Mailer *Ragtime* (1981)

Harold Pinter *Rogue Male* (1976 TV movie)

Damon Runyon *The Great White Way* (1924), *Madison Square Garden* (1932)

John Sayles *Eight Men Out* (1988, as Ring Lardner)

Mickey Spillane *Ring of Fear* (1954), *The Girl Hunters* (1963, as Mike Hammer)

Jacqueline Susann *Valley of the Dolls* (1967)

Mark Twain *A Curious Dream* (1907)

Gore Vidal *Bob Roberts* (1992)

Hugh Walpole *David Copperfield* (1935)

The Jedediah Leland Memorial Award
To 6 Critics Who Lost Their Jobs Because of Their Reviews

None of the critics listed here suffered as badly for their opinions as the unfortunate Mexican film critic who had the temerity to disparage a movie by the notoriously hot-tempered director Emilio (El Indio) Fernández—Fernández shot him. But like Joseph Cotten's Jedediah Leland in *Citizen Kane*, who is fired by Kane after his opera review calls the boss's mistress "a pretty but hopelessly incompetent amateur," each of these critics had to pay a price for writing an honest review.

Sime Silverman While writing for the *New York Morning Telegraph* in 1905, Silverman panned a vaudeville comedy act, Redford & Winchester. When the team retaliated by canceling its Christmas ad in the paper, Silverman was fired. Undaunted, Silverman left to found a new show business trade paper called *Variety*, declaring in the first issue that it "WILL NOT BE INFLUENCED BY ADVERTISING. . . . The reviews will be written conscientiously, and the truth only told." (Silverman's principled stance would lend irony to the actions of *Daily Variety* against another reviewer in 1992—see the final entry.)

Graham Greene *Wee Willie Winkie* (JOHN FORD, 1937). In the London magazine *Night and Day*, Greene wrote that Shirley Temple had become "completely totsy" in the "mature suggestiveness" of her appeal to older men on-screen: "[W]atch the way she measures a man with agile studio eyes, with dimpled depravity." Twentieth Century–Fox sued the magazine and Greene for libel on behalf of Temple. As Greene later wrote, "I kept on my bathroom wall, until a bomb removed the wall, the statement of claim—that I had accused

Twentieth Century–Fox of 'procuring' Miss Temple for 'immoral purposes.'" *Night and Day*, which lost the suit, went out of business and had to pay £3,000 in damages; Greene, unhappily forced to issue an apology to Temple through the magazine's counsel, had to pay £500. Greene's review can be read in its entirety in *The Graham Greene Film Reader* (1994; edited by David Parkinson).

Frank S. Nugent Various Twentieth Century–Fox films in the late 1930s. Fox had been "complaining constantly to the business department about my reviews" in the *New York Times*, Nugent recalled. After he commented favorably on "the omission of Tyrone Power" from *The Story of Alexander Graham Bell* (1939), the studio withdrew its advertising from the paper for almost a year, but the paper backed up its reviewer. Fox production chief Darryl F. Zanuck then devised a clever strategy to remove Nugent from his position. After Nugent wrote a favorable review of John Ford's 1940 Fox film *The Grapes of Wrath*, Zanuck offered him a screenwriting contract. Nugent accepted but spent the next four years critiquing scripts before production and not being allowed to write screenplays. Eventually, Nugent found his niche as a screenwriter with a series of brilliant films for Ford at other studios, including *Fort Apache*, *The Quiet Man*, and *The Searchers*.

Pauline Kael *The Sound of Music* (ROBERT WISE, 1966). Kael's acidic review of this enormously popular musical helped make her *persona non grata* during her brief tenure at *McCall's*. Many readers of the women's magazine objected to Kael's description of *The Sound of Music* as "the big lie, the sugarcoated lie that people seem to want to eat." The magazine's editor, Robert Stein, denied she was fired over that review. "I was quite pleased with it," he claimed, "because that seemed to me to be a very proper thing to be doing in a mass magazine, to deflate something that was that popular." But he felt that "her reviews became more and more uniformly unfavorable—not only to all films, but questioning the motives of the people who made the films. The reviews became less and less appropriate for a mass-audience magazine." "From the beginning I thought I was the wrong person for their readers," Kael responded, "but they were willing to take the risk. I had realized that I would sock the ladies right between the ears, but what the hell is the point of writing, if you're writing banality." Happily for Kael and her followers, she found a far more congenial base at *The New Yorker* in 1968.

Pat Dowell   JFK (OLIVER STONE, 1991). Stone's movie attacking the Warren Commission's single-bullet theory of the Kennedy assassination was described by Dowell in her three-and-a-half-star review as "a brilliantly crafted indictment of history as an official story." But her review never ran in *Washingtonian* magazine, because it provoked the wrath of her editor, Jack Limpert, who considered JFK "the dumbest movie about Washington ever made" and its theory of an assassination conspiracy and cover-up "bizarre, just crackpot, preposterous." After Limpert pulled the review and refused to reconsider his position, Dowell resigned in protest. She later published an essay on Stone in *A Political Companion to American Film* (1994; edited by Gary Crowdus).

Joseph McBride   Patriot Games (PHILIP NOYCE, 1992). My negative review of *Patriot Games* (see "My 13 Least Favorite Movies") prompted Paramount to pull its ads from *Daily Vari-*

ety. That was hardly an unprecedented reaction, but my editor-in-chief, former Paramount executive Peter Bart, reacted by writing a letter to Paramount Communications chairman and chief executive Martin S. Davis apologizing for my review and promising that I would not be allowed to review any more Paramount films. After Bart's letter was leaked to the *New York Times*, I defended my First Amendment right to my opinion. *Daily Variety* tried every possible means of retaliating, such as canceling my assignment to review *A League of Their Own* and assigning me only children's movies until my lawyer forced the paper to let me resume reviewing adult movies. Receiving unanimous public support from my colleagues in the media, I stuck it out for five months before obtaining a financial settlement from *Daily Variety* and resigning to concentrate on writing books.

The Biggest
Electric Train Set
Lists About Directors

10 Great Quotes from Directors

When **John Ford** was asked in 1936 whether he believed in expressing "your point of view in a picture about things that bother you," he replied, "What the hell else does a man live for?"

"A film is like a battleground. It's love—hate—action—violence—death. In one word, emotions."—**Samuel Fuller** appearing as himself in Jean-Luc Godard's *Pierrot le Fou* (1965)

"Photography is truth . . . and the cinema is the truth twenty-four times a second."—**Jean-Luc Godard** (a line spoken by a character in one of his movies, Michel Subor's Bruno in *Le Petit Soldat*, 1960)

"The reason why stars are good, they walk in through a door and they think, 'Everybody wants to lay me.'"—**Howard Hawks**

Whenever an actor asked too many questions, **Alfred Hitchcock** would intone, "It's only a *movie*."

"Because we can't be Stalin, we become movie directors." —**Abraham Polonsky**

"You can't teach film. I don't give a goddamn who says it, *you can't teach film*."—**Nicholas Ray**

"On this earth there is one thing that's terrible—it's that everyone has his reasons."—**Jean Renoir** as Octave in *The Rules of the Game*

"Shooting a film is like taking a stagecoach ride in the Old West. At first you look forward to a nice trip. Later you just hope to reach your destination."—**François Truffaut** as the director in *Day for Night*

At RKO in 1939 working on his abortive film project *Heart of Darkness*, **Orson Welles** exclaimed, "This is the biggest electric train set a boy ever had!"

My 10 Favorite John Ford Moments

Pilgrimage (1933)   After learning that her estranged son has been killed in combat in World War I, Hannah Jessop

(Henrietta Crosman), who vengefully sent him to his death rather than lose him to the girl he loves, sits silently at her desk, her hands reassembling the ripped-up pieces of the boy's photograph.

Young Mr. Lincoln (1939)   Early in his budding political career, Abe Lincoln (Henry Fonda) strolls idyllically along the river with his ill-fated love, Ann Rutledge (Pauline Moore), the one and only time we see her in the film.

How Green Was My Valley (1941)   On her first visit to the Morgan home, Bronwen (Anna Lee), preceded by the awe-stricken young Huw (Roddy McDowall), receives the bows (in pantomime) of four of his older brothers.

The Battle of Midway (1942)   In the midst of the Japanese bombing attack on Midway Island, sailors risk their lives to raise the American flag, as the narrator of this documentary says in a hushed voice, "Yes—this really happened." (The shot was photographed by Ford himself with a handheld 16 mm camera.)

Fort Apache (1948)   As the stagecoach carrying Colonel Thursday (Henry Fonda) and his daughter (Shirley Temple) travels through Monument Valley in the opening sequence, the camera tilts up past the coach so the composition can feature one of the valley's majestic rock formations, or "monuments," Gray Whiskers. This Fordian use of the camera, which so vividly emphasizes the eternal over the temporal, is the moment that made me fall in love with John Ford's movies when I first saw *Fort Apache* on December 23, 1967.

The Quiet Man (1952)   In a warm tableau of an exile's return, the men of Innisfree welcome Sean Thornton (John

Wayne) home by singing "The Wild Colonial Boy" around the bar of Cohan's Pub.

The Searchers (1956)   My favorite shot in all movies: Ethan Edwards (John Wayne) riding toward the Jorgenson homestead at the end of the five-year search, with Debbie (Natalie Wood) in his arms and Laurie Jorgenson (Vera Miles) running joyously to greet his searching partner Martin Pauley (Jeffrey Hunter), her skirt billowing in the desert wind.

The Last Hurrah (1958)   A baby cries from the second story of a Boston tenement; the soundtrack plays the haunting Irish lullaby "The Castle of Dromore." Irish-American Mayor Frank Skeffington (Spencer Tracy) takes his nephew (Jeffrey Hunter) on a nocturnal visit to a cramped, dimly lit alleyway. "I was born here, Adam," the mayor says, looking up toward the sound of the crying child as if peering directly into his own distant past.

The Man Who Shot Liberty Valance (1962)   When saddle tramp Tom Doniphon (John Wayne) dies a forgotten man, the woman he loved and lost, Hallie (Vera Miles), places a cactus rose on his rough wooden coffin. Seeing it there, her husband, Senator Ransom Stoddard (James Stewart), silently realizes that Doniphon is still the man she loves. As Andrew Sarris observes, "Everything that Ford has ever thought or felt is compressed into one shot . . . photographed, needless to say, from the only possible angle." When Ford died in 1973, I made a lengthy search of Los Angeles flower shops for a cactus rose, finally turning up one tiny plant, which I placed next to the altar before the start of his funeral service. Although the bigger floral displays were transported to his grave by the funeral directors, my cactus rose was left behind.

7 Women (1966)   The atheistic Dr. Cartwright (Anne Bancroft) listens with compassionate fascination as her antagonist, the fanatically religious missionary Agatha Andrews (Margaret Leighton), bares her soul in a nocturnal discussion under a tree in the Chinese mission courtyard: "I've always searched for something that . . . isn't there. And God isn't enough. *[Whispers]* God help me. He—isn't enough."

John Ford's 10 Favorite Movies

1. *The Birth of a Nation* (D. W. GRIFFITH, 1915)

2. *The Honor System* (RAOUL WALSH, 1917; A LOST FILM)

3. *3 Godfathers* (JOHN FORD, 1948)

4. *Ninotchka* (ERNST LUBITSCH, 1939)

5. *The High and the Mighty* (WILLIAM WELLMAN, 1954)

6. *Tol'able David* (HENRY KING, 1921)

7. *The Song of Bernadette* (KING, 1943)

8. *Lady for a Day* (FRANK CAPRA, 1933)

9. *Going My Way* (LEO McCAREY, 1944)

10. *The Alamo* (JOHN WAYNE, 1960)

—compiled for *Cinema* magazine in 1964

François Truffaut's Favorite Movies About Children

François Truffaut (1932–1984) directed some of the finest movies dealing with childhood, including *The 400 Blows* (1959), *The Wild Child* (1970), and *Small Change* (1976). He urged Steven Spielberg to make a film about children, a piece of advice that led to *E.T.—The Extra-Terrestrial* (1982). When Todd McCarthy and I interviewed Truffaut for *Film Comment* in 1976, he gave us this list of his favorite movies about children:

Zéro de Conduite (JEAN VIGO, 1933)

Germania Anno Zero (ROBERTO ROSSELLINI, 1947)

Village of the Damned (WOLF RILLA, 1960)

The Innocents (JACK CLAYTON, 1961)

Incompreso (LUIGI COMENCINI, 1966)

Le Avventure di Pinocchio (COMENCINI, 1971)

Directors' Remakes of Their Own Movies

Frank Capra *Lady for a Day* (1933) and *Pocketful of Miracles* (1961); *Broadway Bill* (1934) and *Riding High* (1950)

George Cukor *What Price Hollywood?* (1932) and *A Star Is Born* (1954)

Cecil B. DeMille *The Ten Commandments* (1923 and 1956 versions)

John Ford   *Marked Men* (1919) and *3 Godfathers* (1948); *Judge Priest* (1934) and *The Sun Shines Bright* (1953)

Sidney Franklin   *The Barretts of Wimpole Street* (1934 and 1957 versions)

Howard Hawks   *Ball of Fire* (1941) and *A Song Is Born* (1948)

Alfred Hitchcock   *The Man Who Knew Too Much* (1934 and 1956 versions)

Ernst Lubitsch   *The Marriage Circle* (1924) and *One Hour with You* (1932, codirected with George Cukor); *Kiss Me Again* (1925) and *That Uncertain Feeling* (1941)

Leo McCarey   *Love Affair* (1939) and *An Affair to Remember* (1957)

Jean Negulesco   *Three Coins in the Fountain* (1954) and *The Pleasure Seekers* (1964)

Yasujiro Ozu   *I Was Born, But . . .* (1932) and *Good Morning* (1959); *A Story of Floating Weeds* (1934) and *Floating Weeds* (1959); *Late Spring* (1949) and *Late Autumn* (1960)

Steven Spielberg   *Firelight* (1964) and *Close Encounters of the Third Kind* (1977) (Note: *Close Encounters* is an unofficial remake of Spielberg's first feature, which he made in 8 mm as a teenaged amateur filmmaker in Phoenix)

Raoul Walsh   *High Sierra* (1941) and *Colorado Territory* (1949); *The Strawberry Blonde* (1941) and *One Sunday Afternoon* (1948)

James Whale   *The Kiss Before the Mirror* (1933) and *Wives Under Suspicion* (1938)

William Wyler   *These Three* (1936) and *The Children's Hour* (1962)

20 Memorable Performances by Directors in Other Directors' Movies

1. *John Huston* in *Chinatown* (ROMAN POLANSKI, 1974)

2. *Orson Welles* in *The Third Man* (CAROL REED, 1949)

3. *Victor Sjöström* in *Wild Strawberries* (INGMAR BERGMAN, 1957)

4. *François Truffaut* in *Close Encounters of the Third Kind* (STEVEN SPIELBERG, 1977)

5. *Lee Strasberg* in *The Godfather Part II* (FRANCIS FORD COPPOLA, 1974)

6. *Vittorio De Sica* in *The Earrings of Madame De . . .* (MAX OPHULS, 1953)

7. *Mark Rydell* in *The Long Goodbye* (ROBERT ALTMAN, 1973)

8. *Cecil B. DeMille* in *Sunset Boulevard* (BILLY WILDER, 1950)

9. *Fritz Lang* in *Contempt* (JEAN-LUC GODARD, 1963)

10. *Leni Riefenstahl* in *The Wonderful, Horrible Life of Leni Riefenstahl* (RAY MULLER, 1993 DOCUMENTARY)

11. *Samuel Fuller* in *Pierrot le Fou* (GODARD, 1965)

12. *Woody Allen* in *The Front* (MARTIN RITT, 1976)

13. *Otto Preminger* in *Stalag 17* (WILDER, 1953)

14. *Sydney Pollack* in *Husbands and Wives* (WOODY ALLEN, 1992)

15. *John Cromwell* in *A Wedding* (ALTMAN, 1978)

16. *Martin Ritt* in *The Pedestrian* (MAXIMILIAN SCHELL, 1974)

17. *Elia Kazan* in *City for Conquest* (ANATOLE LITVAK, 1940)

18. *Martin Scorsese* in *Dreams* (AKIRA KUROSAWA, 1990)

19. *Paul Bartel* in *Rock 'n' Roll High School* (ALLAN ARKUSH, 1979)

20. *John Ford* in *Big Time* (KENNETH HAWKS, 1929)

Is There an Auteur in the House?
The Worst Movies by Great Directors

The combination of a unique personal vision with an unfortunate choice of material can produce a uniquely terrible movie.

Robert Altman   *Quintet* (1979)

Michelangelo Antonioni   *Zabriskie Point* (1970)

Ingmar Bergman   *Hour of the Wolf* (1968)

Frank Capra   *Pocketful of Miracles* (1961)

Francis Ford Coppola   *Peggy Sue Got Married* (1986)

George Cukor   *The Blue Bird* (1976)

John Ford   *The Fugitive* (1947)

Jean-Luc Godard   *See You at Mao* (1970)

Howard Hawks   *The Ransom of Red Chief*, a segment of *O. Henry's Full House* (1952), later cut from the film on the (accurate) grounds that it was not funny

Alfred Hitchcock   *Number Seventeen* (1932)

John Huston   *Annie* (1982)

Akira Kurosawa   *Dodes'ka-den* (1970)

Richard Lester   *The Four Musketeers* (1975)

Jean Renoir   *Elena et les Hommes* (1956)

Steven Spielberg   *1941* (1979)

Josef von Sternberg   *Jet Pilot* (1957)

George Stevens   *The Greatest Story Ever Told* (1965)

Oliver Stone   *Natural Born Killers* (1994)

Preston Sturges   *The Beautiful Blonde from Bashful Bend* (1949)

François Truffaut   *Mississippi Mermaid* (1969)

Orson Welles   *The Trial* (1962)

Billy Wilder   *Buddy Buddy* (1981)

The Most Atypical Pictures by Major Directors

Robert Altman's *Countdown* (1968) There are nascent signs of Altman's revolutionary multicharactered, multilayered technique in this efficient movie about NASA astronauts making the first voyage to the moon, but you'd be hard-pressed to identify any Altmanesque themes.

Peter Bogdanovich's (billed as Derek Thomas) *Voyage to the Planet of Prehistoric Women* (1968) When Roger Corman bought a 1962 Russian sci-fi movie, *Planet of Storms*, he assigned aspiring filmmaker Bogdanovich to film some new scenes with Mamie Van Doren and other babes cavorting on the beach in Malibu as Venusian gill-women, wearing cockleshells as brassieres.

Frank Capra's *The Bitter Tea of General Yen* (1933) A moody and powerful drama about an unrequited miscegenatory romance between a Chinese warlord (Nils Asther) and an American missionary (Barbara Stanwyck), *Bitter Tea* was a legendary box-office disaster. In the late '30s, Capra told his soundman Edward Bernds, "I know it didn't make money, but it has more real *movie* in it than any other I did."

Francis Ford Coppola's *Tonight for Sure* (1982) This compilation of footage from various "nudie cutie" movies shot by Coppola in his days as a starving UCLA film student, also incorporating footage he reedited from a German nudie film, was released well after Coppola became celebrated for the *Godfather* movies. The earlier titles of his nudies were *The Peeper*, *The Wide Open Spaces*, *The Playgirls and the Bellboy*, and *Come On Out*.

George Cukor's *Winged Victory* (1944)   As part of his patriotic contribution to the war effort in World War II, Cukor took a break from his customary concentration on women's pictures to film this Moss Hart play about young men training for pilot duty.

John Ford's *Sex Hygiene* (1941 documentary)   At the request of Darryl F. Zanuck, Ford made the U.S. Army's official VD film for World War II troops. *Sex Hygiene* includes graphic close-ups of syphilitic penises, a stentorian lecture about clap and blue balls, and an unintentionally hilarious sequence showing GIs (including George "Superman" Reeves) up to no good in a brothel. Asked by Peter Bogdanovich how he felt about the movie, Ford replied, "I looked at it and threw up."

Howard Hawks's *Land of the Pharaohs* (1955)   Hawks's attempt to jump on the bandwagon of the ancient-epic genre was a bust, although the scenes of building an Egyptian pyramid are impressively mounted. Screenwriter William Faulkner summed up the movie's main problem when he complained to Hawks, "I don't know how a pharaoh talks." Hawks later admitted, "I messed it up, and . . . we didn't know what a pharaoh *did*."

Alfred Hitchcock's *Waltzes from Vienna* (1933)   At what he later remembered as a "low ebb of my career," Hitchcock directed "a musical without music, made very cheaply. It had no relation to my usual work." Comic actor Edmund Gwenn played Johann Strauss the Elder in this British production, released in the U.S. as *Strauss' Great Waltz*.

John Huston's *Annie* (1982)   Huston earned a hefty fee for this clunky, cartoon-based musical, but his black heart was not with the orphan played by Aileen Quinn. Instead he seemed to derive an unholy glee from Carol Burnett's sadistic child-abuser, making *Annie* a truly nasty piece of work.

Fritz Lang's *You and Me* (1938)   Guided by the director of *M* and *Metropolis*, Sylvia Sidney and George Raft starred as ex-cons in love in this Brechtian musical with songs by Kurt Weill. Lang considered *You and Me* "an unfortunate affair from the beginning."

Ernst Lubitsch's *The Man I Killed* (aka ***Broken Lullaby***, 1932)   The master of sophisticated comedy made this passionate, if somewhat stilted, antiwar film about a young World War I veteran (Phillips Holmes) paying penance for killing an enemy soldier.

Sam Peckinpah's *Convoy* (1978)   Near the end of his life, in the period of his sad dissolution, the maker of *The Wild Bunch* hopped on the road-movie, CB, country-music bandwagon with this grandiose, coked-up action spectacle starring Kris Kristofferson and Ali MacGraw.

Martin Scorsese's *Boxcar Bertha* (1972)   A not-bad, sexy, and violent exploitation movie made for Roger Corman, with Barbara Hershey and David Carradine as Depression-era train robbers. After seeing it, however, John Cassavetes told Scorsese to stop wasting his time on commercial "shit," a lesson the young filmmaker took to heart, following *Boxcar Bertha* with the highly personal *Mean Streets*.

Steven Spielberg's *Savage* (1973 TV MOVIE)   The last, and most routine, of Spielberg's early TV movies, *Savage* stars Martin Landau as a crusading TV political journalist, Paul Savage, investigating the blackmailing of a nominee to the U.S.

Supreme Court. The director, who was then under contract to Universal, remembers *Savage* as "an assignment bordering on force majeure. *Savage* was the first and last time the studio ordered me to do something."

Preston Sturges's *The Great Moment* (1944)   This strange comedy-drama starring Joel McCrea is a biopic of the inventor of anesthesia, surely one of the least obviously commercial topics ever devised for a Hollywood movie.

Billy Wilder's *The Spirit of St. Louis* (1957)   Did this stirring saga of the 1927 trans-Atlantic flight of Charles Lindbergh (James Stewart)—the first movie I ever went back to see a second time—appeal to a latent streak of hero worship in the otherwise sardonic director? Wilder later mused that he should have filmed the whole story of Lindbergh. Dramatizing the 1932 kidnap-murder of Lindbergh's son and the aviator's pro-Nazi activities in the years leading up to World War II would have made a far different and far more interesting movie.

It's Either the Best Movie Ever Made or the Worst . . . or BOTH

The Day the Clown Cried (1972)   Jerry Lewis's very own *Schindler's List* is the story of a Jewish clown named Helmut Doork, who unwittingly leads children to the Auschwitz gas chambers. *The Day the Clown Cried* was filmed in Sweden, largely with money supplied by the director-star himself. But the producer failed to secure the rights to the source material, an original screenplay by Joan O'Brien and Charles Denton, and the writers refused to let Lewis release the film. So, we may never find out what it's really like.

Steve Spielberg's Home Movies
10 Amateur Movies by Spielberg
That Should Be Released on Laserdisc

Steven Spielberg has been making movies since 1957, when he was ten and still called himself "Steve." Although a few snippets of his amateur films have been seen on TV specials, he has not seen fit to release them in their entirety (aside from his 1968 short *Amblin'*, which played theatrically before Spielberg bought all rights to the film in 1977). A laserdisc collection of his early work would be a popular collector's item, as well as helping moviegoers understand Spielberg's creative evolution.

The Last Train Wreck (1957) After Spielberg's father ordered him to stop crashing his toy trains into each other, Steve filmed the trains colliding so he could watch the action over and over again.

The Last Gunfight (1958) Spielberg's first story film, a nine-minute Western filmed in the desert outside Phoenix.

Fighter Squad (1960) A fifteen-minute World War II dogfight movie, combining newsreel footage with scenes shot by Spielberg in and around vintage fighter planes at the Phoenix airport.

Steve Spielberg's Home Movies (1960) A series of gags Spielberg put together for his booth at an Ingleside Elementary School Halloween fund-raising carnival in Phoenix.

Escape to Nowhere (1962)   This forty-minute film about World War II, set in North Africa and featuring elaborately staged battle scenes, won Spielberg first prize in an Arizona amateur film contest.

Firelight (1964)   Spielberg's first feature, filmed in 8 mm, was an ambitious sci-fi epic about aliens abducting humans from Arizona with colored "firelights." This 135-minute precursor to *Close Encounters of the Third Kind* had one theatrical showing at the Phoenix Little Theatre on March 24, 1964.

Film About John F. Kennedy (1964–65)   Spielberg and Saratoga (Ca.) High School friend Mike Augustine made this three-minute film tribute to the late President Kennedy, using a mechanical JFK-in-a-rocking-chair figurine playing "Happy Days Are Here Again."

Senior Sneak Day (1965)   A gag-filled movie made about Spielberg's graduating class at Saratoga High School. Shown at the class's graduation party.

Encounter (1965–66)   A twenty-minute film noir shot in 16 mm black-and-white while Spielberg was a student attending California State College at Long Beach.

Amblin' (1968)   This beautifully made 35 mm short, starring Pamela McMyler and Richard Levin as a pair of young hitchhikers, received a theatrical release and won Spielberg his first professional contract with Universal. Spielberg also documented the filming of *Amblin'* with his 8 mm camera.

The Other Side of Orson Welles
His Unseen Movies and TV Shows

Contrary to conventional wisdom, Orson Welles (who died in 1985) was never creatively dormant but in fact was busy directing pictures throughout his lifetime, often using his own money. Unfortunately, many of those movies and TV programs were never completed or released. Parts have appeared in documentaries, however, and some may yet see the light of day in their entirety.

Too Much Johnson (1938)   Forty minutes of silent scenes filmed for a stage production of William Gillette's play but never shown. The only print of this film was lost in a fire in 1970.

Don Quixote (begun in 1955; filming continued into the 1970s)   An adaptation of Cervantes's novel about knight errantry, starring Francisco Reiguera and Akim Tamiroff. A bastardized and incomplete version of this film was released in Spain in 1992.

Moby-Dick—Rehearsed (1955)   A partially completed film of Welles's stage adaptation of Herman Melville's *Moby-Dick*, with a cast including Welles, Gordon Jackson, and Joan Plowright.

Camille, the Naked Lady and the Musketeers (1956)   Half-hour experimental film on the Dumas family.

Portrait of Gina (1958)   Half-hour documentary for ABC-TV on Gina Lollobrigida, filmed as a pilot for a series that would have been titled *Orson Welles at Large*. Rejected by ABC and first shown at the 1986 Venice Film Festival; Lollobrigida obtained an injunction against further screenings.

The Deep (1967–69)   A thriller starring Jeanne Moreau, Laurence Harvey, and Welles, based on Charles Williams's novel *Dead Calm*, later filmed again by Australian director Philip Noyce.

Orson's Bag (1968–70)   An uncompleted CBS special, including a forty-minute condensed version of *The Merchant of Venice*.

The Other Side of the Wind (1970–76)   A satire of Hollywood in the *Easy Rider* era, starring John Huston and Peter Bogdanovich (with the author of this book as the film historian Mr. Pister). The major project of Welles's later years; filming was completed, but not the postproduction process, and the film has not yet been released due to legal and financial complications.

The Magic Show (1976–85)   A compendium of magic acts and lore.

Orson Welles Solo (1978–?)   A self-portrait and cinematic scrapbook.

Television talk show pilot (1978–79)   With Burt Reynolds, Angie Dickinson, and the Muppets. Completed (on videotape) but unsold.

The Dreamers (1980–82)   An adaptation of two stories by Isak Dinesen, starring Welles and Oja Kodar. About twenty minutes was filmed.

Hawks Talks
Advice to Young Directors from the Master, Howard Hawks

1. "A director's a storyteller, and if he tells a story that people can't understand, then he shouldn't be a director."

2. "Most of [my movies] were well written. That's why they last. I've always been blessed with great writers. As a matter of fact, I'm such a coward that unless I get a good writer, I don't want to make a picture."

3. "See, if you're gonna do something, do it with characters. Do 'em a little differently. Every scene's been done. Now, your job is to do 'em a little differently. To get mad a little differently. To steal a little differently."

4. "I must change [the script] to fit the action because, after all, it's a motion picture. Some of the stuff that's handed to you on paper is perfectly good to read, but it isn't any good on the set. . . . If it reads good, it won't play good."

5. "If you'll ever listen to some people who are talking, especially in a scene of any excitement, they all talk at the same time. All it needs is a little extra work on the dialogue. You put a few words in front of somebody's speech and put a few words at the end, and they can overlap it. It gives you a sense of speed that actually doesn't exist. And then you make the people talk a little faster."

6. "Not that you're trying to make every scene a great scene, but you try not to annoy the audience. I told John Wayne when we started to work together, 'Duke, if you can make three good scenes in this picture and don't annoy the audi-

ence the rest of the time, you'll be good. . . . If I make five good scenes in this picture, and don't annoy the audience, I think I'll be good.' "

7. "[T]he dumbest thing in the world is an actor getting serious about himself. For God's sake, don't get so serious about it. . . . true drama is awfully close to being comedy. The greatest drama in the world is really funny. A man who loses his pants out in front of a thousand people—he's suffering the tortures of the damned, but he's awfully funny doing it."

8. "A number of [young European directors] have a great deal of talent, but they're telling pictures that are good for only France, Italy, and Germany. When I go over there I talk to them about it. I say, 'Why don't you fellows widen out, make a picture that is good for the world? You aren't going to get enough money to work with unless you can get it out of universal entertainment.' "

9. "Do something that's entertaining. People seem to like chase scenes. Make a good chase. Make one better than anyone's done." (Hawks gave this advice to William Friedkin, who went out and made *The French Connection*. Confirming Hawks's story, Friedkin told me, "I began to think back on what kind of movies I liked as a kid. . . . What he was saying to me was that a sermon should not fall on deaf ears. Basically, my whole body of work before *The French Connection* is masturbatory.")

10. "I try to tell my story as simply as possible, with the camera at eye level."

—from my 1982 interview book *Hawks on Hawks*

Powers Behind the Thrones
Unsung People Who Were Indispensable
Collaborators with Major Filmmakers

One of the shameful secrets of the movie business is that behind each important filmmaker there usually is someone (or more than one person) who does a great deal of the work but doesn't necessarily get the credit he or she deserves. Sometimes that is the great man's fault, but sometimes it's more attributable to the media's tendency to lionize directors at the expense of their collaborators.

Alfred Hitchcock and Alma Reville

From the beginning of his career as a director in the silent era, Alfred Hitchcock relied greatly on the professional advice of his wife, Alma Reville, whom he married in 1926 after a lengthy courtship. "Well, she's a critic . . . nothing to soft-pedal, you know," he told me. They were born a day apart in 1899, but Alma preceded her future husband into the British movie business by four years, working first as an editor and then as a continuity girl. She and Hitchcock met in 1921, and later that year they first worked together when he assisted director Graham Cutts on *Woman to Woman*. After four more films with Cutts, Alma was at Hitchcock's side in 1924 for the shooting of his first completed film as director, *The Pleasure Garden*. She worked behind the scenes of every subsequent Hitchcock film as well, initially as continuity girl and assistant director, later as occasional screenwriter, sharing writing credit on such films as *The Thirty-Nine Steps*, *Sabotage*, *Suspicion*, and *Shadow of a Doubt*. She helped her notoriously secretive husband choose his material and develop it for the screen, continuing to offer advice during shooting. No more symbiotic moviemaking couple has ever existed than Mr. and Mrs. Hitchcock.

Frank Capra and Robert Riskin

Capra's later tendency to denigrate Riskin's enormous screen-writing contributions to the films they made together became a cause célèbre in the acrimonious debates over the auteur theory. Their close collaboration became troubled over Capra's egocentric refusal to give Riskin his due in the press when they worked together at Columbia or, later, to include him in the name of their joint production company, Frank Capra Productions. Much of the populist approach that became known as "Capraesque" was attributable to Riskin, who, unlike Capra, was a political liberal and a supporter of Franklin D. Roosevelt.

Fred Astaire and Hermes Pan

Although not a director, Astaire was the dominant creative force on his films. His closest friend and collaborator was choreographer Hermes Pan, who even bore a remarkable physical resemblance to the great dancer. So much so, in fact, that Samuel Fuller told me he watched Pan double for Astaire on some long shots while the cameras were rolling at RKO on *Top Hat* (1935)! (The ever-loyal Pan wouldn't admit that when I asked him about it.) During the early stages of their preparation for each film, Astaire and Pan would spend weeks working out the choreography privately together. Pan took the role of Ginger Rogers or other dancing partners until the dance was ready for the actual partner to rehearse.

John Ford and Merian C. Cooper

A remarkable character in his own right, Cooper was an explorer, military man, and filmmaker, best known for producing and directing *King Kong* (1933) with Ernest B. Schoedsack. While serving as production chief of RKO, Cooper brought Ford to the studio to make *The Lost Patrol* (1934). Their teaming at an uncertain juncture in Ford's career helped set the director on the road to the stature he eventually achieved. After World War II, Ford and Cooper became partners in Argosy Pictures, for which Ford directed some of his greatest films, including the Cavalry trilogy, *Wagon Master*, and *The Quiet Man*. Cooper also produced *The Searchers* with C. V. Whitney.

Howard Hawks and the Rosson Brothers

Although Hawks was misleadingly considered an "action" director for much of his career, brothers Richard and Arthur Rosson were among the expert second-unit directors who shot many of the action sequences in Hawks's films while he concentrated on dialogue scenes. Richard Rosson was billed as Hawks's "codirector" on *Scarface* and served as second-unit director on *Tiger Shark*, *Today We Live*, *Come and Get It*, and *Only Angels Have Wings*; he also directed Hawks's 1943 production *Corvette K-225*. Arthur handled second unit for Hawks on *His Girl Friday*, *Ball of Fire*, *Red*

River, and *The Big Sky*. Their brother Harold (Hal) was cinematographer on the first feature Hawks produced, *Quicksands* (directed by Jack Conway, 1923), as well as on the Hawks-directed silent *Trent's Last Case* and the 1967 Western *El Dorado*.

George Cukor and George Hoyningen-Huene

Considering himself primarily a director of actors, Cukor always felt he needed help in the visual realm. He had the modesty and sense to place great trust in the talents of his art directors and in the distinguished still photographer George Hoyningen-Huene, who served as color consultant on Cukor's masterpiece, *A Star Is Born* (1954), as well as on all his other color films with the exception of *My Fair Lady*. Through Huene's influence, Cukor's visual style became increasingly cinematic and subtle, and his use of color increasingly ravishing.

Steven Spielberg and Arnold Spielberg

Steven Spielberg claimed for many years that his father (a pioneer in computer engineering) did nothing but hinder his ambitions to become a director. In fact, Arnold Spielberg, a longtime amateur filmmaker himself, worked closely with his son for several years on their joint filmmaking hobby. Arnold and his wife, Leah, financed Steven's early movies, including his first feature, *Firelight* (1964). Steven's later deprecation of his father's role in his career evidently resulted from Arnold's disapproval of Steven's desire to become a professional filmmaker rather than following him into the computer engineering field. But Arnold continued to help Steven anyway after they moved to southern California together, forming a filmmaking company called Playmount Productions (the Spielberg family name is German for "play mountain"). As Arnold told me in 1996, "I paid some of the bills. Sometimes he paid me back, sometimes not, but it didn't make any difference. I just recently turned over to him all the books that we had. 'Hey, Dad,' he said, 'you really *did* help me out with my career.' "

Ken Russell and Huw Wheldon

Before he turned his primary focus toward feature filmmaking, Ken Russell was a brilliant television director, specializing in imaginative, intensely romantic biographical films for the BBC about famous composers and other artists, including his masterpieces *Isadora Duncan, The Biggest Dancer in the World* (1966) and *Song of Summer,* about Frederick Delius (1968). When I once asked the veteran producer John Houseman why Russell's feature film work never quite reached the same level as his work for TV—and indeed often fell far short of it—Houseman suggested it was due to the collaboration of Huw Wheldon, the producer of BBC's arts program *Monitor,* who restrained Russell's worst tendencies and encouraged his best during their five years of working together (1959–64). Wheldon once said, "Ken needs a strong producer or a strong scriptwriter, or both, because without them his own powers of invention and imagination are so enormous that he's like a bird being driven along on a huge gale." In his 1989 autobiography *Altered States*, which is dedicated to his former producer, Russell writes that Wheldon "always helped polish my rough diamonds till they glittered. And when I disappointed him with a paste job, he worked even harder to make it shine."

Jean-Marie Straub and Danièle Huillet

One of the most glaring examples of sexist injustice in film criticism has been the frequent tendency to write about the films Jean-Marie Straub has made in collaboration with his wife, Danièle Huillet, as if they were Straub's alone.

John Huston and Gladys Hill

When producer Sam Spiegel's assistant, Gladys Hill, was divorced from her husband in 1959, John Huston wrote her, "Since you like to travel and since your job is temporary, why not come to Ireland and work for me forever and ever?" Hill served as his personal assistant and collaborator until her death in 1981, even living with him at his castle in Ireland and his oceanside retreat in Mexico. Since Huston hated solitude, he also hated writing alone. Hill gave such increasingly important help with his screenplays that they eventually began sharing credit. Their finest work together was on *The Man Who Would Be King*, the magnificent 1975 adaptation of Rudyard Kipling's short story, for which they received Academy Award nominations. Hill also was credited on the screenplays of *Reflections in a Golden Eye* and *The Kremlin Letter*.

Orson Welles and Gary Graver

Welles's devoted cinematographer for the last fifteen years of his life, Graver made it possible for the director to keep making his highly personal low-budget films. Often working for no or little pay, and recruiting other young crew members to assist them, Graver helped Welles on every aspect of the production of such films as *F for Fake, Filming "Othello"*; the still uncompleted features *The Other Side of the Wind, The Magic Show*, and *Don Quixote*; and many other, more fragmentary projects.

François Truffaut and Suzanne Schiffman

Schiffman first met Truffaut when they were both seventeen-year-old film buffs and her name was Suzanne Klochendler. She began working with the director as his script girl in 1959 and quickly made herself an indispensable collaborator and professional confidante. Truffaut's assistant director on every film from *The Wild Child* (1970) through the end of his career in 1983, Schiffman was also his screenwriting collaborator on every film from *Day for Night* (1973) onward, with the exception of *The Green Room*. Later she became a director herself.

The Good, the Bad, and the Outré
Lists About Actors

My 17 Favorite Close-Ups in Movies

1. Greta Garbo in the famous ending shot of *Queen Christina* (ROUBEN MAMOULIAN, 1933), described by the director as her "tabula rasa" close-up of the queen looking silently out to sea as she sails for Sweden with the body of the only man she has ever loved.

2. Charlie Chaplin at the end of *City Lights* (CHAPLIN, 1931), smiling hesitantly as the flower girl realizes that her wealthy benefactor actually is a tramp.

3. Setsuko Hara as Noriko in *Tokyo Story* (YASUJIRO OZU, 1953), answering a young girl's anguished question, "Isn't

life disappointing?" with a serene smile, nodding and saying with perfect equanimity, "Yes. It is."

4. Orson Welles as Sir John Falstaff in *Chimes at Midnight* (WELLES, 1966), looking in tearful disbelief at the newly crowned King Henry V (Keith Baxter), who has just ordered him banished.

5. Garbo in *Queen Christina*, lips parted as she leans her head against a pillow, gazing sensuously at her offscreen lover while she goes about "memorizing this room" (also see "The Butter Was on the Toast: The Most Erotic Scenes with the Actors Fully Clothed").

6. Lillian Gish as the battered Lucy Burrows in *Broken Blossoms* (D. W. GRIFFITH, 1919), whirling around uncontrollably inside a closet, terror-stricken, hiding from her abusive father.

7. James Stewart as Scottie Ferguson in *Vertigo* (ALFRED HITCHCOCK, 1958), watching with a stare of glassy-eyed sexual obsession as Judy (Kim Novak) slowly advances toward him, transformed back into the dead Madeleine.

8. John Wayne as Ethan Edwards in *The Searchers* (JOHN FORD, 1956), staring grimly into the recesses of Monument Valley as he slowly wipes the back of his horse, contemplating what the Comanches are doing to his helpless family.

9. Agnes Moorehead as Mary Kane, calling out in controlled pain to her young son in *Citizen Kane* (WELLES, 1941), before signing away his future to a bank.

10. Anthony Perkins as Norman Bates at the end of *Psycho* (HITCHCOCK, 1960), staring fixedly at the camera, eyes gleaming madly, as he says in his mother's voice, "She wouldn't hurt a fly."

11. Mae Marsh as the Dear One in the courtroom scene of *Intolerance* (GRIFFITH, 1916), watching in incredulous horror and twisting her hands in agony as her innocent husband is sentenced to execution.

12. James Mason as Norman Maine in the final scenes of *A Star Is Born* (GEORGE CUKOR, 1954), breaking down in silent sobs as he listens to his wife (Judy Garland) tell her studio boss (Charles Bickford) that she's giving up her career to help him.

13. Victor Sjöström as the elderly Professor Isak Borg in *Wild Strawberries* (INGMAR BERGMAN, 1957), smiling with hard-won content as he closes his eyes to sleep in the final shot of the film.

14. Marcel Dalio as the marquis Robert de La Chesnaye in *The Rules of the Game* (JEAN RENOIR, 1939), displaying his treasured mechanical organ to his guests. Renoir later told Dalio, "I think it's the best shot I've done in my life. It's fantastic. That mixture of humility and pride, of success and doubt."

15. Jean-Pierre Léaud addressing the camera as Antoine Doinel in *The 400 Blows* (FRANÇOIS TRUFFAUT, 1959), matter-of-factly answering an unseen psychologist's questions about his troubled family life.

16. Ronald Colman as the disillusioned Robert Conway, turning back for an agonizing last look at Shangri-La in *Lost*

Horizon (FRANK CAPRA, 1937) as he prepares to leave what he thought was an earthly paradise.

17. François Truffaut as the ufologist Lacombe, exchanging a gentle, brotherly smile with the alien Puck as the mother ship prepares to depart in *Close Encounters of the Third Kind* (STEVEN SPIELBERG, 1977).

The Good, the Bad, and the Outré
The Cinema's Most Extreme Overactors

Inclusion on this list does not necessarily mean that someone is a bad actor, only that his or her acting is very broad indeed. Sometimes—as in the case of George C. Scott's glorious comic performance as General Buck Turgidson in *Dr. Strangelove*—it's *good* to be over the top. (Actors who are primarily comedians, such as Jerry Lewis and Jim Carrey, are not included in this list.)

1. Jack Palance

2. Rod Steiger

3. Shelley Winters

4. Burt Lancaster

5. Anthony Quinn

6. Kirk Douglas

7. Emil Jannings

8. George C. Scott

9. Bette Davis

10. Joan Crawford

11. Jennifer Jason Leigh

12. Charlton Heston

13. (The later) Marlon Brando

14. Laurence Olivier

15. Orson Welles

16. Wallace Beery

17. Ernest Borgnine

18. Anthony Perkins

19. Demi Moore

20. Anne Bancroft (after her marriage to Mel Brooks)

. . . And the Most Extreme UNDERactors

1. *Steven Seagal* (why is this guy in show business? For a possible answer to this question, see "The 15 Strangest Movie Stars")

2. *Gregory Peck* (whom critic Manny Farber described as "an ironing board")

3. *Richard Gere* (of whom *The New Yorker* once observed, "The kind word for his acting is 'minimal' ")

4. *Anouk Aimee* (whose exasperated director George Cukor described her as "A blank, boring wall")

5. *Gary Cooper* (who turned underacting into an art form)

The Energizer Bunny Award
The Longest Screen-Acting Careers*

Milton Berle   84 years (1914–PRESENT). Berle's first film appearance was as a child actor clinging to Marie Dressler's knee in the silent Mack Sennett feature *Tillie's Punctured Romance*.

Fay Wray   79 years (1919–PRESENT)

Lillian Gish   75 years (1912–1987)

Cyril Cusack   75 years (1917–1992)

Helen Hayes   75 years (1910–1985)

Sir John Gielgud   74 years (1924–PRESENT)

Brian Keith   73 years (1924–1997)

Mickey Rooney   72 years (1926–PRESENT)

Sylvia Sidney   69 years (1929–PRESENT)

Luise Rainer   68 years (1930–PRESENT)

Bessie Love   68 years (1915–1983)

Gloria Stuart   66 years (1932–PRESENT)

Gilbert Roland   64 years (1918–1982)

Noah Beery Jr.   62 years (1920–1982)

Claudette Colbert   60 years (1927–1987)

Don Ameche   58 years (1936–1994)

Myrna Loy   56 years (1925–1981)

---

*Some of these actors did their last work on television.

Who, Me?
Movies Stars Would Like to Leave Off Their Résumés

When Paul Newman's first movie, *The Silver Chalice* (1954), began a week's run on a Los Angeles television station in 1963, the star took out a black-bordered advertisement in the *Los Angeles Times* declaring, "Paul Newman apologizes every night this week." Ironically, the ad only prompted more viewers to watch the movie, leading Newman to describe his stunt as "a classic example of the arrogance of the affluent." That may help explain why these other actors haven't followed Newman's example.

Woody Allen   *Casino Royale* (1967)

Ann-Margret   *Kitten with a Whip* (1964)

Anne Bancroft   *Gorilla at Large* (1954)

Geena Davis   *Transylvania 6-5000* (1985)

Richard Dreyfuss   *Valley of the Dolls* (1967)

Faye Dunaway   *The Extraordinary Seaman* (1969)

Clint Eastwood   *Revenge of the Creature* (1955), *Francis in the Navy* (1955), *Lady Godiva* (1955), *Tarantula* (1955), *The First Traveling Saleslady* (1956), *Paint Your Wagon* (1969)

Sally Field   *The Way West* (1967)

Jane Fonda   *F.T.A.*, aka *Fuck the Army* or *Free the Army* (1972)

Teri Garr   *Mom and Dad Save the World* (1992)

Whoopi Goldberg   *Theodore Rex* (1996)

Elliott Gould   *Whiffs* (1975)

Tom Hanks   *Joe Versus the Volcano* (1990)

Katharine Hepburn   *Spitfire* (1934)

Tommy Lee Jones   *Love Story* (1970)

Malcolm McDowell, John Gielgud, Peter O'Toole, and *Helen Mirren*   *Caligula* (1980)

Demi Moore   *Striptease* (1996)

Jack Nicholson   *The Terror* (1963)

Michelle Pfeiffer   *Grease 2* (1982)

Jason Robards   *Mr. Sycamore* (1974)

Roy Scheider   *The Curse of the Living Corpse* (1964)

Arnold Schwarzenegger (as "Arnold Strong")   *Hercules in New York*, aka *Hercules Goes Bananas* (1970)

Tom Selleck   *Myra Breckenridge* (1970), *The Seven Minutes* (1971)

Sylvester Stallone   *A Party at Kitty and Stud's Place* (1968), reissued in 1971 as *The Italian Stallion*

Robin Williams   *Can I Do It . . . Til I Need Glasses?* (1977)

Debra Winger   *Slumber Party '57* (1977)

5 Actors Who Are Never Bad

Although these actors sometimes have been stuck in vehicles unworthy of their talents, and though the first and third men listed are effective only within a limited range, I have never seen any of them doing anything less than good work on-screen. The same cannot be said of such cinematic icons as Marlon (*The Missouri Breaks*) Brando, Cary (*Arsenic and Old Lace*) Grant, Katharine (*Spitfire*) Hepburn, Laurence (*The Betsy*) Olivier, and Meryl (*Heartburn*) Streep.

Ward Bond   In films from 1929 through 1960. Best performances: *They Were Expendable* (John Ford, 1945), *Fort Apache* (Ford, 1948), *Wagon Master* (Ford, 1950), *On Dangerous Ground* (Nicholas Ray, 1952), *The Searchers* (Ford, 1956).

Lillian Gish   In films from 1912 through 1987. Best performances: *The Mothering Heart* (D. W. Griffith, 1913), *Broken Blossoms* (Griffith, 1919), *True Heart Susie* (Griffith, 1919), *The Wind* (Victor Sjöström, 1928), *The Night of the Hunter* (Charles Laughton, 1955).

Gene Hackman   In films from 1961 through the present. Best performances: *Bonnie and Clyde* (Arthur Penn, 1967), *The French Connection* (William Friedkin, 1971), *The Conversation* (Francis Ford Coppola, 1974), *Young Frankenstein* (Mel Brooks, 1974), *Unforgiven* (Clint Eastwood, 1992).

Ben Johnson   In films from 1940 through 1996. Best performances: *She Wore a Yellow Ribbon* (John Ford, 1949), *Wagon Master* (Ford, 1950), *Shane* (George Stevens, 1953), *The Last Picture Show* (Peter Bogdanovich, 1971), *The Sugarland Express* (Steven Spielberg, 1974).

Thelma Ritter   In films from 1947 through 1968. Best performances: *All About Eve* (Joseph L. Mankiewicz, 1950), *The Model and the Marriage Broker* (George Cukor, 1951), *Pickup* *on South Street* (Samuel Fuller, 1953), *Pillow Talk* (Michael Gordon, 1959), *Birdman of Alcatraz* (John Frankenheimer, 1962).

The 15 Strangest Movie Stars

Al Jennings in *The Bank Robbery* (1908) and *Beating Back* (1915) In perhaps the most extreme case of the movies glorifying criminality, Jennings, an actual Western bank and train robber, played himself on-screen. In the 1951 biopic *Al Jennings of Oklahoma*, Jennings was played by Dan Duryea.

George Arliss in *Disraeli* (1921, 1929), etc. This British theater star became a Hollywood leading man even though he looked like Nosferatu. Why he remained popular for years as "The First Gentleman of the Screen" and even received an Oscar (for the sound remake of *Disraeli*) seems somewhat mysterious to modern eyes and ears, but Arliss's rhetorical style was in its time considered the epitome of fine acting. He took himself very seriously indeed. Once, during a court appearance, he described himself as the world's greatest living actor. "You see, I am on oath," he explained.

Rin Tin Tin in *Jaws of Steel* (1927), etc. This canine performer was a major star for Warner Bros. in the silents and early talkies. In the words of studio chief Jack L. Warner, "The dog faced one hazard after another and was grateful to get an extra hamburger for a reward. He didn't ask for a raise, or a new press agent, or an air-conditioned dressing room, or more close-ups." But Rinty left this world in a manner we can all envy—

according to Warner, he died with Jean Harlow cradling his head in her lap.

Liberace in *Sincerely Yours* (1955) Need I say more? Except to note that the campy pianist's only starring role came in a remake of the 1932 George Arliss vehicle *The Man Who Played God.*

Joe Namath in *The Last Rebel* (1971), etc. Of all the many athletes given repeated starring roles in films, "Broadway Joe" perhaps had the least discernible acting talent.

Ray Milland and ***Roosevelt Grier*** in *The Thing With Two Heads* (1972) In what surely must go down as the most bizarre casting idea in film history, the debonair Welsh-born leading man and the hefty African-American ex–football player were stuffed into the same costumes to play the title character in this comedy-drama about a white bigot whose head is grafted onto a black man's body.

Karen Black in *Airport 1975* (1975) Having an eye abnormality isn't necessarily a fatal handicap for an actress—Helen Hayes did quite well being walleyed, thank you—and Karen Black has undeniable strengths as an oddball character actress. But it may have been unwise to cast the cross-eyed Black as the female lead of *Airport 1975*, since the part required her stewardess character to pilot the disabled airliner. As Charlton Heston patiently instructs her over the radio, it's hard not to feel alarmed and disoriented watching Black struggle to make eye contact with the instrument panel. That unintentional sight gag causes an already ludicrous movie to crash and burn.

Truman Capote in *Murder by Death* (1976) The epicene author found that his eccentric personality, which played so entertainingly on TV talk shows, didn't translate so well onto the screen.

Linda Lovelace in *Linda Lovelace for President* (1976)   A performer whose only evident talent was an unusual capacity for oral sex, Lovelace went on from the runaway success of the 1972 porno movie *Deep Throat* to make the would-be mainstream comedy *Linda Lovelace for President*. Joining her in the eclectic cast were such names as Scatman Crothers, Mickey Dolenz of the Monkees, and former JFK impressionist Vaughn Meader. Perhaps Lovelace's most lasting contribution to film history is her impassioned autobiography *Ordeal* (with Mike McGrady, 1980), chronicling her story of abuse in the porno industry. It would make a good movie (with Don Cheadle as Sammy Davis Jr.?), although the bestiality scene alone would draw an NC-17 rating. Lovelace and her coauthor already have written the sequel, *Out of Bondage* (1986).

E.T. in *E.T.—The Extra-Terrestrial* (1982)   Anyone who thinks Steven Spielberg isn't a first-rate director of actors should consider what a moving performance he coaxed from an animatronic puppet.

Steven Seagal in *Under Siege* (1992), etc.   This inexplicable action star talks in a whisper and has one expression, a frown/glower that could be mistaken for a sign of severe constipation. Perhaps the reason he stars in movies has something to do with the fact that he entered the business as then-superagent Michael Ovitz's martial arts instructor.

Quentin Tarantino in *Pulp Fiction* (1994), etc.   Tarantino's talents as a director do not necessarily mean he should appear on camera as frequently as he does. But such is the nature of celebrity in our time that a former video-store geek with only two full-length-feature directing credits became a highly visible actor as a result, as well as the subject of several biographies before he finally got around to directing a third feature, the dreadful *Jackie Brown* (1997).

Pauly Shore in *Bio-Dome* (1996), etc. Maybe it's a sign of advancing age that I don't get this guy's humor, but have you actually *seen Bio-Dome*? If there's such a thing as an Idiots' Anti-Defamation League, they ought to sue Pauly Shore for damaging their image.

Howard Stern in *Private Parts* (1997) The deliberately offensive radio-show personality, who looks like a nastier and more depraved version of Tiny Tim, starred in the film version of his autobiography. He drew large numbers of his fans in the opening weekend, briefly deluding Hollywood into thinking he was a genuine movie phenomenon. But it was all downhill after that for Howard Stern's career as a leading man.

10 Actors We Should See More Often

Eddie Bracken   The quintessential Preston Sturges hero in the classic satires of the American homefront in World War II, *The Miracle of Morgan's Creek* (1943) and *Hail the Conquering Hero* (1944), Bracken was absent from the screen for thirty years following his 1953 appearance in *A Slight Case of Larceny*. No doubt his nebbishy hick persona was more in keeping with an early-1940s satirical take on manly innocence, a concept that would be obliterated by the war and the subsequent disillusionment of what's become known as the film noir period. But Bracken's squirrely charm has survived intact, and he seemed little changed by age when he made a welcome reappearance as the Walt Disneyish theme-park impresario in *National Lampoon's Vacation* (Harold Ramis, 1983). Bracken has played a few more roles since then but still qualifies as a neglected national treasure.

Roscoe Lee Browne   Browne's sardonic, ironic intelligence enlivened several noteworthy films during the 1960s and 1970s, including Alfred Hitchcock's *Topaz* (1969), William Wyler's *The Liberation of L. B. Jones* (1970), and John Wayne's Western *The Cowboys* (Mark Rydell, 1972). But since then he has been wasted, popping up only occasionally in such movies as *Jumpin' Jack Flash* (1986) and *The Mambo Kings* (1992).

Blythe Danner   There are many fervent Blythe Danner fans out there, but we're not being satisfied by her rare appearances in such movies as *The Prince of Tides* (1991), *Husbands and Wives* (1992), and *The Myth of Fingerprints* (1997). If she doesn't get more opportunities in the years ahead, she's in danger of being remembered by most moviegoers as Gwyneth Paltrow's mother.

Jane Fonda   Jane, remember that you're a great actress and stop being a trophy wife to Ted Turner. Since the chameleon-like Fonda essentially reinvents herself every decade or so, there's some hope she will eventually do so.

Pam Grier   This toughest and foxiest of female action stars, a veritable genre unto herself during the "blaxploitation" era, made a welcome splash in Quentin Tarantino's *Jackie Brown* (1997), even though her comeback vehicle (after some forgettable smaller parts) wasn't worthy of her talents.

Donald O'Connor   This tremendous musical-comedy talent, best known for his glorious supporting role in *Singin' in the Rain* (1952), is still vital in his seventies, but he has appeared on screen only intermittently since the musical genre began falling into decline after the 1950s.

Michael Parks   Although he played the father of mankind, Adam, in John Huston's *The Bible . . . in the Beginning* (1966), Parks's intense, subtle acting style often has been squandered in insignificant movies. You have only to witness what he does with the oft-abused role of Robert F. Kennedy in Larry Cohen's little-seen *The Private Files of J. Edgar Hoover* (1977) to realize what we've been missing.

Robert Redford   His absorption in directing and in the Sundance Film Festival, while commendable, unfortunately keeps him from acting more frequently. Although he's lost some of his box-office clout with age, his more mature look only makes this unusually cerebral star more interesting.

Gloria Stuart   After a career as a glamorous leading lady in such 1930s films as James Whale's *The Old Dark House* (1932) and John Ford's *The Prisoner of Shark Island* (1936), Stuart retired from the screen for many years until returning in the 1970s. But she didn't find a worthy role until her haunting, career-crowning performance as the agelessly beautiful Old Rose in James Cameron's *Titanic* (1997).

Sam Waterston   This thoughtful, low-key, sensitive actor makes occasional appearances in such films as *Crimes and Misdemeanors* (1989) and *The Man in the Moon* (1991), but he's more in demand on TV. François Truffaut told me that

Waterston was his favorite contemporary American actor, because "Sam Waterston is not macho." What a shame they never worked together.

30 Great Overlooked Performances

Lillian Gish in *True Heart Susie* (D. W. GRIFFITH, 1919)

Edward G. Robinson in *Tiger Shark* (HOWARD HAWKS, 1932)

Don Ameche in *Heaven Can Wait* (ERNST LUBITSCH, 1943)

Charles Laughton in *This Land Is Mine* (JEAN RENOIR, 1943)

Juano Hernandez in *Intruder in the Dust* (CLARENCE BROWN, 1949)

Stepin Fetchit in *The Sun Shines Bright* (JOHN FORD, 1953)

Doris Day in *Love Me or Leave Me* (CHARLES VIDOR, 1955)

Gregory Peck in *Moby Dick* (JOHN HUSTON, 1956)

Clark Gable in *Band of Angels* (RAOUL WALSH, 1957)

John Wayne in *The Wings of Eagles* (FORD, 1957)

Lee Remick in *Wild River* (ELIA KAZAN, 1960)

Geraldine Page in *Summer and Smoke* (PETER GLENVILLE, 1961)

Jerry Lewis in *The Nutty Professor* (JERRY LEWIS, 1963)

Tippi Hedren in *Marnie* (ALFRED HITCHCOCK, 1964)

Ronald Reagan in *The Killers* (DON SIEGEL, 1964)

Anne Bancroft and *Margaret Leighton* in 7 *Women* (FORD, 1966)

Charlton Heston in *Khartoum* (BASIL DEARDEN, 1966)

Susan Clark in *Tell Them Willie Boy Is Here* (ABRAHAM POLONSKY, 1969)

Dorothy Tutin in *Savage Messiah* (KEN RUSSELL, 1972)

Bernadette Lafont in *Such a Gorgeous Kid Like Me* (FRANÇOIS TRUFFAUT, 1973)

John Huston in *Winter Kills* (WILLIAM RICHERT, 1979)

Anthony Hopkins in *The Elephant Man* (DAVID LYNCH, 1980)

Philip Baker Hall in *Secret Honor: The Last Testament of Richard M. Nixon* (ROBERT ALTMAN, 1984)

Orson Welles in *Someone to Love* (HENRY JAGLOM, 1987)

Irma P. Hall in *A Family Thing* (RICHARD PEARCE, 1996)

Eddie Murphy in *The Nutty Professor* (TOM SHADYAC, 1996)

Timothy Spall in *Secrets & Lies* (MIKE LEIGH, 1996)

Helen Mirren in *Critical Care* (SIDNEY LUMET, 1997)

Debbi Morgan in *Eve's Bayou* (KASI LEMMONS, 1997)

Fake That Tune

by Charles Champlin

When an actor who can play the piano plays the piano in a movie, that's terrific. Think of Jack Lemmon in *Tribute* or Clint Eastwood in *City Heat*. But when the actor who can't play anything is asked to play a musician, the results are mixed, on a scale from awesome to awful.

The Awesome

Geoffrey Rush in *Shine* (1996) practiced a very few bars of Rachmaninoff's Third to perfection so that the camera got brief glimpses of the whole pianist at work, not just somebody else's hands.

Richard Dreyfuss gets two stars for his inspired keyboard fakery in *The Competition* (1980) and *Mr. Holland's Opus* (1996).

Amy Irving also gets a star for *The Competition*.

Robert De Niro in *New York, New York* (1977) looked as if he could join any big band's saxophone section tomorrow.

Steve Allen, an expert pianist, handled a clarinet with utter conviction in *The Benny Goodman Story* (1956).

James Stewart moved the trombone slide authoritatively in *The Glenn Miller Story* (1955) but admitted later he made such terrible noises that his coach put a piece of cork in the mouthpiece so he couldn't make any sounds at all.

The Awful

Fred Astaire and **Burgess Meredith** played rival trumpet players in Artie Shaw's band in *Second Chorus* (1940), wiggling their fingers on the valves without heed to the soundtrack. Who cared, of course, except disgruntled trumpet players?

Kirk Douglas in *Young Man With a Horn* (1950) played the doomed trumpeter soulfully, but his fingers did not match what Harry James was doing on the soundtrack.

CHARLES CHAMPLIN is arts editor emeritus of the *Los Angeles Times* and the author of such books as *Back There Where the Past Was, The Movies Grow Up: 1940–1980, George Lucas: The Creative Impulse*, and *Hollywood's Revolutionary Decade: Charles Champlin Reviews the Movies of the 1970s*. His interviews with filmmakers appear on the Bravo cable series *Champlin on Film*.

14 Actors Who've Played Fictitious U.S. Presidents

Walter Huston in *Gabriel Over the White House* (1933)

Franchot Tone in *Advise and Consent* (1962)

Peter Sellers in *Dr. Strangelove or: How I Learned to Stop Worrying and Love the Bomb* (1964)

Henry Fonda in *Fail-Safe* (1964)

Polly Bergen in *Kisses for My President* (1964)

Fredric March in *Seven Days in May* (1964)

James Earl Jones in *The Man* (1972)

Bob Newhart in *First Family* (1980)

Donald Moffat in *Clear and Present Danger* (1994)

Michael Douglas in *The American President* (1995)

Bill Pullman in *Independence Day* (1996)

Jack Nicholson in *Mars Attacks!* (1996)

Harrison Ford in *Air Force One* (1997)

Morgan Freeman in *Deep Impact* (1998)

. . . And Some Unusual Castings as Actual American Presidents

Nikolai Cherkasov as Franklin D. Roosevelt in the U.S.S.R.'s World War II film *The First Front* (1949)

Harry Carey Jr. playing the West Point cadet Dwight D. Eisenhower in John Ford's *The Long Gray Line* (1955)

Pat McCormick as Grover Cleveland in Robert Altman's satirical *Buffalo Bill and the Indians, or Sitting Bull's History Lesson* (1976)

Philip Baker Hall recreating his one-man stage performance as Richard Nixon in Robert Altman's *Secret Honor: The Last Testament of Richard M. Nixon* (1984)

Nick Nolte as Thomas Jefferson in the Merchant Ivory film *Jefferson in Paris* (1995)

Anthony Hopkins as Richard Nixon in Oliver Stone's *Nixon* (1995) and John Quincy Adams in Steven Spielberg's *Amistad* (1997)

Nigel Hawthorne as Martin Van Buren in *Amistad*

Movie Actors Who Became Political Figures

It could be argued that the actor who had the most impact on politics was John Wilkes Booth—at least until Ronald Reagan was elected president in 1980. Although Reagan hardly was the first movie figure to hold government office, few people ever had thought an actor could advance so far in politics. The story goes that in 1966, when Jack L. Warner was told Reagan was running for governor of California, Reagan's former studio boss said, "No, no, no. *Jimmy Stewart* for governor—Ronald Reagan for best friend."

Rex Bell   The cowboy actor, who was married to actress Clara Bow, was elected lieutenant governor of Nevada as a Republican in 1954 but lost a 1958 bid for governor. His last film was John Huston's *The Misfits* (1961).

Shirley Temple Black   After entering Republican politics in the 1960s and running unsuccessfully for Congress, the former child star became a U.S. representative to the United Nations, ambassador to Ghana and Czechoslovakia, and U.S. chief of protocol.

Sonny Bono   Cher's former husband and performing partner, who made his film debut with her in William Friedkin's first feature, the 1967 *Good Times*, was mayor of Palm Springs, California, before being elected to the U.S. House of Representatives as a Republican in 1994. He served in that post until his death in a 1998 skiing accident.

Chiang Ch'ing   Chairman Mao Zedong's third wife was a former movie actress in Shanghai. After marrying Mao in the early 1940s, she headed the film office of China's Propaganda Department. In 1969–70 she served as a member of the Politburo, the central committee of the Communist Party. After Mao's death in 1976, she was expelled from the party, charged with being a "counter-revolutionary" plotting to usurp power with the help of her fellow members of the so-called Gang of Four (not the punk rock group).

Helen Gahagan Douglas   The star of *She* (1935) served three times as a California Democratic congresswoman before being defeated by Richard Nixon in his Red-baiting 1950 U.S. Senate race. Married to the actor Melvyn Douglas, Douglas was grandmother of the actress Illeana Douglas.

Clint Eastwood   The Man with No Name served as mayor of Carmel, California, from 1986 to 1988.

Glenda Jackson   The distinguished stage and screen actress who won Academy Awards for *Women in Love* (1969) and *A Touch of Class* (1973) retired from acting in 1992 when she was elected to Britain's House of Commons as a member of the Labour Party.

Grace Kelly After marrying Prince Rainier of Monaco in 1956, this Hollywood leading lady assumed the title of Her Serene Highness Princess Grace. She made no further acting appearances, turning down many offers, including the title role in Alfred Hitchcock's *Marnie* (1964), but narrated documentaries including *The Children of Theatre Street* (1978).

John Lodge Marlene Dietrich's handsome leading man in Josef von Sternberg's *The Scarlet Empress* (1934) later served as a Republican U.S. congressman and governor of Connecticut and as U.S. ambassador to Spain, Argentina, and Switzerland.

George Murphy The song-and-dance man who appeared in such movies as *Broadway Melody of 1940* (1940), *Little Nellie Kelly* (1940), and *For Me and My Gal* (1942) was a founder of the Hollywood Republican Committee in 1947 and served as a U.S. senator from California from 1965 through 1971.

Patricia Ryan Nixon Before marrying Richard Nixon, the future first lady of the United States briefly pursued an acting career, working as an extra in RKO and MGM movies during the mid-1930s. She had only one speaking role, a single line of dialogue in the first three-strip Technicolor feature, Rouben Mamoulian's *Becky Sharp* (1935), but it was cut from the movie.

Eva Duarte Perón The Argentinian movie actress married Juan Perón and became first lady of her country. Her story was told in the stage and screen musicals *Evita*. (See "The

Ultimate Movie Collectible: 4 Actors Whose Bodies Were Stolen.")

Nancy Davis Reagan Before becoming first lady of the United States in 1981, Davis had a Hollywood acting career and costarred with her husband in *Hellcats of the Navy* (1957).

Ronald Reagan After acting in such movies as *Kings Row* (1942), *Bedtime for Bonzo* (1951), and *The Killers* (1964), Reagan served as Republican governor of California from 1967 through 1975 and as president of the United States from 1981 through 1989.

Fred Dalton Thompson This character actor, whose film credits include *The Hunt for Red October* (1990), *Cape Fear* (1991), and *In the Line of Fire* (1993), is now a Republican U.S. senator from Tennessee. Before becoming an actor, he practiced law and served as House Minority Counsel during the Watergate hearings. Thompson's movie career was born when he played himself on-screen in *Marie* (1985), as the defense counsel for a Tennessee government whistle-blower (Sissy Spacek).

"The Most Complete Actor-Personality in the American Cinema"*
James Stewart's 15 Greatest Performances

1. *Mr. Smith Goes to Washington* (FRANK CAPRA, 1939)

---

* Critic Andrew Sarris's description of Stewart.

2. *Vertigo* (ALFRED HITCHCOCK, 1958)

3. *It's a Wonderful Life* (CAPRA, 1946)

4. *The Spirit of St. Louis* (BILLY WILDER, 1957)

5. *Winchester '73* (ANTHONY MANN, 1950)

6. *Rear Window* (HITCHCOCK, 1954)

7. *The Shop Around the Corner* (ERNST LUBITSCH, 1940)

8. *Call Northside 777* (HENRY HATHAWAY, 1948)

9. *Anatomy of a Murder* (OTTO PREMINGER, 1959)

10. *The Man Who Shot Liberty Valance* (JOHN FORD, 1962)

11. *Harvey* (HENRY KOSTER, 1950)

12. *Destry Rides Again* (GEORGE MARSHALL, 1939)

13. *The Philadelphia Story* (GEORGE CUKOR, 1940)

14. *The Man Who Knew Too Much* (HITCHCOCK, 1956)

15. *The Flight of the Phoenix* (ROBERT ALDRICH, 1965)

Feo, fuerte y formal
John Wayne's 12 Greatest Performances

"I would like to be remembered—well, the Mexicans have an expression, Feo, fuerte y formal. *Which means: 'He was ugly, was strong and had dignity.' "*
　　　　　—John Wayne, 1970

1. *The Searchers* (JOHN FORD, 1956)   As Ethan Edwards, the deranged Indian hater searching for his niece, kidnapped by Comanches

2. *She Wore a Yellow Ribbon* (FORD, 1948)   As Captain Nathan Brittles, the retiring cavalry officer who wants to bring peace on his final mission

3. *Red River* (HOWARD HAWKS, 1948)   As Tom Dunson, the tyrannical Texas rancher who battles his adopted son on an epic cattle drive

4. *The Shootist* (DON SIEGEL, 1976)   As J. B. Books, the legendary gunfighter dying of cancer

5. *Rio Bravo* (HAWKS, 1959)   As John T. Chance, the Western sheriff who needs but doesn't ask for help to hold his jail against a band of outlaws

6. *The Wings of Eagles* (FORD, 1957)   As Frank W. (Spig) Wead, the reckless Navy flier who turns to screenwriting after being paralyzed

7. *The Man Who Shot Liberty Valance* (FORD, 1962)   As Tom Doniphon, the man who shot a notorious outlaw but let another man take the credit

8. *The Quiet Man* (FORD, 1952)   As Sean Thornton, the American boxer who quits the ring after killing a man and returns to Ireland, the land of his birth

9. *El Dorado* (HAWKS, 1967)   As Cole Thornton, an aging gunfighter crippled by a bullet lodged against his spine, who comes to the aid of an old friend

10. *Stagecoach* (FORD, 1939) As The Ringo Kid, the noble outlaw who saves a stagecoach full of pilgrims

11. *Fort Apache* (FORD, 1948) As Captain Kirby York, the Army man whose respect for Apaches leads him to defy his commanding officer

12. *Rio Grande* (FORD, 1950) As the aging Lt. Col. Kirby York, coping with rebellious Indians and trying to reconcile with his estranged Southern wife

That'll Be the Day
Movies in Which John Wayne Dies

In one of *Mad* magazine's classic "Scenes We'd Like to See," an Indian was shown waving a rifle over his head and exulting, "John Wayne is dead!" But that earth-shaking event occurred only a few times in the Duke's long screen career. His attitude on the subject was succinctly expressed in John Ford's *The Searchers*. When an exasperated Jeffrey Hunter tells him, "I hope you die!" Wayne sardonically replies, "That'll be the day."

Reap the Wild Wind (CECIL B. DEMILLE, 1942) Wayne is crushed to death by a giant squid

The Fighting Seabees (EDWARD LUDWIG, 1944) Killed in battle with the Japanese

Wake of the Red Witch (LUDWIG, 1948) Dies trying to recover gold from his sunken ship, the *Red Witch*

Sands of Iwo Jima (ALLAN DWAN, 1949)   While smoking a cigarette, he is shot by an unseen Japanese sniper

The Alamo (JOHN WAYNE, 1960)   As Davy Crockett, he is run through with a lance by a Mexican soldier, then he blows himself up along with the Alamo's powder supply

The Man Who Shot Liberty Valance (JOHN FORD, 1962) Dies offscreen, evidently of natural causes

The Cowboys (MARK RYDELL, 1972)   Gunned down by outlaw Bruce Dern

The Shootist (DON SIEGEL, 1976)   Dying of cancer, he is shot to death in a gunfight with three men in a saloon

The Best Performances by Child Actors

1. *Roddy McDowall* in *How Green Was My Valley* (JOHN FORD, 1941)

2. *Jean-Pierre Léaud* in *The 400 Blows* (FRANÇOIS TRUFFAUT, 1959)

3. *Christian Bale* in *Empire of the Sun* (STEVEN SPIELBERG, 1987)

4. *Jackie Coogan* in *The Kid* (CHARLES CHAPLIN, 1920)

5. *Patty Duke* in *The Miracle Worker* (ARTHUR PENN, 1962)

6. *Mickey Rooney* in *Boys Town* (NORMAN TAUROG, 1938)

7. *Brigitte Fossey* in *Forbidden Games* (RENÉ CLÉMENT, 1951)

8. *Joan Carroll* in *The Bells of St. Mary's* (LEO MCCAREY, 1945)

9. *Bobby Henrey* in *The Fallen Idol* (CAROL REED, 1948)

10. *Natalie Wood* in *Miracle on 34th Street* (GEORGE SEATON, 1947)

11. *Brandon de Wilde* in *Shane* (GEORGE STEVENS, 1953)

12. *Peggy Ann Garner* in *A Tree Grows in Brooklyn* (ELIA KAZAN, 1945)

13. *Eamonn Owens* in *The Butcher Boy* (NEIL JORDAN, 1997)

14. *Anna Paquin* in *The Piano* (JANE CAMPION, 1993)

15. *Margaret O'Brien* in *Meet Me in St. Louis* (VINCENTE MINNELLI, 1944)

16 & 17. *Hideo Sugawara* and *Tokkan Kozo* in *I Was Born, But . . .* (YASUJIRO OZU, 1932)

18. *Jackie Cooper* in *The Champ* (KING VIDOR, 1931)

19. *David Bennent* in *The Tin Drum* (VOLKER SCHLÖN-DORFF, 1979)

20. *Jean Simmons* in *Great Expectations* (DAVID LEAN, 1946)

21. *All the children* in *Small Change* (TRUFFAUT, 1976)

Joan Crawford's 10 Tips for Gracious Living

1. "After a catastrophe I take a deep breath, pin on a grin, and get on with something else."

2. "Above all be sure that you're very fond of the people you ask to come and stay. Some beautiful friendships have been shipwrecked over a long weekend."

3. "Hot food must be on hot plates. . . . I think it's an insult to a guest to offer meat on a plate that's come right out of the cupboard."

4. "Scrubbing, for me, is the greatest exercise in the world. It gives me rosy cheeks, and I just have a ball."

5. "I always pack in daylight. In artificial light when I'm in a hurry it's too easy to grab the wrong accessories and find myself in Kansas City or San Juan with a hot pink dress and a shocking pink hat—and that's a catastrophe."

6. "I sit on hard chairs—soft ones spread the hips."

7. "I love massage. It won't replace sex, but it's a luxurious feeling."

8. "I avoid chintz."

9. "Regular exercise, all alone, can be boring. . . . Get all those pleasingly plump pals together *regularly* at a certain hour on certain days of the week—and compete. A woman will give up anything—from a fudge sundae to a dry martini or a grilled cheese sandwich—to beat her fellow club members to a slim finish. She may lose a friend or two, but she'll gain loveliness, and her husband's pride and admiration. *That's* worth a couple of fat friends!"

10. "I've always thought, too, that 'father' and 'mother' are words that mean disciplinarian. I like the word 'friend'

instead. We wouldn't have, or adopt, children if we weren't anxious to be their greatest friends."

—from Crawford's 1971 book *My Way of Life*

"Vy you are smilink?"
Strange Ethnic Castings

1. *John Wayne* as Genghis Khan in *The Conqueror* (1956)

2. *Katharine Hepburn* as Trigger Hicks, the Ozark hillbilly in *Spitfire* (1934); as a Chinese in *Dragon Seed* (1944); and as a Russian in *The Iron Petticoat* (1956, in which she asks Bob Hope, "Vy you are smilink?")

3. *William Daniels* and *Elizabeth Wilson* as Dustin Hoffman's parents in *The Graduate* (1967)—as Mort Sahl put it, "No wonder that kid's screwed up. He's a Jewish kid with gentile parents"

4. *Marlon Brando* as an Okinawan in *The Teahouse of the August Moon* (1956)

5. *Mickey Rooney* as a Japanese in *Breakfast at Tiffany's* (1961)

6. *Spencer Tracy* and *John Garfield* as Mexicans in *Tortilla Flat* (1942)

7. *Goldie Hawn* as the Russian title character in *The Girl from Petrovka* (1974)

8. *Alec Guinness* as the Indian Professor Godbole in David Lean's 1984 film of E. M. Forster's *A Passage to India*, a

casting choice Guinness himself considered "absolute madness"

9. *Katharine Ross* as a Native American (Morongo tribe) in *Tell Them Willie Boy Is Here* (1969)—the only blot on an otherwise great film, this is just one of many such egregious castings throughout the history of Hollywood (remember Don Ameche in *Ramona* [1936], Robert Taylor in *Devil's Doorway* [1950], and Burt Lancaster in *Apache* [1954]?)

10. *Frank Sinatra* singing "Ol' Man River" in a white suit in *Till the Clouds Roll By* (1946)

The Film Performance I'm Most Relieved We Never Saw

James Stewart in *The Good Earth*   As a contract player at MGM in the 1930s, Stewart was made up and screen-tested for a role in the studio's lavish adaptation of Pearl Buck's novel. In a 1966 interview with Peter Bogdanovich, Stewart recalled that the role he tested for "was . . . as a *Chinaman*! They gawt me all made up—took all morning—an' gawt me together with Paul Muni and . . . there was just . . . just one thing . . . wrong . . . I was too *tall*! So they dug a trench and I walked in it and Muni walked alongside . . . an' I . . . I didn't get the part. I didn't. . . . They gave the part to a Chinaman!"

The Butter Was on the Toast
The Most Erotic Scenes with the Actors Fully Clothed

The sexiest scenes are often those in which the sex is implicit rather than explicit, more inside the heads of the actors and the audience than right up there on the screen. To borrow Judith Crist's description of Billy Wilder's *Kiss Me, Stupid*, what results from such suggestive ellipticism is the equivalent of a scene in which "Only the characters' clothes separate them from their counterparts in a stag movie."

Flesh and the Devil (CLARENCE BROWN, 1927) Greta Garbo and John Gilbert exchange lingering kisses in a shadowy garden, lit by a single flame; from their faces we can tell that these actors were actually falling in love while making this movie.

The Smiling Lieutenant (ERNST LUBITSCH, 1931) Maurice Chevalier and Claudette Colbert exchange double entendres over breakfast following their (unseen) night of lovemaking. Billy Wilder commented on this delicious Lubitsch touch: "Ah, but regard how they are sucking their coffee and how they are biting their toast: this leaves no doubt in anybody's mind that other appetites have been satisfied. In those days, the butter was on the toast and not the ass, but there was more eroticism in one such breakfast scene than in all of *Last Tango in Paris*."

Queen Christina (ROUBEN MAMOULIAN, 1933) While caressing objects in the room where they have spent the night together, Garbo leans her head on a pillow and looks longingly at Gilbert. "I have been memorizing this room," she tells him. "In the future, in my memory, I shall live a great deal in this room."

The More the Merrier (GEORGE STEVENS, 1943)   After walking Jean Arthur home, Joel McCrea sits with her on the steps of her brownstone apartment in wartime Washington, D.C. As they talk, she keeps rearranging his hands as they explore various parts of her body in and out of the audience's view. Frank Capra called this "probably the sexiest and the funniest scene I've ever seen in any picture. Their words talked government, their hands talked something else."

Notorious (ALFRED HITCHCOCK, 1946)   Kissing constantly as they navigate her Rio apartment in intimate two-shots, Ingrid Bergman and Cary Grant discuss the romantic dinner they're about to eat together.

The Ghost and Mrs. Muir (JOSEPH L. MANKIEWICZ, 1947) As white-haired Gene Tierney dies of old age, ghostly sea captain Rex Harrison takes her hand, and she rises from her chair rejuvenated, walking off with him into the afterlife.

A Place in the Sun (STEVENS, 1951)   Their faces filling the screen in breathtakingly tight over-the-shoulder close-ups, illicit lovers Elizabeth Taylor and Montgomery Clift share urgent confidences at an elegant upper-class party.

Some Like It Hot (BILLY WILDER, 1959)   In a low-cut skintight dress milkily lit to make her look almost topless, Marilyn Monroe mournfully sings "I'm Through with Love" at a nightclub as musician Tony Curtis accompanies her in drag, guilt-ridden for deceiving her.

Tom Jones (TONY RICHARDSON, 1963)   Albert Finney and Joyce Redman (who's later revealed to be his mother) gaze lustily at each other while wolfing down a dinner climaxed by their suggestive ingesting of oysters.

Persona (INGMAR BERGMAN, 1967)   With mingled excitement and shame, psychiatric nurse Bibi Andersson tells her patient (Liv Ullmann) the detailed story of her uninhibited sexual experience with three youths on a beach. As Bergman put it, the scene "must have a suggestive effect on you, enable you to experience it all deep down inside you, in your own cinematograph—much more drastically, brutally, honestly, and voluptuously than I could ever show. Imagine a dissolve there, and the whole story told in pictures—what a horrible anticlimax!"

Ma Nuit Chez Maud (ERIC ROHMER, 1969)   Françoise Fabian and Jean-Louis Trintignant spend an intimate night together chastely but passionately discussing intellectual subjects.

Always (STEVEN SPIELBERG, 1989)   Holly Hunter, in skintight white "girl clothes," dances in her living room to "Smoke Gets in Your Eyes," not knowing she is accompanied by the ghost of her late lover (Richard Dreyfuss).

Ghost (JERRY ZUCKER, 1990)   The clay-smeared bodies of Patrick Swayze and Demi Moore intertwine as they work together at a potter's wheel (this scene was hilariously spoofed by Leslie Nielsen and Priscilla Presley four years later in *Naked Gun 33 1/3: The Final Insult*).

Basic Instinct (PAUL VERHOEVEN, 1992)   Brazenly taunting an aroused Michael Douglas, Sharon Stone and Leilani Sarelle, as lesbian lovers, dance provocatively together in a nightclub.

15 Great Movie Monologues

Charles Laughton in *Ruggles of Red Gap* (LEO MCCAREY, 1935) An American immigrant in the Old West, a former English butler who has started his own restaurant, proclaims his love for his adopted country by reciting Lincoln's Gettysburg Address.

Lew Ayres in *Holiday* (GEORGE CUKOR, 1938) A rich young alcoholic explains to his sister (Katharine Hepburn) why he prefers to spend his life getting drunk.

James Stewart in *Mr. Smith Goes to Washington* (FRANK CAPRA, 1939) Senator Jefferson Smith stands alone to deliver a filibuster about American democracy and "lost causes."

Charles Chaplin in *The Great Dictator* (CHAPLIN, 1940) The filmmaker steps out of character to deliver his passionate cry of alarm for the fate of world civilization as it is confronted with the Nazi menace.

Henry Fonda in *The Grapes of Wrath* (JOHN FORD, 1940) Saying farewell to his mother (Jane Darwell), Tom Joad tells her, "Wherever there's a fight so hungry people can eat, I'll be there. Wherever there's a cop beatin' up a guy, I'll be there."

Richard Bennett in *The Magnificent Ambersons* (ORSON WELLES, 1942) Major Amberson muses philosophically about life and death and how the meaning of everything "must be in the sun."

Walter Huston in *The Treasure of the Sierra Madre* (JOHN HUSTON, 1948) A grizzled old prospector in a Mexican flophouse talks about "what greed does to men's souls."

Orson Welles in *Moby Dick* (HUSTON, 1956)   Father Mapple uses nautical metaphors to give a sermon about the battle between good and evil for the soul of man.

Spencer Tracy in *The Last Hurrah* (FORD, 1958)   Mayor Skeffington tells his nephew (Jeffrey Hunter) how his Irish immigrant mother, while working as a maid, was fired for stealing food from her employer.

Orson Welles in *Compulsion* (RICHARD FLEISCHER, 1959)   A lawyer defending two rich young thrill killers gives a passionate and eloquent argument against the death penalty.

Spencer Tracy in *Guess Who's Coming to Dinner* (STANLEY KRAMER, 1967)   In his last screen appearance, Tracy talks about the woman he loves (Katharine Hepburn).

Boris Karloff in *Targets* (PETER BOGDANOVICH, 1968)   An aging horror-film star tells the story of a man who had an appointment with death in Samarra (before the camera rolled, Bogdanovich asked Karloff to "think of your own mortality").

Ben Johnson in *The Last Picture Show* (BOGDANOVICH, 1971)   As the wintry Texas sun goes in and out of the clouds, Sam the Lion tells the boys about the time he went skinny-dipping with a young woman in a water tank.

Laurence Olivier in *Love Among the Ruins* (CUKOR, 1975 TV MOVIE)   Defending his former lover (Katharine Hepburn) against a breach-of-promise suit brought by a young gigolo, a barrister wears his heart upon his sleeve.

Anthony Hopkins in *Amistad* (STEVEN SPIELBERG, 1997)   Defending the Amistad African captives before the U.S.

Supreme Court, former President John Quincy Adams declares that the nation must live up to its credo, the Declaration of Independence.

12 Electrifying Telephone Scenes

Don Ameche and *Henry Fonda* in *The Story of Alexander Graham Bell* (IRVING CUMMINGS, 1939)   Ameche invents the telephone: "Mr. Watson, come here, I need you!" This scene became so famous that for years afterward, a telephone was called an "ameche."

Joan Fontaine in *The Women* (GEORGE CUKOR, 1939)   As a young married woman reconciles over the phone with her estranged husband, the audience can actually witness Fontaine —so gauche in previous screen appearances—becoming a star and rapturously realizing her own acting abilities.

John Wayne and *Donna Reed* in *They Were Expendable* (JOHN FORD, 1945)   The wartime romance of a U.S. Navy PT boat skipper and an Army nurse in the Philippines is abruptly ended when her field telephone is commandeered for use by two generals (Wayne snaps, "Hope what those generals had to say was important").

James Stewart and *Donna Reed* in *It's a Wonderful Life* (FRANK CAPRA, 1946)   George Bailey angrily declares he'll "never get married ever to anyone" before dropping the phone and capitulating to his love for Mary Hatch, in what Capra called "one of the best scenes I've ever put on the screen."

Barbara Stanwyck in *Sorry, Wrong Number* (ANATOLE LITVAK, 1948)   The film version of Lucille Fletcher's radio play about a bedridden woman overhearing a telephone discussion of a plot to kill her.

Anna Magnani in *Una Voce Umana*, half of the two-part film *L'Amore* (ROBERTO ROSSELLINI, 1948)   In this screen version of Jean Cocteau's play *La Voix Humaine (The Human Voice)*, Magnani gets *her* opportunity for a telephone tour de force as a woman talking up a storm with her lover.

Doris Day and ***Rock Hudson*** in *Pillow Talk* (MICHAEL GORDON, 1959)   In a cleverly risqué device circumventing and mocking censorship restrictions, images of Doris and Rock in separate bathtubs are combined on a split screen as they talk on the telephone and play footsie together.

Laurence Harvey in *The Manchurian Candidate* (JOHN FRANKENHEIMER, 1962)   A voice on the phone triggers a hidden mechanism in the brainwashed Raymond Shaw when it suggests he "play a little game of solitaire." (See Don Siegel's far less compelling 1977 thriller, *Telefon*, starring Charles Bronson, for an elaboration on the same device.)

Tippi Hedren in *The Birds* (ALFRED HITCHCOCK, 1963)   Hedren's nightmarishly claustrophobic torture as she's attacked by birds while taking refuge in a phone booth was aptly compared by Andrew Sarris to Lillian Gish's celebrated closet scene in D. W. Griffith's *Broken Blossoms*.

Peter Sellers in *Dr. Strangelove or: How I Learned to Stop Worrying and Love the Bomb* (STANLEY KUBRICK, 1964)   Hoping to avert all-out nuclear war, U.S. President Merkin Muffley (Sellers) places a call on the hot line to Russian Premier Kissoff, who's drunk as a skunk ("Who should we call, Dimitri? . . . What? I see—just ask for Omsk information").

Anne Bancroft and *Sidney Poitier* in *The Slender Thread* (SYDNEY POLLACK, 1965) This film from the height of the civil rights era offered many moments of taut human drama while playing on the irony that race is irrelevant to a woman on the telephone with a stranger trying to convince her that life is worth living.

Mia Farrow in *Rosemary's Baby* (ROMAN POLANSKI, 1968) In an agonizing long take, the bedevilled Rosemary frantically calls for help from a New York phone booth, while a stranger (the film's producer, William Castle) hovers ominously outside.

Oops!
7 Stars Who Did NOT Appear in Frank Capra's It Happened One Night

It Happened One Night (1934) was the first movie to win all five major Academy Awards—for best picture (to Columbia Pictures chief Harry Cohn), director (Frank Capra), screenwriter (Robert Riskin), actor (Clark Gable), and actress (Claudette Colbert). But no one expected such glory from a $325,000 movie that went into production with the title *Night Bus* (it was based on a *Cosmopolitan* story of that title by Samuel Hopkins Adams). Even Capra's crew had little faith in the project. As Capra's nephew, sound recordist Joe Finochio, admitted, "We were all joking with one another, 'Hell, let's get this stinking picture over with.' "

"Nobody wanted to play in *It Happened One Night*," Capra remembered with only slight exaggeration. "Actors don't like comedies much. They're not dynamic like melodramas—nobody gets hurt, nobody gets killed, nobody gets raped."

1. ***Robert Montgomery***   Riskin wrote the male lead for MGM's dapper leading man, an expert in sophisticated romantic comedy, but the studio refused to loan Montgomery to Columbia, which was still struggling to escape its Poverty Row origins (and would do so only with the success of *It Happened One Night*). Instead, MGM's Louis B. Mayer punished Clark Gable, who was making what the studio chief considered extravagant money demands, by sending him to Columbia to star in *It Happened One Night* for a mere $10,000.

2. ***Myrna Loy***   Turned down the lead female role. She later explained that "they sent me the worst script ever, completely different from the one they shot."

3. ***Miriam Hopkins***   Also turned down the lead female role.

4. ***Margaret Sullavan***   Ditto.

5. ***Carole Lombard***   Passed on *It Happened One Night* because of a scheduling conflict. Lombard later turned down Capra's *Mr. Deeds Goes to Town* as well.

6. ***Constance Bennett***   Bennett offered to buy the script for herself, but when she was refused, she turned down the part.

7. ***Bette Davis***   Davis, who later had an unhappy experience working with Capra in his last feature, *Pocketful of Miracles* (1961), wanted to appear in *It Happened One Night*. But Warner Bros. was feuding with her over her insistence

on being loaned to RKO to make *Of Human Bondage* and punished her by refusing to loan her to Columbia.

Note: The actress who starred in *It Happened One Night*, Claudette Colbert, initially rejected Columbia's offer partly because she had not enjoyed working with Capra on her first movie, *For the Love of Mike*, in 1927. She also was accustomed to glamorous roles at Paramount and was not eager to appear "a little seedy" in a bus movie at such a déclassé studio as Columbia. But Colbert finally accepted an offer of $50,000, insisting she took the part "mostly to work with Clark."

Ye Gods!
The 15 Least Appropriate Castings in Historical Roles

1. *John Wayne* as Genghis Khan in *The Conqueror* (1956)

2 (tie). *Hedy Lamarr* as Joan of Arc, *Dennis Hopper* as Napoleon, and *Peter Lorre* as Nero in *The Story of Mankind* (1957)

5. *Jack Palance* as Fidel Castro in *Che!* (1969)

6. *Omar Sharif* as Che Guevara in *Che!* (1969)

7. *Ronald Reagan* as George Armstrong Custer in *Santa Fe Trail* (1940)

8. *Wallace Beery* as Pancho Villa in *Viva Villa!* (1934)

9. *Jeffrey Hunter* as Jesus in *King of Kings* (1961)

10. *Richard Burton* as Leon Trotsky in *The Assassination of Trotsky* (1972)

11. **Mickey Rooney** as Lorenz Hart in *Words and Music* (1948)

12 (tie). **John Wayne** as The Centurion, **Shelley Winters** as the Woman of No Name, **Sal Mineo** as Uriah, and **Pat Boone** as Young Man at the Tomb in *The Greatest Story Ever Told* (1965)

The Ultimate Typecasting
21 People Who Have Played Themselves in Movies

Muhammad Ali in *The Greatest* (1977)

Lord Baden-Powell in *Boys of the Otter Patrol* (1918), *The Man Who Changed His Mind* (1928), *The Woodpigeon Patrol* (1930)

George Washington Carver in *George Washington Carver* (1940)

Sir Arthur Conan Doyle in *The $5,000,000 Counterfeiting Plan* (1914)

Zane Grey in *White Death* (1936)

Arlo Guthrie and **Police Chief William Obanhein (Officer Obie)** in *Alice's Restaurant* (1969)

Jack Johnson in *Jack Johnson's Adventures in Paris* (1913)

Helen Keller in *Deliverance* (1919)

Sophia Loren in *Sophia Loren: Her Own Story* (1980 TV MOVIE)

Mickey Mantle and *Roger Maris* in *Safe at Home!* (1962)

Marshall McLuhan in *Annie Hall* (1976)

Barney Oldfield in *Barney Oldfield's Race for Life* (1916)

Pablo Picasso in *Le Mystère Picasso* (1956 DOCUMENTARY) and *Le Testament d'Orphée* (1959)

Jackie Robinson in *The Jackie Robinson Story* (1950)

Babe Ruth in *The Pride of the Yankees* (1942)

Margaret Sanger in *Birth Control* (1917)

Frank Wills (Watergate Hotel security guard) in *All the President's Men* (1976)

Florenz Ziegfeld and *Adolph Zukor* in *Glorifying the American Girl* (1929)

The Jeff Bridges Life Achievement Award
13 Very Good Movies with Jeff Bridges

Jeff Bridges (b. 1949) has long been one of the American cinema's best and most underrated actors. His unusually good taste in choosing roles has not often guaranteed commercial success, but his body of work is all the more impressive for not being built on ephemeral hits. Bridges's keen intelligence, sense of humor, and essentially good-natured charm sometimes coexist with a streak of brutality and embittered meanness.

Writing about his 1975 movie *Hearts of the West*, Pauline Kael identified the essence of Bridges's youthful appeal as his "ability to transform the commonplace. He appears to be an average, good-looking, burly, blond American boy, yet he sensitizes us to the boy's feelings to such a degree that this average kid seems like the most wonderful kid we've ever seen." As Bridges matured, David Thomson observed that he is "as close as the modern era has come to Robert Mitchum. Which is to say that Bridges works steadily, without any show of self-importance or dedication, his natural sourness or skepticism picking up weariness with the years. . . . Bridges's reliability, his skill and his hangdog, wounded grace are very appealing in an era of self-glorying superstars."

The Last Picture Show (PETER BOGDANOVICH, 1971)   Timothy Bottoms's Sonny was supposed to be the central character of Bogdanovich's black-and-white elegy to the pre-television era (based on Larry McMurtry's novel), but Jeff Bridges ran away with the picture in the star-making part of Duane, his Texas roughneck friend. Duane's more jaundiced take on the social changes occurring around him occasionally makes him behave loutishly, but he seems far more intelligent and vital than the ethereally sensitive, self-pitying Sonny.

Fat City (JOHN HUSTON, 1972)   Huston's own early experiences as a boxer helped make *Fat City* one of the most authentic depictions of boxing ever filmed. This melancholy, grittily unsentimental drama based on a novel by Leonard Gardner stars Jeff as a talented but green fighter who drifts into the care of a punched-out veteran (Stacy Keach).

Bad Company (ROBERT BENTON, 1972)   Jeff Bridges and the broodingly intellectual, ill-fated Barry Brown make an engaging pair of rascals living by committing robberies during the Civil War. Benton and David Newman wrote the picaresque screenplay for this mordant comedy-Western, graced with somber imagery courtesy of cinematographer Gordon "The Prince of Darkness" Willis.

The Iceman Cometh (JOHN FRANKENHEIMER, 1973)   An uneven but intermittently brilliant cast was assembled for this monumental American Film Theater version of Eugene O'Neill's tragedy set in a 1912 working-class saloon. Jeff plays Parritt, admirably holding his own among such veterans as Robert Ryan (great in his last film role), Fredric March, and Lee Marvin as Hickey.

Hearts of the West (HOWARD ZIEFF, 1975)   "I come all the way out here and what happens? The place goes crazy," says Jeff in the role of a starry-eyed Iowa farm boy who travels to Hollywood during the Depression to become a writer of Western fiction and winds up a movie star. One of the rare movies about Hollywood that isn't overwhelmingly tragic or just plain nasty, *Hearts of the West* is an affectionate tribute to the modest virtues of the Gower Gulch B Westerns.

Rancho Deluxe (FRANK PERRY, 1975)   An uproariously witty screenplay by Thomas McGuane keeps this contemporary Western comedy constantly and slyly off-kilter. Jeff is amiably involved in Montana cattle rustling with a hip, ironic Native American buddy (Sam Waterston, of all people), while the supporting cast includes a sensational turn by Elizabeth Ashley as a jaded married lady pining for some "Gothic ranch action."

Stay Hungry (BOB RAFELSON, 1976)   This offbeat comedy about bodybuilding performed the near-miraculous feats of rescuing Sally Field from her Flying Nun image and launching Arnold Schwarzenegger on his acting career, but it wouldn't have worked without Jeff solidly anchoring the cast as a

wealthy young Alabama real-estate speculator who goes slum-
ming. Rafelson's customarily quirky direction is just right for
the funky Southern milieu.

Winter Kills (WILLIAM RICHERT, 1979)   An astounding,
audacious black comedy, *Winter Kills* barely was released, but
its cynical send-up of the Kennedy assassination (based on a
novel by Richard Condon) plays as a pointed commentary on
conspiracy theories and political corruption. Jeff's essential
decency makes him perfect to play the audience surrogate figure, the slain president's idealistic but gradually disillusioned
younger brother.

Heaven's Gate (MICHAEL CIMINO, 1980)   Hands down the
most unfairly maligned American movie of the modern era (if
not of *any* era), *Heaven's Gate* is a sprawling, beautiful, and
vastly ambitious Western epic. It may have disturbed people
because its view of American history—focusing on a land war
between cattlemen and immigrant Wyoming settlers—is so
relentlessly downbeat, with unmistakably Marxist implica-
tions. As "John Bridges," Jeff costars with Kris
Kristofferson and Christopher Walken.

Starman (JOHN CARPENTER, 1984)   Columbia was ridiculed for passing on *E.T.* to make
Starman instead, but *Starman* is nothing to be
ashamed about, except financially. It's a charming and poetic love story between an Earth woman from Wisconsin (Karen Allen) and the sensitive alien (Jeff) who takes on
the human form of her late husband.

Tucker: The Man and His Dream (FRANCIS FORD COPPOLA,
1988)   When Coppola's longtime dream project reached the

screen, its darker edges had been softened somewhat by an overlay of Capracorn imposed by producer George Lucas. But Jeff is simply wonderful as the indefatigable visionary Preston Tucker, whose dream of a fuel-efficient car for the masses was squashed by the big Detroit automakers.

Texasville (BOGDANOVICH, 1990) Audiences and most reviewers angrily rejected this sequel to *The Last Picture Show* because it so little resembles the original movie. But how could it? Like America in the intervening years, Jeff's Duane (who has made and lost an oil fortune) has gone to pot both physically and morally, along with most of the other characters. In its tragicomic compassion toward its large cast of aimless characters, *Texasville* is a worthy successor to Renoir's *The Rules of the Game*, to which it bears more than a passing resemblance.

The Big Lebowski (JOEL COEN, 1998) As an aging, terminally laid-back hippie who calls himself "The Dude," Jeff Bridges gets into some really heavy shit in this Coen brothers comedy. Jeff shows deliciously subtle comic timing as he gets lost in his own rambling sentences, playing a character whose biggest problem at the outset is explaining to people what he does for a living. The Dude does have one accomplishment to boast about: "I was one of the authors of the Port Huron Statement—the original Port Huron Statement, not the compromised second draft." Somehow The Dude's blinkered innocence enables him to survive involvement in a nonsensical crime caper with a deranged Vietnam veteran buddy (John Goodman). Moments of genuine emotion sneak up on the viewer in Jeff's portrayal of a man with a stubbornly offbeat sense of integrity. As he sums it up at the end, "Yeah, well, The Dude abides."

The Ultimate Movie Collectible
4 Actors Whose Bodies Were Stolen

John Barrymore   As a gag, Barrymore's body was spirited away from a funeral home in 1942 by several drinking buddies, including Peter Lorre, Humphrey Bogart, and director Raoul Walsh, who bribed the mortuary to let them borrow it. Walsh later confirmed to Peter Bogdanovich that the body was taken to Errol Flynn's home in the Hollywood Hills and propped up on a couch. Flynn's reaction when he returned home drunk and saw the corpse? "Jumped out of his skin!" Walsh laughed. "Almost made him quit drinking—almost."

Charles Chaplin   After his death in 1977, Chaplin was buried in the village cemetery of Corsier-sur-Vevey, Switzerland. Two months later, a pair of grave robbers shocked the world by abducting his coffin and holding it for ransom. Chaplin's widow, Oona, refused to pay them, but seventy-six days after the coffin was stolen, it was found buried in a field ten miles from the cemetery. The grave robbers, Galtcho Ganav and Roman Wardas, were later convicted. The bizarre incident has caused the burial places of some other movie stars to be kept secret or unmarked.

Eva Duarte Perón   The first lady of Argentina, a former movie actress whose life was portrayed in the stage and screen musicals *Evita*, died of cancer in 1952, at age thirty-three. Like Lenin's body, Evita's was mummified. A quasi-religious icon, her corpse was privately displayed for special guests in a chapel at the new national headquarters of the unionists in Buenos Aires, the *Confederacion General del Trabajo*. But after her dictator husband, Juan Perón, was deposed in 1955, the Argentinian military junta feared that Evita's body would be deified and become the focus of a new Peronist movement. Thus, it was decided, "The cadaver had to be excluded from the political scene." Evita's body was kidnapped and secretly kept in military buildings, before being buried later under another name in Milan, Italy. Removed in 1971 to Madrid, where her exiled husband was living, Evita was returned to Argentina in 1974 and finally reburied in Buenos Aires two years later.

George Tobias   Tobias was one of the most amusing and endearing character actors in the Golden Age of Hollywood; his films include *Ninotchka*, *Sergeant York*, and *Yankee Doodle Dandy*. So it's oddly fitting that what happened to his body following his death on February 27, 1980, resembled a scene from an old slapstick comedy. Tobias's remains were being transported in a station wagon from a hospital to a mortuary when the mortuary's driver became involved in a minor traffic accident in Hollywood on Sunset Boulevard and stopped to exchange information with the other driver. Two young men jumped into the station wagon and drove off with it, but within three blocks they panicked when they discovered Tobias's body on a gurney in the back, covered with a blanket. Police reported that the hijackers "ran screaming" from the station wagon, leaving it with its engine running and doors ajar. The body was safely recovered and later was transported to New York City for burial.

What I Really Want to Do Is Direct
25 Movies Directed by Actors Who Did Not Direct Again

There are various reasons why these actors never returned (or, in some cases, haven't yet returned) to directing. Lillian Gish is reported to have said (in the 1920s) that directing was no job for a lady, although Gish was such a feminist pioneer that the remark sounds apocryphal. (For another explanation, see "10 Important Lost Movies.") Others found that their debut films were commercial failures. Some perhaps managed to get directing out of their systems. The saddest case was that of character actor Steve Ihnat, who played a memorable villain in Don Siegel's *Madigan* (1968) but died of a heart attack at the Cannes Film Festival four years later while promoting the first and only film he directed. But two of these actors directed films that have come to be widely regarded as classics— Charles Laughton and Marlon Brando.

Dan Aykroyd   *Nothing but Trouble* (1991)

Anne Bancroft   *Fatso* (1980)

Marlon Brando   *One-Eyed Jacks* (1961)

James Cagney   *Short Cut to Hell* (1957)

Bud Cort   *Ted & Venus* (1991)

Albert Finney   *Charlie Bubbles* (1968)

Lillian Gish   *Remodeling Her Husband* (1920)

Tom Hanks   *That Thing You Do* (1996)

Laurence Harvey   *The Ceremony* (1964)

Steve Ihnat   *The Honkers* (1972)

Charles Laughton   *The Night of the Hunter* (1955)

Jack Lemmon   *Kotch* (1971)

Barbara Loden   *Wanda* (1970)

Peter Lorre   *Die Verlorene* (1951)

Karl Malden   *Time Limit* (1957)

Walter Matthau   *Gangster Story* (1961)

Roddy McDowall   *Tam Lin*, aka *The Devil's Widow* (1971)

Toshiro Mifune   *The Legacy of the 500,000* (1963)

John Mills   *Sky West and Crooked* (1965)

Anthony Quinn   *The Buccaneer* (1958)

Ralph Richardson   *Home at Seven*, aka *Murder on Monday* (1952)

Joan Rivers   *Rabbit Test* (1978)

Peter Sellers   *Mr. Topaze* (1961)

Talia Shire   *One Night Stand* (1995)

Frank Sinatra   *None But the Brave* (1965)

Final Takes . . .

My 25 Favorite Movies

1. *The Quiet Man* (JOHN FORD, 1952)   The quintessential romantic fantasy of every Irish-American male is to move to Ireland, buy a cottage in Connemara, and marry a woman who reminds him of Maureen O'Hara. Imagine my consternation when I married an Irish woman named O'Hara who told me she hated *The Quiet Man*! Although people in Ireland get their Irish up over what they consider to be the movie's corny ethnic stereotypes (see Ruth O'Hara's list, "No More Blarney: Understanding the Irish Through Movies"), while visiting the places where *The Quiet Man* was filmed in County Mayo with my new bride in 1985, I found that everybody there behaves *exactly* like a character out of *The Quiet Man*.

2. *Chimes at Midnight* (ORSON WELLES, 1966)   The moment to which all of Welles's previous work leads is the climax of the coronation sequence in *Chimes at Midnight*, when the aged Sir John Falstaff (Welles) is coldly banished by his former boon companion, King Henry V (Keith Baxter). In this culmination to his career-long obsession with

the theme of male betrayal, Welles achieved an emotional nakedness that he never equaled before or after. His majestic adaptation of Shakespeare's history plays about the Falstaff-Hal relationship revolves around the director's incarnation of what he called "the greatest conception of a good man, the most completely good man, in all drama." Welles's Falstaff is the performance of a lifetime.

3. *Trouble in Paradise* (ERNST LUBITSCH, 1932)   "As for pure style," Lubitsch wrote shortly before his death, "I think I have done nothing better or as good as *Trouble in Paradise*." When I first saw *Trouble in Paradise*, it was also the first Lubitsch movie I had ever seen, but I felt certain I had encountered the director's masterpiece. After viewings of many other wonderful Lubitsch movies, I still have the same conviction while watching this most elegant, sophisticated, and gracefully poignant of all romantic comedies.

4. *The Searchers* (FORD, 1956)   I'm more ambivalent than I once was about Ford's portrayals of Indians in this great Western about an obsessive racist (John Wayne), but that ambivalence acknowledges the fact that no other film looks so profoundly into the heart of American darkness. Ford's haunting visual and dramatic poetry in *The Searchers* is the cinematic equivalent of D. H. Lawrence's observation that "white men have probably never felt so bitter anywhere, as here in America, where the very landscape, in its very beauty, seems a bit devilish and grinning, opposed to us." (See "Scarred for Life: The Seminal Influence of *The Searchers*.")

5. *The Magnificent Ambersons* (WELLES, 1942)   See "Flyover Movies: 13 Ways of Looking at the Midwest."

6. *Tokyo Story* (YASUJIRO OZU, 1953)   See "Family Values: My 14 Favorite Movies About Families."

7. *Mr. Smith Goes to Washington* (FRANK CAPRA, 1939) Despite his many declarations in later years that his best movie was *It's a Wonderful Life*, Capra acknowledged to me in 1984 that he considered *Mr. Smith Goes to Washington* a better film: "It's a stronger story and a story about our government; a lot of the internal workings of our government are revealed. I suppose that's why I like it better than the other ones—it's *big*." More realistic and astringent than *Wonderful Life*, *Mr. Smith* doesn't resort to the supernatural to save James Stewart's Senator Jefferson Smith, even if the happy ending is made barely credible only by Capra's directorial sleight of hand. The eloquent, impassioned screenplay by Sidney Buchman (a radical leftist whom Capra informed against during the blacklist era) gave Capra his most fitting vehicle to express his own deeply ambivalent feelings about his adopted country.

8. *Jules and Jim* (FRANÇOIS TRUFFAUT, 1962)   In my early manhood, when I embraced *Jules and Jim* as one of my favorite movies, I saw in Jeanne Moreau's Catherine all the alluring qualities I admired in women. A boldly sensual adventuress, Catherine tries to live with utter freedom and passion, even if life ultimately disappoints her. Returning to *Jules and Jim* years later, after my youthful romanticism had been tempered by experience, I was stunned to realize that Catherine not only commits a crime of passion, but also is an obvious sociopath. How could she have come to be regarded as a feminist icon? Even more disturbing, how could I have been so taken with this woman, whose behav-

ior toward men is so deranged? Perhaps the answer is that Truffaut's Catherine is *both* the woman I was attracted to when I was young, and the woman I was repelled by when I was older and (somewhat) wiser. As Truffaut suggests with his hypnotic zooms and tracks around a statue of a Sphinxlike woman, Catherine embodies all the conflicting feelings men have toward women.

9. *Schindler's List* (STEVEN SPIELBERG, 1993) When I learned that Steven Spielberg finally had decided to go ahead with his much-delayed plans to make a film about the Holocaust, that was all I needed to go ahead with my biography of Spielberg. I knew he had taken the final, irrevocable step to full personal and artistic maturity.

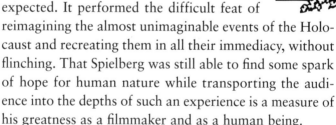

And, as a longtime admirer of his work, I was confident that he had the emotional depth to deal with such a harrowing subject responsibly, without minimizing any of its impact. But *Schindler's List* turned out to be even more powerful than I could have expected. It performed the difficult feat of reimagining the almost unimaginable events of the Holocaust and recreating them in all their immediacy, without flinching. That Spielberg was still able to find some spark of hope for human nature while transporting the audience into the depths of such an experience is a measure of his greatness as a filmmaker and as a human being.

10. *Citizen Kane* (WELLES, 1941) Suffice it to say that when I saw *Citizen Kane* in the fall of 1966 at the age of nineteen, I lost (at least for quite a while) my ambition to become a novelist, deciding instead to write about movies

and, some day, to make movies myself. "You've seen *Kane* forty times?" Welles asked me in astonishment when I met him in 1970. "How could you see *any* movie forty times?" "Well," I replied, "you watched *Stagecoach* forty times in one year while you were preparing to make *Kane*. I was emulating you." "Yes," said Welles, "but I didn't really *watch Stagecoach* every time. Every night for more than a month, I would screen it with a different technician from RKO and ask him questions all through the movie." Eventually, I came with regret to a similarly distanced vantage point in my appreciation of *Kane*. I have trouble watching it straight through now, because after more than seventy-five viewings, I can play it in my head. But even if other movies now hold a greater claim to my attention, like François Truffaut I still regard *Kane* as "the Film of Films."

11. ***Wagon Master*** (FORD, 1950)   Here's what I've always imagined moviemaking should be like—going out in the desert with a small group of friends, making a movie with a modest budget, and telling a simple story with larger overtones and complex undertones, a gloriously photographed Western that serves as a vessel for the filmmaker's greatest joys and deepest feelings. *Wagon Master* is the movie that comes to my mind, with mingled admiration and regret, whenever I hear someone say, "They don't make 'em like that anymore."

12. ***Some Like It Hot*** (BILLY WILDER, 1959)   In 1956, *Time* magazine put Marilyn Monroe on its cover. Inside was a photo that seemed extremely risqué at the time, even shocking—a shot of the young Marilyn, in loose blouse

and pants, unzipping her fly and giving the camera a side-long glance that somehow was simultaneously lewd and innocent. The caption read, "NORMA JEANE AT 17." I kept that issue of *Time* in my family's dim, dusty garage for several of my childhood years and held many a secret rendezvous with that photo. That will help explain why seeing *Some Like It Hot* for the first time when I was twelve was such an eye-opening and liberating event. Not only was our ultimate 1950s fantasy goddess up there on the screen in her most alluring and yet most three-dimensional role, but there were so many other audacious elements for a Catholic kid from that repressed era to assimilate—the movie's black-comedy treatment of violence, its outrageous gender-bending humor, and, perhaps above all, its feminist theme, fully ten years ahead of its time. *Some Like It Hot* literally taught men what it was like to walk in women's shoes. My gratitude to Billy Wilder for acting as a one-man sexual revolution can best be expressed by quoting what the Spanish director Fernando Trueba said when he received an Academy Award in 1994: "I would like to believe in God in order to thank him, but I just believe in Billy Wilder, so . . . thank you, Mr. Wilder."

13. *The 400 Blows* (TRUFFAUT, 1959)   The best movie ever made about childhood, Truffaut's semiautobiographical story strikes a chord with anyone who cannot look back on the early stages of life with romantic nostalgia. As direct as a punch in the mouth, *The 400 Blows* captures all the claustrophobic misery of an unhappy childhood, from the intolerable home situation Antoine Doinel (Jean-Pierre Léaud) flees by turning delinquent, to the

Dickensian reform school he runs from at the end. But as the famous freeze-frame ending graphically demonstrates, for Antoine there is no escape from the suffering of childhood.

14. *Psycho* (ALFRED HITCHCOCK, 1960)   I didn't see *Psycho* until seven years after it was released, so I missed out on the initial shock it created. In the interim, so much about the social climate had changed: President Kennedy had been assassinated, the war in Vietnam had escalated, and riots had occurred in America's inner cities. But *Psycho* still stunned me. Not only for its shower scene and its other horrifying acts of violence, but also for a scene I find even more disturbing, although nothing happens in it but talk. It's the scene of Norman Bates (Anthony Perkins) quietly sharing his psychological torment as he has a nighttime snack with Marion Crane (Janet Leigh) in his motel office, not long before he stabs her to death. "We're all locked in our private traps," he tells her. "We scratch and claw, but only at the air, only at each other, and for all of it we never budge an inch. . . . We all go a little mad sometimes. Haven't you?" That these two lost people share a few moments of emotional communion beforehand makes the shower scene infinitely more poignant, by heightening its terrible sense of futility and missed opportunities.

15. *La Grande Illusion* (JEAN RENOIR, 1937)   When asked once what films dealing with peace and war he found most effective, Renoir responded, "In 1936 I made a picture called *La Grande Illusion* in which I tried to express all my deep feelings for the cause of peace. This film was

very successful. Three years later the war broke out. That is the only answer I can find to your very interesting enquiry." That ironic spirit, both melancholy and humble, informs *La Grande Illusion*, demonstrating the filmmaker's awareness that the gallantry and brotherhood he so stirringly depicts between Frenchmen and Germans during World War I may be only a pipe dream. The title suggests as much, although it also refers to the illusory glory of war. No other film has been so passionate in exploring the reasons why mankind persists in annihilating its own kind, despite its own better judgment.

16. *City Lights* (CHARLES CHAPLIN, 1931) It's fashionable today for critics to venerate Buster Keaton at the expense of Chaplin, but why must we prefer one silent-comedy genius to the other? While I list *City Lights* among my twenty-five favorite movies, I could just as easily list Keaton's *The General*. But there's something ineffably moving about the tramp's relationship with the flower girl (Virginia Cherrill) in *City Lights* that makes its romance seem disturbingly real today in a way that other silent comedies never approached. As Andrew Sarris has observed, "What, after all, is the final close-up of *City Lights* but the definitive image of a man who feels tragically unworthy of his beloved?" (Also see "My 17 Favorite Close-Ups in Movies.")

17. *7 Women* (FORD, 1966) See "My 20 Favorite Underrated Movies."

18. *Close Encounters of the Third Kind* (SPIELBERG, 1977 ORIGINAL EDITION) Rationally, perhaps, one has to prefer *Schindler's List* to *Close Encounters* because of

the gravity of the later film's themes and our awareness of how many possible pitfalls Spielberg so masterfully avoided. Still, I feel that while another director also could have made a great film out of *Schindler's List*—probably not as great as Spielberg's—no one else could have made *Close Encounters* . . . at all. This urgently felt fantasy of escape from the mundane reality of Midwestern suburbia is the most personal of all Spielberg's films, expressing the Jewish director's deep-seated identification with the transforming power of the alien. He had the story on his mind from 1957, when he saw a meteor shower in the desert with his father shortly after the family moved to Phoenix. Spielberg's first feature, *Firelight* (1964), a wildly ambitious amateur undertaking in 8 mm, was a rough draft for *Close Encounters*. The dazzling creative excitement and the infinitely tender sense of hope that Spielberg brought to *Close Encounters*, his youthful masterpiece, are something to cherish forever.

19. *The Godfather Part II* (FRANCIS FORD COPPOLA, 1974)
At the ball following the 1975 Academy Awards ceremony, I spotted Coppola holding his Oscar as best director for the *Godfather* sequel, and impulsively told him, "They gave you the award for the wrong movie." I meant *The Conversation*, that gem of a thriller which also came out in 1974. But I was dead wrong, as Coppola's frowning, dumbstruck response to my rude remark should have told me. With a Tolstoyan range of emotion and style, effortlessly moving backward and forward in historical eras, Coppola made one of the

great American movies, an immigrant family saga that, by extension, encompasses all the hopes and tragedies of our national life in the twentieth century.

20. *Shock Corridor* (SAMUEL FULLER, 1963) See "High Anxiety: The 12 Best Mental Hospital Movies" and "The Greatest Bad Line in the History of Movies."

21. *Dr. Strangelove or: How I Learned to Stop Worrying and Love the Bomb* (STANLEY KUBRICK, 1964) The first time I sat through *Dr. Strangelove*, I didn't understand that it was supposed to be funny—that's how radical a departure it was. But my friend Dick Benka, who cracked up all through the movie, convinced me to stay for a second viewing. *Then* I got it. The paradigm shift *Dr. Strangelove* required in all of our attitudes toward government, world survival, and human nature left us permanently altered, almost as if Kubrick had tampered with our common genetic framework. Only a handful of movies in anyone's lifetime will do that. Black comedy suddenly became the hippest, most serious mode of dealing with the absurd, out-of-control nature of reality in the nuclear age.

22. *Let There Be Light* (JOHN HUSTON, 1945) Also see "High Anxiety: The 12 Best Mental Hospital Movies." One of my most gratifying achievements was helping liberate this documentary in 1980. With the support of producer Ray Stark and Motion Picture Association of America President Jack Valenti, I conducted a campaign in *Daily Variety* that put public pressure on the U.S. Army to declassify Huston's overwhelmingly powerful wartime documentary about shell-shocked soldiers. The campaign

succeeded thanks to a direct appeal by Vice President Walter Mondale to the Carter administration's enlightened secretary of the Army, Clifford Alexander.

23. *French Cancan* (JEAN RENOIR, 1955)   See "You Ain't Heard Nothin' Yet: 10 Underrated Movie Musicals."

24. *Singin' in the Rain* (GENE KELLY, STANLEY DONEN, 1952) See "Two Cheers for Hollywood: 15 of the Best Movies About Movies."

25. *Titanic* (JAMES CAMERON, 1997)   Not only the greatest disaster movie and greatest special-effects movie ever made, *Titanic* presents a rich canvas of 1912 society from high to low, enabling us to experience the profound emotional impact of one of history's most awesome human tragedies. This is moviemaking on the grandest of scales, the kind that made us love movies when we were kids, but that most directors today would consider themselves too sophisticated to attempt. Bravo to Cameron for boldly flying in the face of moviemaking fashion, while resurrecting the epic genre, bringing a keen intelligence to bear on the class and gender inequities of the early twentieth century, and in the process, making the film of his lifetime.

My 13 Least Favorite Movies

1. *Eraserhead* (DAVID LYNCH, 1977)   In my *Daily Variety* review of Lynch's first feature, I called it "a sickening bad-taste exercise. . . . *Eraserhead* consists mostly of a man sitting in a room trying to figure out what to do with his

horribly mutated child. . . . [T]he pic has good tech values (particularly the inventive sound mixing), but little substance or subtlety. The mind boggles to learn that Lynch labored on this pic for five years." Although *Eraserhead* since has acquired cult status among Lynch acolytes, I haven't changed my mind. I'm willing to sit through some gut-wrenching stuff in the name of cinematic art, but *Eraserhead* is the only movie I've ever seen that actually made me turn my face to the wall on several occasions. As John Wayne says in *3 Godfathers*, "I'm a tough bird, an awful tough old bird, but I'm not goin' back in there."

2. *Myra Breckenridge* (MICHAEL SARNE, 1969)   If only for the mind-blowing sight of film critic Rex Reed masturbating in wide-screen color, intercut with the moppet Shirley Temple being squirted in the face and giggling as she milks a goat, this chaotic film by young British director Michael Sarne would represent the ultimate act of indulgence in what became known as Hollywood's *Easy Rider* era (see number 10). But Sarne's mangling of Gore Vidal's satirical novel about transsexualism is a nonstop parade of offensive idiocy and waste.

3. *The Story of Mankind* (IRWIN ALLEN, 1957)   So ridiculous that it's oddly enjoyable, this movie actually seems to be taking itself seriously at some points as it rushes through the millennia, illustrating landmark human events with clips from old Hollywood movies and cameos by grotesquely inappropriate stars. Ronald Colman certainly plays it straight in the lead role as he debates with the devil (Vincent Price, of course) whether mankind should survive. But when the Marx Brothers appear to reenact the purchase of

Manhattan Island from the Indians, it's clear that even the director couldn't take this nonsense too seriously.

4. *Dodes'ka-den* (1970)   Akira Kurosawa's phantasmagoria about the aimless lives of slum dwellers in modern Japan is a literally maddening piece of work. The title, a sound approximating the noise made by a streetcar, is repeated endlessly by the craziest of the film's characters, whose voice makes the sound of fingernails scraping on a chalkboard seem harmonious by comparison. Much of the film takes place in and around the city dump. I had to force myself to sit through this god-awful mess, which vividly reflects the Japanese filmmaker's disintegrating mental state at that time in his life. Is this the worst film ever made by a great director?

5 & 6 (a virtual tie). *Pocketful of Miracles* (FRANK CAPRA, 1961) and *Here Comes the Groom* (CAPRA, 1951)   Which of these dispirited, leadenly unfunny, and mind-numbingly insincere tearjerkers represents Capra's nadir? It's hard to decide, but in my biography *Frank Capra: The Catastrophe of Success* (1992), I chose *Pocketful of Miracles*, which Gore Vidal aptly described as "one of the all-time bad pictures."

7. *Won Ton Ton, the Dog Who Saved Hollywood* (MICHAEL WINNER, 1976)   See "The 5 Worst Movies About Movies" and "Where Have You Gone, Nathanael West?: The Strangest Event I've Ever Witnessed in All My Years of Covering Hollywood."

8. *The Car* (ELLIOT SILVERSTEIN, 1977)   Among the many *Exorcist* rip-offs made by Hollywood in the '70s, this has

to be the pits—a horror movie about an automobile possessed by the devil. The scene that stands out in my memory has Kathleen Lloyd, playing a schoolteacher, facing down the evil car as it growls and rumbles at her. Poor Ms. Lloyd: she was a promising actress, but I've never seen her on-screen again. One reason I put *The Car* on this list is that immediately after seeing it in a Universal screening room, I had to go to lunch with the director to interview him for *Daily Variety*. We managed to spend a pleasant two hours together without either of us mentioning the film, and I never wrote up the interview.

9. *The Graduate* (MIKE NICHOLS, 1967)
The Graduate represents everything loath- somely smug and narcissistic about my baby-boomer generation, which liked to claim (on scant evidence) that it was "the greatest generation in history." The enor- mous popularity of this movie helped alienate me from my peers for many years. In its ruthlessly condemnatory portrait of Anne Bancroft's sexually predatory older woman, Mrs. Robinson, *The Graduate* is also one of the ugliest pieces of cinematic sexism released since World War II. As the critic Robin Wood once told me, "If I ran a movie theater, I would program a double bill of *The Graduate* with *The Last Picture Show*, to show people how mean Mike Nichols really is."

10. *Easy Rider* (DENNIS HOPPER, 1969) I put *Easy Rider* on this list because it had such a deleterious effect on American filmmaking, becoming such an unexpected hit

that it set off an orgy of misguided attempts by the studios to exploit the growing youth market. Hopper's addlepated ode to two itinerant cocaine dealers (played by himself and an equally spaced-out Peter Fonda) gave birth to many of the druggy, self-indulgent clichés of anti-establishment filmmaking, from technical gimmicks such as rack-focusing and flash-forwards to thematic elements such as a knee-jerk hostility to Middle America and a mindless celebration of rebellion for the hell of it.

11. *Star Wars* (GEORGE LUCAS, 1977)   As my friend Jon Davison remarked at the time, "*Star Wars* would be my favorite movie if I were six years old." I remember walking out of the press screening of this landmark movie at the Academy of Motion Picture Arts & Sciences theater feeling extremely depressed, even while everyone around me was raving about it. I realized that I had just seen the future of the movies—noise and mayhem and spectacular special effects linked to a story of stupefying banality, with cardboard characters, juvenile themes, and reactionary politics. Sadly, my worst fears have been proven correct.

12. *Showgirls* (PAUL VERHOEVEN, 1995)   This moronic soft-core sex extravaganza, written by Joe Eszterhas and directed by Verhoeven with all the wit and sophistication of a horny ten-year-old, has the temerity to act morally superior to lap dancing. Any movie so embarrassingly rotten that it made the Creative Artists Agency drop the star (Elizabeth Berkley) from its client list deserves a special place in film history. To be able to have sex again with a straight face, one must put *Showgirls* out of one's mind.

13. *Patriot Games* (PHILIP NOYCE, 1992) To quote my *Daily Variety* review, *Patriot Games* is an "ultraviolent, fascistic, blatantly anti-Irish" adaptation of Tom Clancy's novel, "a right-wing cartoon of the current British-Irish political situation." I stand by my review. (See "The Jedediah Leland Memorial Award: To 6 Critics Who Lost Their Jobs Because of Their Reviews.")

My 20 Favorite Underrated Movies

True Heart Susie (D. W. GRIFFITH, 1919) This unassuming rustic comedy-drama has long been neglected because of its subject matter and perhaps also because of its title, neither of which is calculated to appeal to highbrow tastemakers. But Lillian Gish gives one of her finest performances as the title character, whose spirited devotion to longtime beau Robert Harron weathers even his ill-fated marriage to another woman. Griffith's elegiac direction avoids sentimentality with its awareness of the emotional repression and sacrifice involved in small-town life.

Make Way for Tomorrow (LEO MCCAREY, 1937) In all of American cinema, there is no more devastating indictment of society's indifference to elderly people than *Make Way for Tomorrow*. It stands with Ozu's *Tokyo Story* in starkly dramatizing the way grown children too often neglect their responsibilities to their parents (see "Family Values: My 14 Favorite Movies About Families"). The concluding sequence of *Make Way for Tomorrow*, showing the forced separation of the old married couple (Beulah Bondi and Victor Moore) after they relive the events of their honeymoon in New York

City, is made bearable to watch only by the counterpoint of McCarey's comedic skills.

Japanese War Bride (KING VIDOR, 1952)   When I complimented King Vidor on *Japanese War Bride*, he looked a bit startled and said, "But that's one of my minor movies." This movie's modesty is actually one of its virtues, for in telling the story of a good-hearted but naive G.I. (Don Taylor) who brings home to his bigoted community a Japanese wife (Shirley Yamaguchi), Vidor returned to the emotional simplicity of his best silent work, such as *The Crowd*.

Glen or Glenda (EDWARD D. WOOD JR., 1953)   aka *I Changed My Sex, I Led 2 Lives, He or She*. Ed Wood is usually cited as the worst director who ever lived, and this is one of his most ridiculed films, an earnest, often absurd plea for tolerance toward transvestites (starring the director in an angora sweater). But even the artless simplicity of the film works for it by giving *Glen or Glenda* the emotional urgency of a cri de coeur. Aside from the fact that Wood acts under a pseudonym, this is personal filmmaking at its most undisguised and unashamed, and for that it deserves high praise indeed.

The Sun Shines Bright (JOHN FORD, 1953)   Some viewers can't see beyond the presence of Stepin Fetchit in a movie released only a year before the U.S. Supreme Court issued its landmark decision in the case of *Brown v. Board of Education*. But Ford made *The Sun Shines Bright* because he wanted a second chance to show Kentucky Judge William Pittman Priest standing up against a lynch mob. The first time he shot such a scene, with Will Rogers for *Judge Priest* (1934), Fox cut it from the movie. In that version of the stories by Irvin S.

Cobb, Stepin Fetchit played the black man saved by the judge from lynching; this time the aging, unfairly maligned character actor is at the side of Charles Winninger's Judge Priest to defend a black youngster against many of the town's white citizens. A commercial flop, *The Sun Shines Bright* was Ford's own favorite of all his movies, a complex, often satirical, strangely moving portrait of a man rising above his bigoted background to stand up for justice. The videotape version released by Republic without fanfare in 1990 is Ford's original cut, ten minutes longer than the release version. The restored material, which makes the film's social canvas even richer, includes an opening sequence delineating Stepin Fetchit's brotherly relationship with the judge and other scenes involving African-American characters, aptly described by Ford as "climatic scenes."

Wild River (ELIA KAZAN, 1960)   Ironically, it was only after he informed on his colleagues to the House Committee on Un-American Activities that Kazan's films became more subtly shaded in portraying the gray areas of human behavior. *Wild River* is his masterpiece, a finely balanced story about a stubborn old woman (Jo Van Fleet) forced to leave her island when the Tennessee Valley Authority brings progress in the form of a dam. The film's melancholic viewpoint stems from its awareness that there are no easy solutions to this real-life dilemma.

The Intruder (ROGER CORMAN, 1961)   One of the rare Corman films that lost money, *The Intruder* failed to attract audiences even after he retitled it *I Hate Your Guts!*. Not coincidentally, *The Intruder* is also Corman's most serious film, a tough, unsentimental black-and-white drama about an itinerant rabble-rouser (William Shatner) stirring up smoldering racial hatred in small Southern towns. Shot on location, this low-budget movie has a ripped-from-the-headlines urgency that makes it an important time capsule of the civil rights era.

Kiss Me, Stupid (BILLY WILDER, 1964)   A corrosive satire of American sexual hypocrisy and materialism, *Kiss Me, Stupid* was reviled by the shortsighted critics of its day, and it proved a devastating blow to Wilder's career in Hollywood. But its audacious wit and undercurrent of bittersweet romanticism earn this *film maudit* a special place in my affections. As Wilder pointed out, "Peculiarly enough, the theme of *Kiss Me, Stupid* was human dignity and the sanctity of marriage." The only contemporary critic who understood what the movie was really about was novelist Joan Didion, who wrote in *Vogue* (of all places) that Wilder "is not a funnyman but a moralist, a recorder of human venality. . . . The Wilder world is one seen at dawn through a hangover, a world of cheap double entendre and stale smoke and drinks in which the ice has melted: the true country of despair." After reading that review, Wilder wrote a note to Didion: "I read your piece in the beauty parlor while sitting under the hair drier, and it sure did the old pornographer's heart good. Cheers. Billy Wilder."

Fahrenheit 451 (FRANÇOIS TRUFFAUT, 1966)   When I first saw Truffaut's film version of the Ray Bradbury novel about a futuristic society that burns books, college students and townspeople in the Madison, Wisconsin, audience took turns endorsing their own favorite brand of fascism. The McLuhanite college kids greeted the immolation of hated literary works with cheers and whistles, while the townies responded with a frightening round of applause when the Gestapo-like authorities gave a forced haircut to a long-haired youth. Could there have been a worse time for Truffaut to have made this impassioned fable about the joys of reading and nonconformity? But I was heartened when Jean Renoir told me that the ending in the snow with the "book people" reciting their memorized texts was "one of the most beautiful things I've ever seen." I expressed my own appreciation for *Fahrenheit 451* in my essay for Philip Nobile's 1973 anthology *Favorite Movies: Critics' Choice*.

Isadora Duncan, The Biggest Dancer in the World (KEN RUSSELL, 1966 TV MOVIE)   Breathtaking in its stylistic audacity and its expressively elliptical approach to narrative—so perfectly suited to its subject matter—Russell's BBC biographical film boasts a marvelous performance by Vivian Pickles as the grand but somewhat ridiculous pioneer of modern dance. Isadora's outsize, ungainly body mirrors her ambitions and pretensions in Russell's empathetic presentation, which never descends into facile mockery. His nimble-footed version of Duncan's life is far superior to Karel Reisz's turgid and heavy-handed 1968 theatrical film *Isadora*, which shamelessly plagiarized some of Russell's best directorial touches, such as the staging of her death scene and its accompaniment with "Bye Bye Blackbird."

7 Women (FORD, 1966)   "The last champions of John Ford have now gathered around *7 Women* as a beacon of personal cinema," wrote Andrew Sarris in his 1968 book *The American Cinema*. Sarris was echoing the mood of apocalyptic finality in Ford's last feature film, a dark vision of chaos overrunning a Christian mission in 1935 China, counterbalanced by the heroic sacrifice of a humanistic and atheistic doctor (Anne Bancroft). MGM had so little faith in *7 Women* that the New York opening took place on 42nd Street, on the lower half of a double bill with Burt Kennedy's *The Money Trap*. Most American reviewers responded in kind, but French and British critics had more understanding of the bleakness of Ford's valedictory statement, which stood in poignant contrast to the communal values of his earlier films about isolated fortresses.

Bye Bye Braverman (SIDNEY LUMET, 1968)   Lumet's little-seen masterpiece, a movie about death that somehow manages to be joyously comical throughout, *Bye Bye Braverman* follows four Jewish intellectuals (George Segal, Jack Warden, Joseph Wiseman, and Sorrell Booke) on their bittersweet journey through New York City to the funeral and burial of an old friend. How could I resist a movie whose characters include a writer (Booke) working on a study of John Ford, and another played by a member of the Ford Stock Company (Warden)? Lumet's interweaving of tragedy and farce is very Fordian, as are his use of a black cab driver (Godfrey Cambridge) as an ironic chorus and the *Stagecoach*-like long shots of the men's little red Volkswagen wending its way through the canyons of New York.

Targets (PETER BOGDANOVICH, 1968)   Appropriately enough, I first watched this movie at a Chicago theater while taking a break from being teargassed in the streets during the 1968 Democratic Convention. There was very little audience in Chicago or elsewhere for this alarmingly believable portrait of a wholesome young California suburbanite (Tim O'Kelly) who snaps and goes on a shooting spree (the character was based on Texas sniper Charles Whitman). Perhaps the real-life violence in the streets and in Vietnam made audiences recoil from the hard truths about American life contained in Bogdanovich's bravura directorial debut. *Targets* also features a moving performance by Boris Karloff as an over-the-hill horror-movie star whose life fatefully intersects with the young killer's (see "15 Great Movie Monologues").

The Comic (CARL REINER, 1969) A bittersweet look back at the heyday of silent comedy, *The Comic* resembles Billy Wilder's *Sunset Boulevard* in refusing to sentimentalize the ruthless egomania of stars who helped bring about their own destruction. Dick Van Dyke is chillingly on target as the comedian who alienates everyone in his life except his former partner, Cockeye (a great supporting performance by Mickey Rooney). The ending is a heartbreaking commentary on the differences between life and the movies.

Tell Them Willie Boy Is Here (ABRAHAM POLONSKY, 1969) This somber, elegantly choreographed chase movie was described to me by Polonsky as "a pavane for an early American." Polonsky's return to directing following twenty years on the blacklist employs the fatalistic rhythms of the Western chase to critically examine genre conventions, while expressing the tragic interrelationship between whites and Indians at the closing of the frontier.

The Twelve Chairs (MEL BROOKS, 1970) Brooks's most emotional film, a fable about greed set ten years after the Russian Revolution, is also laced with raucous black comedy. In one of several cinematic adaptations of the Russian novel by Ilf and Petrov, Ron Moody hilariously plays the dispossessed aristocrat driven mad by his search for lost family jewels; Dom De Luise is sublime as the venal Father Fyodor ("O God, you're so *strict*!"). The critics weren't kind to *The Twelve Chairs*, but most people who bought tickets loved the movie. When I watched it with an African-American audience in San Bernardino, a spectator reacted to Moody's deranged snarling by calling out, "He's a ba-a-a-d motherfucker!"

Avanti! (WILDER, 1972)   My lonely appreciation of *Avanti!* in *Film Heritage* was titled "The Importance of Being Ernst," for this is Wilder's most Lubitschean film, a moving blend of romantic comedy and drama of which the master himself, Ernst Lubitsch, would have been proud. Wilder's seriocomic exaltation of an old couple's illicit romance over the shabby antiromanticism of the present seemed hopelessly "out of it" to the audience of its day.

Exorcist II: The Heretic (JOHN BOORMAN, 1977)   Viciously maligned by critics and audiences alike, then mutilated by the director in a misguided attempt to placate the yahoos, *The Heretic* is a deeply moving, almost avant-garde film about evil's tendency to attack examples of the greatest goodness. Boorman's commercial "sin" was twofold: he used a poetic, nonlinear narrative, and he implicitly criticized the obscene debasement of a child in William Friedkin's 1973 blockbuster *The Exorcist*.

Somewhere in Time (JEANNOT SZWARC, 1980)   This ravishingly beautiful time-traveling romance, starring Christopher Reeve and Jane Seymour and set on Michigan's Mackinac Island, has become a cult classic, but it largely was ignored on its initial release. A recent book about *Somewhere in Time* contains the surprising and gratifying information that my review in *Daily Variety* was the only positive review the movie received!

Rosewood (JOHN SINGLETON, 1997)   Unaccountably pooh-poohed by most critics, this searing, beautifully crafted docudrama about the destruction of a prosperous African-American town by white racists in 1920s Florida also was largely ignored by the moviegoing public. Perhaps the subject matter was too painful for many black viewers and too threatening for most whites.

The 10 Best Films Not Available on Video

by Leonard Maltin

It's difficult to isolate just ten films that aren't yet on video, because any "want list" of this sort is bound to be dictated by personal taste. There are many silent films, foreign films of more recent vintage, bread-and-butter pictures from the 1930s, and cult favorites from the '50s (many in CinemaScope) that could swell this list to at least five times its current length. But, if I'm pinned to the wall for ten titles, these are the ones that stand out to me.

1. *Trouble in Paradise* (1932) may be the single greatest American film not yet available on video. It's a pinnacle of sophisticated, romantic comedy about a pair of elegant jewel thieves who (against their better judgment) find themselves falling in love. It was directed by the great Ernst Lubitsch at the height of his powers, but its ideally cast stars (Kay Francis, Miriam Hopkins, and Herbert Marshall) are no longer household names,

and this may be what's kept it on the shelf until now. Happily, a Lubitsch boxed laserdisc set—including *Paradise*—was finally released in 1997 by Image, which made a half dozen of the Master's best films available to laser collectors, but for those with only VHS machines, it's no sale.

2. *Song of the South* (1946)   This is the Disney film that combines live action and animation to tell the tall tales of Uncle Remus, a black storyteller in the antebellum South. Its characters include Brer Rabbit, Brer Fox, and Brer Bear, and it features the Oscar-winning song "Zip-A-Dee-Doo-Dah." I'm quite fond of this film—as are many other people—but it's become a hot potato for the Disney company in this era of political correctness. What a shame. (A Japanese laserdisc pressing has found its way into some American collectors' hands, however.)

3. *Annie Get Your Gun* (1950)   Betty Hutton and Howard Keel star in this splashy, colorful MGM adaptation of Irving Berlin's Broadway musical hit about Annie Oakley, which introduced such memorable songs as "There's No Business Like Show Business." Unfortunately, the rights reverted to the Berlin estate some years ago, and Mr. Berlin insisted on keeping the movie under wraps in the hopes of mounting a remake. Since this has never come to pass, one can only hope that a deal will finally be made to bring the movie back into circulation.

4. *Counsellor-at-Law* (1934)   John Barrymore gives an electrifying performance—perhaps his best, at least on

film—as a busy, successful New York lawyer (and assimilated Jew). One of William Wyler's first great achievements as a director, this was adapted from the Broadway play by Elmer Rice. Its pace is astonishing, its outsize art deco sets are knockouts, and Wyler somehow makes you forget you're watching a photographed stage play. What a shame that people who read about Barrymore (or see him portrayed by Christopher Plummer onstage) can't follow up by seeing this great performance.

5. *Adventures of Robinson Crusoe* (1952)   Irish-American actor Dan O'Herlihy earned an Oscar nomination for his performance in this colorful, entertaining interpretation of Daniel Defoe's classic story about a resourceful shipwreck victim. This is no ordinary literary adaptation, however, as it was directed by Luis Buñuel, who brought his distinctive point of view to the material. Rights problems have plagued this film in recent years.

6. *Images* (1972) is one of Robert Altman's most intriguing and original movies, filmed in Ireland, a difficult but fascinating story of a troubled woman (Susannah York) who tries to sort out her life, amidst a clash of reality and fantasy. This film seems to have slipped through the cracks since its debut at the New York Film Festival years ago. It's not for every taste, but I remember liking it quite a lot. It hasn't been revived in any medium, so far as I know, in many years.

7. *The Old-Fashioned Way* (1934)   Every one of W. C. Fields's films ought to be on video—and should be

required viewing for young people as an antidote for some of the alleged comedies on TV today. This is one of The Great Man's better vehicles, from his peak period, and not only includes one of his classic encounters with Baby LeRoy, but also features his peerless juggling routine—which originally made him a star in vaudeville.

8. *The Good Fairy* (1936) William Wyler again, directing a delicious Preston Sturges screenplay, based on a fairy-taleish comedy by Molnár about a wide-eyed young woman who decides to act as a kind of good fairy to a struggling lawyer. Herbert Marshall and Frank Morgan costar. It's easy to see why Wyler fell in love with leading lady Margaret Sullavan while making this film; we do, too.

9. *Swiss Family Robinson* (1940) was made by many of the same craftsmen who worked on the same studio's *Citizen Kane*; in fact, it opens with uncredited narration by Orson Welles! It's a serious, thoughtful, often dark version of the Johann Wyss story, quite different from the entertaining slapstick version Walt Disney later fashioned. Thomas Mitchell stars as the man who decides to move his family to Australia, to live a purer life; Edna Best, Freddie Bartholomew, and Tim Holt costar.

10. *The High and the Mighty* (1954) Perhaps the single most-requested film not on video—or TV, or theatrical release, for that matter. John Wayne heads a stellar cast in this multicharacter aviation saga, a forerunner of *Airport* and other such films. It's not what

any critic would call a "great movie," but it is a great piece of Hollywood entertainment, directed by William Wellman, and not to be taken lightly on that level. Although it used to air on television, and even made it to HBO, it's been under wraps with the Wayne estate (along with a handful of other titles) for many years. Michael Wayne continues to promise that we'll see it sometime soon. But we're still waiting.

LEONARD MALTIN is best known for his appearances on television's *Entertainment Tonight*, and as the editor of the annual paperback reference guide *Leonard Maltin's Movie & Video Guide*. He has written many other books on film, including *Of Mice and Magic: A History of American Animated Cartoons*, *The Art of the Cinematographer*, *Selected Short Subjects*, *The Great Movie Comedians*, and *The Disney Films*. He appears regularly on the STARZ! and Encore cable networks, and hosts a daily syndicated radio program.

10 Important Lost Movies

Many (no one really knows the exact number) of the movies made on nitrate film—before the introduction of safety film in 1949—have been lost. Following are just a few of the major missing titles. Some may yet turn up in archives or private collections, as have, in recent years, such long-lost silents as a 1912 adaptation of Shakespeare's *Richard III*, John Ford's 1918 Harry Carey Western *Hell Bent*, and Frank Capra's 1928 comedy *The Matinee Idol*.

The Honor System (RAOUL WALSH, 1917)   This story about a furloughed convict (Milton Sills) who is kidnapped while trying to get back to an Arizona prison to uphold its honor system was listed by John Ford in 1964 as his favorite movie after D. W. Griffith's *The Birth of a Nation* (see "John Ford's 10 Favorite Movies").

The Greatest Thing in Life (D. W. GRIFFITH, 1918)   A drama about a young Southerner (Robert Harron) who fights in World War I, *The Greatest Thing in Life* was described by its female star, Lillian Gish, as "one of Mr. Griffith's best films and one of his most neglected." Gish particularly regretted that modern-day audiences repelled by Griffith's racial attitudes in his 1915 Civil War epic *The Birth of a Nation* could not see Harron kissing a dying black soldier who is calling for his mother on the battlefield.

The Prince of Avenue A (JOHN FORD, 1920)   This is just one of many early Ford films for Universal that are no longer known to exist. *The Prince of Avenue A*, the director's first non-Western, was a movie about Irish-American politics and starred the celebrated boxing champion Gentleman Jim Corbett.

Remodeling Her Husband (LILLIAN GISH, 1920)   The only film the great actress ever directed, *Remodeling Her Husband* was a romantic comedy with titles by Dorothy Parker. It starred the director's sister, Dorothy Gish, and James Rennie (Dorothy's future husband). After the difficult experience of directing it, Gish found herself "cured of any desire to make films. I had acquired a new respect for directors."

Hollywood (JAMES CRUZE, 1923)   Among the silent movies about the movie business (including Cruze's own 1924 *Merton* *of the Movies*), *Hollywood* sounds as if it must have been one of the most fascinating. Liberally blending actuality with fiction, Paramount's satiric tale of an Ohio girl (Hope Drown) who tries to break into the movies includes appearances by such stars as Charlie Chaplin, Gloria Swanson, Mary Pickford, Douglas Fairbanks, Will Rogers, and even Roscoe (Fatty) Arbuckle, whose ostracism from Hollywood is poignantly conveyed in a scene of a casting director's window slamming shut in front of his eyes.

Greed (ERICH VON STROHEIM, 1925)   The original eight-hour director's cut of *Greed* is considered the Holy Grail of lost movies. It was shown privately at MGM before the film was cut by the studio from forty-two to ten reels. Even that butchered version is one of the masterpieces of silent cinema.

The Road to Glory (HOWARD HAWKS, 1926)   Otherwise unrelated to his 1936 film of the same title, Hawks's first feature as a director sounds fascinatingly unlike his later work. The Fox release starred May McAvoy in a somber story about a young woman blinded in an auto accident who regains her sight through prayer.

For the Love of Mike (FRANK CAPRA, 1927)   This low-budget independent comedy about three men who join forces to raise an adopted son (Ben Lyon) was made in New York and marked the film debut of Claudette Colbert. Capra considered it the worst movie of his career. When it was completed, there was no money left to pay the director, so he had to hitchhike back to Hollywood.

The Patriot (ERNST LUBITSCH, 1928)   Lubitsch received his first Academy Award nomination for directing this spectacle about Czar Paul I of Russia (Emil Jannings). Some crowd scenes from *The Patriot* were used in Josef von Sternberg's *The Scarlet Empress* (1934). Ironically, Lubitsch, then head of production at Paramount, chastised Sternberg for his extravagance when he saw these lavish scenes, not realizing they were his own footage.

The Magnificent Ambersons (ORSON WELLES, 1942)   While Welles was in South America directing *It's All True*, a good-will documentary undertaken at the request of the U.S. government, RKO heavily recut *Ambersons* and had some scenes reshot following a disastrous preview. The cut footage was later destroyed by the studio. However, Welles preserved frame enlargements of some of the missing shots, and a few snippets of the footage can be glimpsed in the trailer for the film, which runs on Turner Classic Movies. For descriptions of the missing scenes, see my book *Orson Welles* (1996 revised edition) and the appendix by Peter Bogdanovich and Jonathan Rosenbaum in the 1992 interview book by Bogdanovich and Orson Welles, *This Is Orson Welles*.

Where Have You Gone, Nathanael West?
The Strangest Event I've Ever Witnessed in All My Years of Covering Hollywood

When Paramount held a studio premiere party for *Won Ton Ton, the Dog Who Saved Hollywood* on April 26, 1976, guests were invited to bring along their dogs. As I arrived with my girlfriend, Laurel Gilbert, we were greeted by the stars of TV's *Laverne and Shirley*, Penny Marshall and Cindy Williams, two smart ladies who looked embarrassed by this assignment.

A publicist asked to borrow Laurel's dog, Doobie, so Ernest Borgnine could be seen arriving in a vintage automobile with a dog. Doobie was thus introduced to the TV cameras as Borgnine's dog "Marty." Borgnine called Doobie a "ham," which, coming from him, probably was meant as a compliment. Doobie behaved better than Marisa Berenson's dog, which did its business on her dress. During the screening and dinner, the dogs were tied up on Stage 11. When we retrieved Doobie afterward, we found all the dogs sitting miserably in pools of their own waste, being serenaded by a boom box playing classical music.

The inedible food served to the human guests at the party—stringy shrimp and tough, scrawny hot dogs—was on a par with the movie, that witless, unrelentingly cynical mockery of 1920s Hollywood by the world's worst director, Britain's Michael Winner. (When I was an extra in Winner's 1982 movie *Death Wish II*, I watched the crew openly laughing at him while he screamed orders, a sight I've never seen on a set before or since.) Many of the beloved old performers callously misused by Winner in *Won Ton Ton* cameo roles were in attendance at the party. They included the mouth-popping comic character actor Fritz Feld, who sat at our dinner table with his wife, actress Virginia Christine, better known as Mrs. Olsen on the Folger's Coffee commercials.

The mind-boggling topper to the evening came when the dog who starred in the movie was brought out onstage during dinner. Ushered onto a red-and-gold throne, the dog watched curiously as the octogenarian Mae West tottered out, squeezed into one of her trademark skintight gowns, primping and undulating as in days of yore when she was Paramount's greatest box-office attraction. As the dog stared at Miss West, his eyes became glassy, his tongue hung out of his mouth, and he pulled a huge, bright-red erection. Miss West, whose eyesight had faded, seemed mercifully oblivious. Otherwise she would have had a perfect setup for her immortal line, "Is that a pistol in your pocket, or are you just glad to see me?"

The next person brought out onto the stage was none other than the legendary founder of Paramount Pictures, the wizened, 103-year-old Adolph Zukor. Poor Mr. Zukor, whose mental faculties weren't what they once were, saw the animal sitting in the throne and became visibly confused and upset. No doubt he wondered why a dog had taken his rightful place at Paramount.

That incredible triumvirate of the tumescent dog, Mae West, and Adolph Zukor has lingered in my memory ever since as the strangest sight I've seen in Hollywood, a tableau as surreal as anything in Nathanael West's *The Day of the Locust*.

Index

About the Author

Joseph McBride is the author of twelve other books, including the acclaimed 1992 biography *Frank Capra: The Catastrophe of Success*, *Steven Spielberg: A Biography* (1997), and *High and Inside: An A-to-Z Guide to the Language of Baseball* (Contemporary Books, 1997). His books on filmmakers also include *Orson Welles*; *John Ford* (with Michael Wilmington); and the Howard Hawks interview book *Hawks on Hawks*, which was chosen by the Book Collectors of Los Angeles as one of the "100 Best Books on Hollywood and the Movies." A former reporter and critic for *Daily Variety* in Hollywood, McBride currently reviews films for *Boxoffice* magazine.

McBride also wrote the American Film Institute Life Achievement Award specials on CBS-TV honoring James Stewart, Fred Astaire, Frank Capra, John Huston, and Lillian Gish. He was twice nominated for Emmy Awards for those scripts and won the Writers Guild of America Award in 1983 for the Huston tribute. McBride was one of the writers of the cult classic movie *Rock 'n' Roll High School*, and he coproduced the American Movie Classics/MCA Home Video documentary *Obsessed with "Vertigo": New Life for Hitchcock's Masterpiece* (1997).